3ᵒⁿ

Waiting for America

Waiting for America

A STORY OF EMIGRATION

Maxim D. Shrayer

 Syracuse University Press

Syracuse University Press, Syracuse, New York 13244-5160
Copyright © 2007 by Maxim D. Shrayer
Individual sections copyright © 1998, 1999, 2002, 2003, 2007 by Maxim D. Shrayer.

First Edition 2007

07 08 09 10 11 12   6 5 4 3 2 1

The paper used in this publication meets the minimum requirements
of American National Standard for Information Sciences—Permanence
of Paper for Printed Library Materials, ANSI Z39.48–1984.∞™

For a listing of books published and distributed by Syracuse University Press,
visit our Web site at SyracuseUniversityPress.syr.edu.

ISBN-13: 978-0-8156-0893-6   ISBN-10: 0-8156-0893-4

Library of Congress Cataloging-in-Publication Data

Shrayer, Maxim, 1967–
   Waiting for America : a story of emigration / Maxim D. Shrayer. — 1st ed. 2007.
    p. cm.
   ISBN 978-0-8156-0893-6 (hardback : alk. paper)
  1. Immigrants—United States. 2. Jews—United States. I. Title.
PG3487.R34W35 2007
818'.603—dc22   2007031391

Manufactured in the United States of America

for Karen and Mirusha,
with all my love

MAXIM D. SHRAYER was born in Moscow, in 1967, to a Jewish-Russian family. With his parents, the writer and medical scientist David Shrayer-Petrov and the translator Emilia Shrayer (née Polyak), he spent almost nine years as a refusenik. He and his parents left the USSR and immigrated to the United States in 1987, after spending a summer in Austria and Italy.

Shrayer was educated at Moscow University, Brown University, Rutgers University, and Yale University. He is presently professor of Russian and English and chair of the Department of Slavic and Eastern Languages at Boston College, where, in 2004, he cofounded the Jewish Studies Program.

Among Shrayer's books are the acclaimed critical studies *The World of Nabokov's Stories* and *Russian Poet/Soviet Jew,* and three collections of Russian poetry. A bilingual author and translator in English and Russian, he recently edited and cotranslated the two-volume *Anthology of Jewish-Russian Literature: Two Centuries of Dual Identity in Prose and Poetry* and the collection *Autumn in Yalta: A Novel and Three Stories,* by David Shrayer-Petrov.

Shrayer's English-language prose, poetry, and translations have appeared in *Agni, Kenyon Review, Massachusetts Review, Partisan Review, Southwest Review,* and other magazines. He has been the recipient of a number of fellowships, including those from the National Endowment for the Humanities, the Rockefeller Foundation, and the Bogliasco Foundation.

Shrayer lives in Chestnut Hill, Massachusetts, with his wife, Dr. Karen E. Lasser, and their daughter, Mira Isabella Shrayer.

Waiting for America is Shrayer's first book-length literary work in English.

Contents

Acknowledgments

I started this book in Boston, in 1996, and resumed working on it in 2001, after a hiatus of four years. A portion of it was completed in November and December 2002 at the Rockefeller Foundation's Study and Conference Center in Bellagio, Italy, and I thank the foundation for its support. A fellowship from the Bogliasco Foundation and the staff of the Centro Studi Ligure per le arti e le lettere (Bogliasco, Italy) enabled me to write a section of this book while on a Boston College Faculty Fellowship in October and November 2004. The rest of the book was completed in my home in Chestnut Hill, Massachusetts, in 2004–6.

I am grateful to the editors of the following magazines, where several sections of this book originally appeared: *Agni* (a section of chapter 1), *Boston College Magazine* (a section of chapter 5), *Brown Alumni Monthly* (a section of chapter 3), *Massachusetts Review* (a section of chapter 2), and *Southwest Review* (sections of chapters 3 and 9; a section of chapter 7).

I would like to thank Mary Selden Evans for believing in this book, and all my friends at Syracuse University Press for welcoming it and giving it a warm American home.

Linda Cuckovich copyedited the book with attention to my authorial whims. Stephen Vedder and Michael S. Swanson of Boston College's Media Technology Services have done a splendid job with the cover design. Daniel Oliver Bachmann, Anna Bliss, Ellen S. Goodman, Sean Keck, Luba Ostashevsky, and Christopher Springer read and commented on different drafts of this book. My heartfelt thanks go to all of them.

My wife, Karen E. Lasser, and my parents, Emilia Shrayer and David Shrayer-Petrov, took time from their important work to read and critique drafts of this book. My father taught me to write (I haven't been a good student, papa), and my mother taught me English (still working on it, mama). My wife has opened my eyes, my ears, my heart, and my whole body to more American and immigrant worlds than there are words either in my native Russian or in my adopted English.

Our daughter Mira Isabella Shrayer was born on 9 February 2006, as I was finishing a draft of this book. Mirusha is more perfect than anything I will ever write.

Preface

In our time, when the critical climate of U.S. culture encourages readers and publishers to engage in vicarious scrutiny of the relationship between the raw material of so-called "real life" and the final literary product, I feel it necessary to make several advance observations about my book and the story it tells.

Waiting for America: A Story of Emigration is a creative product of memory and imagination. I altered and changed names to protect the identities of the individuals and the institutions that have informed the characters and circumstances described in these pages. Furthermore, the very nature of reconstructing the past and presenting it in narrative form demanded that, in places, I relinquish control of the writing and let the muses fill the sails of my story with their fervent breath.

Fictionalization and poetization, I believe, are not—and should not be regarded as—the opposites of narrative truth-telling; rather, documentary homebrew is aged, purified, and given an artistic vintage by the writer's conscious use of language, style, and narrative structure. Trying to discern where precisely the writer has strayed from the double phantom of verity and authenticity strikes me as a losing proposition for the reader, as it threatens to rob the reader of the pleasure of artistic revelation. As far as I am concerned, as the author of *Waiting for America,* everything in this story "really" happened.

28 January 2007   M. D. S.
Chestnut Hill, Mass.

My enormous and morose Mademoiselle is
all right on earth but impossible in
eternity. Have I really salvaged her
from fiction?

        —Vladimir Nabokov

The only time I spoke Italian then was
when my father and I would visit the
raven in the Borghese Gardens and feed
him peanuts.

        —John Cheever

PART ONE | Flight

1

Wienerwald

In early June 1987, two days after I turned twenty, my family left the Soviet Union for good. We'd been trying to emigrate for nine years, struggling, losing hope, and regaining hope. I was ten when my parents decided to emigrate, and I was a junior in college by the time we were finally leaving.

It rained during our last night in Moscow, and as my parents and I walked out of our former apartment building early in the morning, the streets and sidewalks lay under a blanket of poplar fuzz, a Russian summer snow. We rode to the airport in a black BMW with diplomatic license plates. Our friend and protector, a cultural affairs officer at the American Embassy, personally drove us to Sheremetyevo-2, Moscow's international airport, and delivered us to the terminal. This was done to safeguard my parents and me from any surprises that the KGB was saving for the last.

In the midst of airport chaos I said goodbye—forever, I thought at the time—to my whole world. Traveling with us were my grandmother, my mother's younger, divorced sister, and her eleven-year-old daughter. My grandmother was a robust blue-eyed seventy-three-year-old widow with wavy amber-dyed hair. In her coriander skirt and blouse of a pale tulip yellow silk, my grandmother looked a lot younger than her Soviet age. With both hands she clung to an over-sized brown leather purse. In Moscow my grandmother, aunt, and little cousin had always shared an apartment and formed a nuclear family. Now they were the first to go through customs. A tall female sergeant, who in another life might have been cutting women's hair in the antechambers of concentration camps, separated my grandmother from her daughter and granddaughter and led her away for a "personal inspection." At this point my little cousin, as if realizing the finality of our leaving, started bawling, smearing large tears across her high cheeks and frenetically waving over the divide to her father, my aunt's long-divorced husband, who was staying in Russia with his new family. It was impossible to watch this innocent creature in a polka-dot dress, with pale curls sheared like those of a little lamb, say goodbye forever to her own father. I was almost glad to be summoned over to the customs booth.

"Where you going, pal?" a leery customs lieutenant asked me as he strangled my blue backpack into submission. "Down south or to the States?"

I didn't answer and looked down at my new shiny black wingtips, pretending that I wasn't sure what the lieutenant was asking. Of course I knew that "down south" referred to Israel and was meant to provoke me.

I was a different person back then, in June of 1987, when I was leaving Russia for good. I was braver, more brazen, more desperate, but also less sensitive, less tolerant, and much more judgmental. I was accustomed to finding antisemitic behavior everywhere and was ready to defend my honor with fists. I sincerely believed Ronald Reagan was good because he fiercely opposed the "evil" Soviet Empire. I was thinner and looked lankier with a full head of hair that I cut short and wore straight down over the brow, à la jejune Pasternak. I was also generously self-absorbed.

"What's in your pockets?" the customs lieutenant asked, growing impatient with my defiant silence. One by one, I emptied onto the counter the contents of all the pockets of my new glen plaid suit. They included a small leather-bound notebook where I jotted down lines for future poems, a tape measure, two handkerchiefs, a treasured roll of color film, and a chocolate bar someone had just given me at the airport. My nice suit was a present that my father's Uncle Pinya had mailed from Israel. Mother, father, and I were dressed in our finest clothes and wanted to look our best as we entered a new life.

After we had passed through customs and then through the turnstile of Soviet passport control, we lingered and marched in place, taking one more and yet another glance at the small crowd of friends and relatives who were seeing us off. There they were, my dear friends, a magic circle broken: Misha Zaychik, growing his first sandstone beard; Tanya Apraksina, with her stupendous legs and ballerina posture; Alik Frayerman, a Levantine live wire under normal circumstances but now frozen with stupor; Lenochka Borisova, with mascara bleeding along her Slavic cheekbones; the phlegmatic aristocrat Fedya Bogolepov, fishing for a handkerchief in the fathoms of his corduroy jacket; Lana Bernshteyn, with her Jugendstil haircut, perfectly chiseled nose, and refined hands. No girlfriend was seeing me off; at the time we didn't have girlfriends or boyfriends in the American sense of the word, only girls or boys we dated now and then. Lana Bernshteyn had been my first love, never my "girlfriend." Some of my dearest people were now standing on that side of the turnstile, waving. Will I ever see them again? I thought as an Aeroflot steward escorted us to the empty first class lounge.

We were flying first class because it had been much easier to get the tickets, and after nine years of living in refuseniks' limbo, we didn't want to stay in Russia even for an extra day. In English, the term *refusenik* corresponds to the Russian word *otkaznik* and means "one who was refused, denied permission" to leave the Soviet Union. But in its English rendition, the term has acquired an ambiguity, whose irony was hardly intentional: The Soviet authorities, not the Jews, were *refusing.* The only thing refuseniks themselves had refused was a ticket to Soviet paradise.

While we waited in the first class lounge for our drinks and a tray with black caviar canapés, my mother and father hugged me feverishly. My mother sipped her tonic and shivered, fighting back tears.

"Are you cold? Do you want my jacket?" my father asked her.

"Wait, I can't speak," mother whispered, resting her head on my father's shoulder and fumbling for a cigarette and matches in her suede purse.

At forty-seven, my mother had ash-gold hair; later, from unremembering the Soviet past, her hair would succumb to quicksilver. In summer, my mother's straight, thick hair would grow wavy and pale, almost blonde, and her large blue eyes, piercingly perceptive, ever ready to laugh and humor and subvert, would be saturated with aquamarine blueness—a miracle of water, salt, and sun. But the salt in her eyes now came from withheld tears, and the luster was from sleeplessness and the fluorescent lights of the first class lounge.

"We got you out, son. Finally we got you out," said my father. A strange mixture of shrewdness, ferocity, distrust, and naïveté lurked in his bloodshot, gray-green eyes, framed by his rectangular tortoise-shell glasses. Father couldn't sleep the night before we left Moscow and walked around our neighborhood until dawn, saying goodbye. And with breakfast father had had some cognac with his good friend, the poet G. S., who came over to bid us farewell.

My long-limbed father, a former athlete, was fifty-one at the time. An American TV journalist who had interviewed my parents in Moscow and later stayed in touch told me many years later that my father looked younger at sixty-one than at fifty-one. Over a year before our leaving, father had suffered a heart attack from two months of being hunted by the KGB—after a novel of his had come out abroad. The wounds of his heart had healed, but the memories were healing more slowly. That morning in the airport, to look his best, my father was wearing a navy sport coat of the sort that we used to call "club jacket" after some forgotten British fashion, gray gabardine pants, and cordovan shoes. On his knees he held a black and brown briefcase with all our papers.

"We got you out," father repeated, and he kissed me and my mother on our chins, noses, temples, like a blind person missing lips and cheeks.

That was my family at the doorstep of the West, unprepared, as we would soon discover, despite the years of waiting, for what emigration held in store for us.

Half an hour later we boarded an Ilyushin 86. The Aeroflot stewardesses, navy-clad creatures with movie star looks, no longer treated us as their own—as fellow subjects of the Soviet Empire. Which meant they treated us better. The "emigrants" in their eyes were almost as good as Westerners and deserving of proper service. In the air flying over Ukraine and Czechoslovakia, my parents and I toasted with champagne our deliverance and yet waited anxiously for the plane to touch down outside the boundaries of the Eastern Bloc. Our whole lives' belongings had been packed in five suitcases. Our proofs of identity were Soviet-issued exit visas with black-and-white frenzied photos. We'd been stripped of our Soviet citizenship. Refuseniks we had been, kept hostage by the state for nine years, and now we became refugees, stateless persons loosely protected by international conventions. All we knew about our future was that we were Jews bound for America.

IN THE VIENNA AIRPORT, blue-gray uniforms escorted our group of about twenty-five Soviet refugees to some concourse or hall (this part is a panicky blur), where we all stood, huddled together, waiting for the first separation.

"To Israel? Anybody going to Israel?" a tall suntanned woman called out in Russian. She was a representative of the Israeli Ministry of Absorption and looked like a lady warrior.

Dropping his briefcase, my father shuddered and jerked forward, unclasping his hands and unlocking his dry lips as though he wanted to motion to or say something to the Israeli woman. My mother gave him a scornful look.

"Please don't start again," she whispered, and her leaden whisper reached the ears of others in our small crowd of refugees.

Waiting right next to us was another refugee, formerly a classics professor. His name was Anatoly Shteynfeld. Back in 1980 he had lost his university position. My parents knew him superficially, the way many members of the Moscow refusenik community knew one another, and never particularly cared for him because of his chronic superciliousness. As a refusenik, Shteynfeld taught history in a night-extension school for factory workers. He was in his mid-forties and twice divorced. He left a teenage daughter in Moscow. A polyglot, Shteynfeld was mainly known in the Moscow refusenik circles for two things. Although he had never set foot outside the Soviet Union, he was said to be fluent in English, German, French, Italian, and Spanish. Shteynfeld's second claim to fame was his closeness to a Moscow Russian Orthodox priest of Jewish origin, Father M., who made it his life's work to convert to Christianity as many Jewish intellectuals and artists as there were crenellations on all of the Kremlin walls. Under Father M.'s influence, Shteynfeld was baptized some time in the late 1970s; later he began to spread among refuseniks the message that Jewish Christians were "doubly chosen" and supposedly fulfilled a double mission. Shteynfeld sported a Caesar cut and cultivated a disdainful pallor on his flabby cheeks and double chin.

"Who would want to go to Israel?" Shteynfeld uttered, loud enough for our whole group of refugees to hear despite the competing noises of the terminal. "It's a police state." And he smirked.

Like a bull who is shown a red rag, my father was incapable of ignoring Shteynfeld's poisonous remark.

"Listen, Shteynfeld," my father said, swaying on the feet that still remembered the boxing rings of his youth. He had to stop boxing in medical school, when the doctors told him he would otherwise go blind. "Listen, Shteynfeld," father repeated, bringing his head and torso closer to Shteynfeld. "Where we all go is our personal business. But don't stand here besmirching Israel. Without Israel you'd still be teaching the French Revolution to a bunch of drunks and delinquents."

Mother pulled father by the elbow of his club jacket.

"Without your charming wife you'd be quite the Zionist, wouldn't you, Mr. Writer?" Shteynfeld said, bowing his oily chin.

"Anybody to Israel?" the Israeli Amazon asked, this time like a bartender announcing last call.

"Yes, here," shouted a girl of about twenty, as she started vehemently waving at the Israeli woman. "Ken!"

Ken means "yes" in Hebrew, and after our small crowd of Soviet refugees heard it, we split our ranks, leaving the girl and her family in the middle. The girl had been traveling from Moscow with her father, a veteran refusenik, and his younger, second wife and their two young children. The girl's mother had died of leukemia while they were refuseniks, and the father remarried.

"Well, papa," said the girl, taking her father's hands in hers. "Good luck with everything in America!" She kissed her father on the brow. Then she kissed her little half-brothers, but not her father's second wife.

"Let's go, my dear," the Israeli woman said, putting her arm around the young Zionist. "You'll miss your connection to Tel Aviv."

"Anya," the girl's father said imploringly and reached out his tottering hand, as if trying, for the last time, to dissuade her. "Anechka, wait!" But the Israeli Amazon was already leading his daughter toward an aluminum door on the opposite side of the small concourse.

"No one else—to Israel?" asked a skinny bald man who had materialized out of nowhere and was now standing in front of our group. Dressed in a white linen derby, yellow shirt, and white slacks, he looked about sixty and spoke a shtetl sort of Russian, not unlike that of my father's late auntie from Minsk, except more heavily Yiddish-accented and misstressed. On the open palm of his left hand he held a leather-bound notebook, and he was tapping on it with a thick silver fountain pen. "Too hot for you down there?" The quick-eyed man gave all of us a collective wink and then removed a cap from his silver pen.

"You can all hear me, right?" he asked, taking another step toward us.

"Yes. We can. Yes," came several voices from our group.

"Swell. Slansky's my name," he said loudly, hissing on the sibilants like an old grass snake. "I work for JIAS, which stands for Jewish Immigrant Aid Society. I'm from Poland originally, from outside Warsaw. Me and my wife," and he turned his head to his left where a blonde lady of about fifty, dressed in a sequined blouse and a white skirt, swayed on high heels. "Her name is Basia. We've been here in Vienna for over twenty-five years, and we've been working for JIAS for almost as long. So don't worry, we'll get you started and deliver you to your hostels. You'll ask all the questions when we're riding from the airport. We have three minivans. I drive one, my lovely wife drives another one, and there's a Romanian guy, Popescu, who works with us. He also speaks Russian. So now, dear refugees, let's please get going. We need to collect your bags. There are bathrooms in the baggage-claim area."

After the baggage was claimed, Slansky and his wife wrote down everyone's name and began to divide us into three groups of eight to ten. As the Slanskys animatedly discussed in Polish how to break us into groups according to the number of vacancies in the hostels and hotels for refugees, I began to inch my way out of the fog of cognitive paralysis into which I had sunk after stepping off the plane in Vienna. The Moscow-Vienna flight had only lasted about three hours, but it amounted to a passage from being within the Soviet Bloc to being without it. During the first hours after the arrival in Vienna, I felt numb and could barely talk or make eye contact with those around me.

It sometimes happens that in the most shocking or heart-rending moments our memory shoots and stores irrelevant footage. My eyes came upon a group of six that stood out from the other Jewish departees. They waited like a family at a provincial photographer's studio of yore. In the center of the group was a smug-looking man in his late forties, wearing a black suit and an oversized woolen derby of the sort known in Russian as "airfield" and associated with men from the Caucasus; the broad collar of his striped cream shirt spread over the extra broad collar and lapel of the coat. A smoldering cigarette hung like a marionette out of the corner of his mouth. On his arm the man in the oversized derby held a woman with lush black hair covered with a transparent kerchief of golden gauze. She wore a dress embroidered in gold thread and smiled in fits and starts. To their left stood a girl of about ten or eleven, already showing buds of femininity as young girls from the Middle East, Central Asia, and the Caucasus often do at that age. She held the hand of a young man who was also dressed in a black suit and sported a dark crimson tie. The girl looked like she was trying to tell the young man something funny, to get him to laugh or smile, but he just stood beside her, like a dummy, letting her play with his listless hand. His downcast eyes studied the marble squares of the terminal floor, still unlittered at this hour. On his shoulder the young man had a narrow black carrying case with a zipper. To the right of the smoking man and the gilded woman, on an beat-up brown fiberglass suitcase, sat, arm in arm, a old couple of escapees from a museum of ethnography. The old man was in his seventies, sinuous and small, his face bristling with steel wire. On his feet he had what looked to me like riding boots. Over a jacket the old man wore a belted coat of thick gray wool with rows of narrow long pockets for bullets stitched on either side of his chest. Coats like that are the traditional garb of men in the mountains of the Caucasus. Atop the head of the old warrior, a tall black astrakhan rose like a water tower over a small town's central square. The face of the old man reflected nothing but contempt for his surroundings, contempt with an admixture of fierceness and bravery. His goitrous wife, who clung to his side like a hen to her perch, had porcelain saucers for eyes and was clad in all black, except for her gauze kerchief, which had silver beads. Despite the obvious differences in temperament (which can sometimes overshadow the phenotypical similarity), all three men in this family looked alike: shortish, with hooked noses, black wavy hair, and tyrannical eyebrows. Every now and then, the old man said something in a shrieky voice to his wife, in a language that sounded a bit like Tadjik. Father sensed my curiosity and explained:

"Oh, they are Tats. Mountain Jews. They speak Tat, a Judeo-Iranian language."

"Papa, how do you know all this?" I asked.

"Well, I met some Tats in the military, and later in Azerbaijan, in the '60s. And I once translated a Tat poet, Kukullu, into Russian," he answered.

Suddenly the young man with the narrow black case came up to me. Tenderly laying his small hand on my elbow, he said, "Hello, friend, my name is Aleksandr. I'm from Baku, from the sunny Azerbaijan."

I looked at the young musician without saying anything.

"Friend, where are they taking us? Do you know?"

"Some hotel, or hostel, or dormitory for refugees," I answered, without any intonation.

"I've never lived in a dormitory," the young man said with passion. "Back home, in Baku, we had a grand apartment. Four rooms. You know, friend," he said looking me right in the eye, "I still don't understand why we left. There was never any prejudice against us in Baku. Or against anyone else. We all lived like brothers—Azeris, Jews, Armenians, Russians."

By some strained effort I recalled reading in high school about massive anti-Armenian violence in Baku around 1900 to 1910, but I didn't feel like arguing with the homesick flautist. I just patted him on the back, lightly, and soon our family name was called.

From the airport we rode in a long silver-blue van. Popescu had rolled his window down and tossed cigarette butts at the smooth surface of the freeway. Riding there with us were my grandmother, aunt, and cousin, as well as two complete strangers. One of them was Mrs. Perelman, a plump old lady who was on her way to Calgary to be reunited with her son and his family after eight years of living apart. She told us that her husband, an aeronautical engineer, had died in Russia without ever seeing his "Canadian" grandchildren. The other fellow traveler was a single man in his early thirties, a dentist with a thick Cossack mustache who told us that his girlfriend, an American of two years, was coming from St. Louis to meet him in Italy. All the while, as we drove out of the airport through lilac dusk striated with neon signs, the windswept dentist made comments like this: "Wow, that's what I call a highway!" Or this: "Everything looks so new and clean!"

About thirty minutes later the van delivered us to a refugee hostel in the town of Gablitz, about five miles outside Vienna. The hostel was a three-story stucco building with balconies and a red roof. The owner, a sickly looking creature in her late forties, greeted the Romanian driver in German and signed some papers he placed on the reception counter.

"This lady's name is Charlotte," the Romanian driver explained to us in his formidable Russian. "She runs this place. Very tough lady. No smile, all discipline. Like all of them here, you know."

"How do we get in touch with you if there's an emergency?" asked the dentist.

"What emergency?" Popescu replied, sneering. "Relax, my friend, you're in the free world." At the door he turned around and added, "Don't forget, tomorrow morning the Slanskys will come to take you to Vienna. The other families from your group are staying in the center of Vienna, so we don't need to drive them around. You get to stay in the country and we drive you around—it's a great deal."

Charlotte the hostel proprietress was dressed in pink jeans and a white lacy blouse. She had sallow skin, unkempt hair, and a long waxen nose. "Long nose," I whispered to my mother in Russian.

Barely acknowledging our presence, Charlotte studied her register for a couple of minutes.

"You and you," she finally said, pointing her index finger at my parents. "No. 5." And she gave my father a key.

"You, you, and you," she pointed at my aunt, grandmother, and cousin. "All together. No. 12."

"What about me?" I asked.

"You." Long Nose brought her yellow finger close to my chin. "No. 17. Attic."

We carried all of our luggage up the stairs and then hauled most of our relatives' luggage, except my aunt's very heavy trunk, which we left in a storage room on the ground floor. By the time we had finished supper, which was served in the dining room downstairs, we were all so exhausted that going out to tour the environs of the hostel was out of the question. I don't even remember returning to my garret and falling asleep.

IN THE MORNING AFTER our arrival in Austria I woke up and looked outside the narrow window of my garret. I saw the lush treetops of Wienerwald. In Soviet grade school I had soloed in a chorus performance, and the refrain was stuck in my memory: "The Vienna Woods (tra-la-la), the world of miracles (tra-la-la)." I showered in a hallway bath, dressed, and went out for a stroll. I passed a wine garden and a tiny post office. I followed the bends of a narrow roadway, eventually turning left onto a rural asphalt road veined with cracks. The road continued up a slope, past a deserted house with a gable roof and a large fruit orchard, also forsaken and grown wild. The gray tower of a distant castle showed through the verdure of beeches, oaks, and elms. A stork of an old gentleman dressed in a black three-piece suit, a white shirt with a crimson bow, and a Tyrolese hat, greeted me with a squeaky "Grüss Gott!" and stepped back into his century. An oriole whistled its fluty song. A red doe crossed the road and vanished in the shady underbrush. Three clouds hung motionless over my head. Having just escaped from a country where privacy was utterly impossible, I was now miraculously alone. I was a person of no country, a tired wanderer through the Vienna Woods.

After a continental breakfast, Slansky, the JIAS representative, picked us up and drove us to Vienna in a sparkling red Opel.

"First off," he said to my father, "you as head of the family will have an interview with the Israelis. There's an arrangement between JIAS and the Israelis—they get to have another round with you."

"Arm-twisting?" my mother asked.

"You said that, dear lady, not I." Slansky laughed like a satyr. "Just listen and politely say 'no.' There's nothing they can legally do to you."

"We're not going to Israel," said mother. "What happens after the interview?"

"After that, the dog ate the cat," Slansky retorted, very pleased with his knowledge of limericks. "Patience, my dear lady. You're not in the Soviet Union anymore."

My mother turned chalk-white but said nothing.

Slansky dropped us off in the center of Vienna, in front of a building that employed caryatids to support its windows and top floors. "When you're finished here, go to this address. That's the Vienna office of JIAS. Second floor, they'll show you where." And he handed us a poorly photocopied map of the center of Vienna with two places circled in black ink.

Mother and I waited for about an hour and a half outside an office door through which my father had been accompanied by a man with copper hair and a scar across his brow. When my father finally came out, he had his jacket off; the knot of his striped gray and blue tie was loose. He looked pale and spent, his forehead and bald spot glistening with the dew of resistance.

"Let's go," he told us through his teeth.

When we walked into the street busy with late morning traffic, father told us about his grueling talk with representatives of the Israeli Ministry of Absorption who had tried to persuade him to make *aliya* instead of going to America.

"They were pressuring me. Shaming me. 'A Jewish writer and a sufferer like you belongs in Israel.' And what's worse, a part of me agreed with what they said. Both of them came from Russia as young men in the early 1970s and love Israel. They'd served in the army. One of them, the one with the scar, was wounded in 1973. He read my novel soon after it came out in Israel. It was hard to look them in the eye."

"Well, it's over now," mother said.

Father nodded silently.

"What did they say about our relatives?" mother asked impatiently.

"Well, they knew about my cousin, Uncle Pinya's son. They said he's a famous artist in Israel."

"Didn't they know any of my father's cousins?!" mother asked. "My aunt is well known over there—she used to be dean of a nursing school at Hadassah Hospital. And my uncle Hayim—"

"—I'm thirsty and hungry," said my father, changing the subject.

At the airport, Slansky had given each family a token amount of money for incidentals, just for the next few days. Walking in the direction of the JIAS office, where we were going for our next interview, we stopped at a sandwich shop and spent almost all of our shillings on two sandwiches and two bottles of orange juice that we shared three ways.

The Jewish Immigrant Aid Society had its headquarters in New York City. JIAS took care of the Jewish refugees from the point of arrival in Vienna until the touch-down in America. In Vienna all of us needed to fill out the initial paperwork that was required to apply for refugee status.

After waiting in a large, noisy hall that resembled a newsroom, we were taken to an office with pulled-down blinds and an antique floor lamp with a bright yellow shade.

A self-absorbed JIAS official delivered his lines in an operatic falsetto while petting a Pekinese dog sitting in his lap. To all three of us he said: "Aha, Muscovites. The elite!"

"So I understand you speak fluent English?" he said to my mother without tearing his myopic eyes off the paperwork in front of him on the desk.

"I used to teach at a university. I was fired when we applied for exit visas," my mother replied.

"What did you expect, that they would keep you working while you waited for an exit visa?" the official remarked, oozing caustic delight.

"You're quite the philosopher, aren't you?" my father retorted, still his dissident self, still ready to fight for justice.

"One more comment like that," the official yelped at my father, a venomous green light twitching in his eyes, "and you'll get thrown out of here." In Russian he literally said "and you'll *fly* out of here" *(i vy otsyuda vyletite)*. I remember sitting there and thinking, what a foolish man! We had just flown in here. We hadn't been in the West a week, and some dwarfish tyrant was already kicking us around. Even after so many years of living freely abroad, this caricature of a man hadn't lost the small-time meanness of a petty Soviet civil servant he might have become had he stayed in the Soviet Union.

My father made a jerking motion to get up, like a horse venturing to shake off an arrogant rider, and only my mother's stroking hands helped rein in his anger. For the next few minutes my father sat on the edge of his chair, studying the faded carpet and fretting.

Apparently the official sensed he'd gone too far and said to my father, in a conciliatory tone: "I think I've read something of yours, a novel? A poem? One of those things. Something about Lot's wife, perhaps? I tell you, it's a good thing you're also a physician—they have more writers in America than they have house cleaners."

He studied us silently, as we sat under his gaze in uncomfortable chairs. Then he said, to all three of us: "Old refuseniks, huh? Haven't seen many of you in a long time. So when did you first apply? Let me guess—'78? '79? Yeah, I know, got stuck because of Afghanistan. Many of you people with advanced degrees got stuck. And what did you expect?"

He studied his notes for a couple of minutes, then turned his buttery eyes back at us.

"Let's see now. . . . Going where?"

"Washington, D.C., or perhaps Philadelphia. We aren't sure," my mother answered.

"Not sure? Why not? You'd better be sure when you get to Italy."

As a child, he told us, he had been in a concentration camp with his parents. In the 1950s they went to Israel.

"But I've been here in Vienna for many years," the official said. "My wife's a Hungarian Jew. Also a survivor. She doesn't know Russian. We speak Yiddish and Hungarian at home." He turned a picture frame on his desk in our direction.

"You say you took natural sciences in Moscow. What do you want to study in America?" he asked me at the very end of the interview.

"Literature," I replied.

"Literature? Why not medicine, business, or law?" A desk fan was reflected in his gold teeth. "Do you know what your last name means?" the official asked me. "Screamer!" His Russian had a thick patina of a Yiddish accent. He issued us a cash allowance for the week.

"Don't do anything stupid, like ride the metro without a ticket," he warned us. "In about a week," he said mysteriously, "you will be traveling to Italy by night train. Be prepared."

The allowance made it possible for us not to feel desperately poor in Vienna that afternoon. We toured the former Hapsburg living quarters and stood in front of the crown that had once united Spain and Austria. A horseman myself, I had talked my parents into going to see the performing stallions at the Spanish Riding School. We had a late lunch in an open-air café. After lunch we slowly walked around Judenplatz, the center of the old Jewish ghetto where a synagogue had been destroyed by a raging mob during a mid–fifteenth-century pogrom. A pogrom it was, although the Russian word somehow felt odd and barbaric when used in connection with Vienna, here in the middle of the square where Mozart had once lived. A pogrom in Vienna? This contraposition stirred and quivered in my head, but there was too much beauty and cordiality around to suggest anything but happiness and peace to a family of Jewish refugees from the Soviet Union who were spending their second day in the West.

We came back to Gablitz by bus, just in time to catch supper at our hostel. The following day we didn't go to Vienna. We rested and took an excursion to the center of Gablitz. It was an innocuous town with shops and restaurants that were prohibitively expensive to us at the time. The town's main attractions were a Roman gravestone and a local history and art museum. Located in the grade school building, the museum was a succession of cavernous rooms and nooks, filled to the brim with porcelain knickknacks, portraits of the local aristocrats and their hunting dogs, tapestries, oleographs, and watercolors representing vistas of the Vienna Woods in different seasons and times of day, manuscripts of Austrian writers who had stayed in Gablitz, and, unavoidably in such museums, an arsenal of swords, sabers, helmets, and armor, an arsenal so large that one could arm the town's entire population. There was nothing in the museum about Austria and the town of Gablitz during the Nazi era.*

My parents and I walked aimlessly about the picture-perfect Austrian town, partaking of its serenity, window shopping, trying to unburden ourselves of the turmoil of the previous two months, the turmoil of leaving Russia. We were still in some sort of daze.

On the way back to our hostel, we took a different route and discovered a little food market. The abundance of foods stacked on the shelves and in glass-door refrigerators was astounding, and the market to us was more of a museum than the one we had just visited in the center of Gablitz. The smiling store owner with large ruddy cheeks and meaty hands, a blue apron tied around his waist, kept casting cursory glances at the three of us as we picked up and weighed in our hands various packages and tins while also examining the prices.

We ended up buying a loaf of delicious aromatic rye bread, smoked turkey breast, tomatoes, bananas, and five or six different custards and

---

*About three weeks later, already in Italy, I would read Vladimir Nabokov's third collection of Russian stories, *Spring in Fialta*. In it there's a story entitled "The Visit to the Museum." In this phantasmagoria, a Russian émigré visits a local history museum, in a town on the French Riviera, and loses himself in the cavernous corridors of history. Reading Nabokov's story on the hot black sand of a Tyrrhenian beach in the Italian town of Ladispoli, I would be reminded of the Gablitz museum, of the serene absurdity of its exhibit, of its mounted antlers and hunting scenes, and of its selective suppression of the past.

fruit yogurts in plastic containers. There was a picnic table outside the store, and we had a feast under the canopy of an old elm tree.

In the vicinity of the food market we also discovered a swimming pool surrounded by a wire fence and a rectangle of shrubs. We walked up to the entrance and peeked in through a half-open gate. An old man slept in his chair, having dropped a newspaper onto the ground. Children were jumping into the water and screaming with delight. Topless women—were they the children's mothers?—sat in chaise lounges and sipped from tall narrow bottles.

"It's probably private. Let's go," said my father.

"Why don't we ask?" said my mother as she went through the gate. She came back in a little while, smiling. "I spoke to a lifeguard. Very friendly. This is actually a community pool. The daily fee is only three shillings."

We went back to the hostel, quickly changed, and went back to the pool. As we walked there, the sun hid itself behind hefty clouds, and it started raining. We ended up returning and spending the rest of the day in our rooms and the hostel's sitting room. At one point in the afternoon long-nosed Charlotte yelled out our last name from the reception area in her shrill voice; our Russian friends had called from Rhode Island.

JIAS had arranged for the refugees to be served free breakfast and supper. Supper was at seven. In the hostel dining room we shared a table with Mrs. Perelman, the plump old lady from Moscow.

"You've met Charlotte, the owner?" Mrs. Perelman loudly whispered to us as soon as we had settled at the table.

"You mean Long Nose?" I asked.

"Well, that's not very nice, young man," the old lady admonished me.

"But it's true!"

And to all three of us Mrs. Perelman said: "You wouldn't believe what I heard this afternoon!"

"Dear Mrs. Perelman, let me guess," my father said playfully. "She's actually a man in disguise."

"But how can you say that? You're a doctor, an educated man! Not like some of the crude types staying here." Mrs. Perelman looked down at the vast majority of our fellow refugees, who came not from large Russian cities but from smaller cities and towns in the former Pale of Settlement, and who were culturally very different from us.

Mrs. Perelman removed a lacy handkerchief from her purse and continued. "Charlotte is such a nice, pleasant hostess. The poor thing, she's suffering so much. She'd been having . . . you know, a liaison."

"An affair? She's uglier than sin!" said my mother.

"Of course, she's no beauty," Mrs. Perelman replied. "But, as they say, ' . . . not by beauty alone.' I met a nice lady from Kiev. She's been here three weeks. This lady has a bad heart, so she's not going to Italy, like most of us, but directly to Brooklyn, where her daughter lives. So this nice lady told me Charlotte had been involved with some horrid man from Western Ukraine."

Mrs. Perelman tempestuously blew her nose and took a sip of hot cocoa.

"So who's this man?" my mother asked.

"A nothing, a provincial. A real swindler, too, I've heard. He's got poor Charlotte twisted around his finger. By the end of the week, I'm told, he had her bringing him breakfast in bed. Unbelievable!"

"So where's the Carpathian gigolo now?" my father asked.

"Oh, he left a few days ago, before we arrived. And supposedly it has turned out he was two-timing Charlotte with another woman, a refugee. Oh, the poor girl. What was she thinking—getting involved with this swindler? Well, I should be going. Good night to all of you!"

The old lady got up and waddled toward the door, leaving us with a vague aftertaste of anxiety—what about, we couldn't yet tell.

THE NEXT MORNING our plan was to have breakfast and head to Vienna to do more sightseeing. We were hoping to hitchhike; our allowance was too small for us to afford daily bus fares. We'd brought with us several tins of beluga caviar; back in Moscow we'd been told that it was easy to sell caviar to delicatessens or restaurants in Vienna.

The hostel's small dining room had dark wood paneling and flowery curtains around the windows. At the far end of the room there was a counter, behind which stood Long Nose, vigilantly watching the refugees. When we came down that morning, from the frozen expressions on the faces of the refugees I gleaned that something was going on. Long Nose gave us a skimming glance and turned to the two women who were helping her serve breakfast. These women, twin sisters in their sixties, came from the town of Czernowitz, in North Bukovina, an area that used to be part of the Austro-Hungarian Empire and later Romania before it was annexed by the Soviet Union and added to Ukraine. The sisters had been at the hostel for over a week. They spoke German and for a few shillings helped Charlotte with the serving and cleaning.

We joined Mrs. Perelman at our regular table, greeting her with a cheery "good morning," but she only nodded, without lifting her turtle head from the plate. The sisters brought each of us a cup of coffee, a roll, and a soft-boiled egg in a porcelain egg holder.

"What's wrong, Mrs. Perelman? Are you not feeling well this morning?" my father asked, ignoring the foreboding silence at the other tables.

"Just don't say anything," Mrs. Perelman whispered. "She's very angry today."

"She who?" my mother asked.

"The owner," said Mrs. Perelman, obviously avoiding Charlotte's name. "Please don't look at her!"

At that point I turned around in my chair to catch a glimpse of Long Nose, who stood behind the counter like a wax effigy. While turning, I touched the egg holder with my elbow and knocked it over. Issuing a loud peal, the egg holder broke into many small shards. The egg split open and the yolk, glossy and bright yellow, trickled across squares of beige tile.

Just picture the whole scene. Before I even had a chance to get up and pick up the egg mess from the floor, Long Nose screamed something in German and raced toward our table. She planted her stick legs apart and stood right in front of us. She stood so close to me that it seemed that the tip of her repulsive nose touched the rim of my cup. Her skinny finger pointed down to the floor, where the remains of the egg lay enmeshed with porcelain shards. She stood like this for what felt like a long time, silently staring at me, her finger, adorned with chipped oxblood nail polish, still pointing at the floor. Then she started walking back and forth across the narrow dining room, waving about her skinny, pale arms. Long Nose was shouting, first in German, then in English. She shouted in her disgusting, ringing voice right into the faces of the terrified refugees as they hastily gulped their coffee and swallowed their breakfasts.

It was hard to imagine that a scene as repugnant as that could be happening in the West, in the free world, and not in the Soviet Union, from which our group of Soviet Jews had just escaped. Why did she yell? Why did she throw this ugly scene? Was it a residual something, something going back to the time when her father, a young SS soldier green out of training, participated in the deportations of the Jews of Vienna to Teriesenstadt? Though probably just the fiction of an impressionable twenty year old, this altogether different scenario did cross my mind. Was it the word *Juden*, the flesh-creeping word *Juden*, which pulsated through Long Nose's head as she stood there, screaming about the high cost of hot water, the large outlay of energy in the rooms, the constant ringing of the telephone from America and Canada, and the "idle refugees" always watching TV in the common room?

My parents and I got up and walked out in the middle of breakfast. We wanted to get away, leaving behind Gablitz, the hostel, the humiliation of being at the mercy of shrieking Long Nose. For a while, as we stood on the curb of the highway trying to hitchhike, memories of Long Nose continued to hurt our eardrums. Gradually it all dissolved in the highway's hum. We waited for at least half an hour before someone finally stopped for us.

The car that had pulled over was a silver-gray Jaguar. Did we look miserable enough in our best Soviet clothes? How had its owner managed to discern through our poisoned smiles that we had been mauled, violated, humiliated? The owner of the Jaguar asked us, first in German, then in English, where we were going. (Where? Anywhere, away from this shame!) He smiled compassionately. He moved his things from the back seat into the trunk. And during the ride to Vienna, he didn't barrage us with intrusive questions.

Half an hour later my parents and I were sitting in soft velour chairs in a café on Kärtner Ring. Or was it Kärtner Strasse? We weren't sure, we didn't know; the flight from Gablitz had been a small miracle. The owner of the Jaguar, whose name was Günter W., had not only brought us to the center of Vienna, but also insisted that we join him for a cup of coffee and dessert.

And so there we were, sitting with Günter W. at a fancy *Koffeehaus* with gilded mirrors and gallant waiters, all four of us having a drink called *Kapuziner*. For each of us, Günter had ordered apple strudel and *Sachertorte*.

"You absolutely must try these," said Günter. "They're classic Viennese deserts."

The strangest thing was that Günter, an Austrian, enjoyed the coffee and pastries no less than we did. We had never tasted such a splendid coffee drink before. Ka-pu-zi-ner! It was weightless in the throat. It must have been made from a wispy summer cloud.

"Here, in Vienna, in the most unassuming place, they serve many, many different kinds of coffee," Günter sang out, whistling through a little coquettish sip.

Günter's portrait: of average height, fiftyish, stout, and lively. His head and the folds of his neck move all the time. When laughing he shakes, and his shiny cheeks turn deep crimson. He speaks in a purring, quiet voice, the sounds drifting up from his earthy vocal cords. He wears a summer jacket with yellow and beige checks and a pair of navy slacks.

Sitting in the Viennese café, I felt an urge to call him "Uncle Günter." Dear Uncle Günter. Good gnome Günter. Several times I also felt like pinching myself, in case I was daydreaming! Just an hour ago, Long Nose had been smashing dishes and yelling at us in her disgusting, ringing voice, and now Günter was treating us to divine coffee and celestial pastries at this luxuriant Viennese café.

After ordering us coffee and dessert, Günter gently pressed his right hand on top of my father's. "My dear friend," he said, "I understand what it's like to be a refugee."

He told us that in May 1945 his wife's family escaped from Southern Bohemia, in Czechoslovakia, where they had been living for centuries—when it was still part of the Austro-Hungarian Empire. They got into their Opel—parents, grandparents, Günter's wife, and her sister—and all drove across the border to Austria, abandoning everything. Günter said they were "fearful of the Red Serpent." He said it, and my parents and I solemnly nodded at the bloody image of Soviet Russia conjured up by this kindly Austrian.

Not until we were almost finished with our coffee and pastries did Günter inquire about our long-term plans.

"America?" Günter pursed his lips. "Why are you going there? There is no antiquity there, too little culture. How old is that church? So it dates back to the time of Mickey Mouse? Ho-ho-ho!" Günter giggled at his own joke.

What could we say? And why shouldn't we have laughed at Günter's impression of Americans? Uncle Günter with his marvelous Kapuziner, his gentle manner of talking, and his jovial laughter was the best medicine for our Soviet wounds.

"I'm afraid I must be going," Günter said in a guilty tone of voice. "Otherwise I'll be late for a meeting with some clients."

"If I may so inquire," my mother gathered the courage to ask in her textbook-perfect English, "what do you do?"

"Oh, how silly of me. I own a leather company. Belts, wallets, briefcases, lady's purses."

We exchanged addresses, or, actually, we traded our promise to write from the New World for Günter's card with an ornate weave of letters. The first to get up from his velour chair, Günter W. bent at the waist and kissed my mother's hand, gently gripping her wrist. He shook my father's hand for a long time. And he tapped me on the shoulder.

"Good luck in your studies, young fellow," he told me. "And be good to your parents! They are lovely people."

Then Günter smiled, a confused or culpable smile. Together the four of us walked out of the café. A few minutes later, already without Günter, we were strolling down Kärtner Strasse. Reaching in his side jacket pocket for a handkerchief, my father discovered an orange envelope with "Bon voyage" scribbled across the middle. Dear sweet gnome Günter! A real Austrian romantic, in whose nature German barley sentimentality was mixed with the Italian capacity to hearken to every moment's revelation. With trembling fingers, my father removed a mauve bank note from the orange envelope. One thousand shillings!

In a short while, after we had collectively figured out how much one thousand shillings was worth in American dollars, I parted with my parents for the day. I was wearing a pair of faded blue jeans, brown suede sneakers, and a cotton shirt with green, pale blue, and white squares. I had just enough money to get back to Gablitz from Vienna. On my back danced a nylon blue backpack containing a sweater and three tins of beluga caviar I was hoping to sell to some restaurant or delicatessen. I headed toward the long-legged consumptive steeple of St. Stephan, which beckoned me from afar. Soon I ended up in a pedestrian area, Graben, where every building was a fancy store or a restaurant. I entered three restaurants in a row but was too embarrassed to offer my goods. Elegant middle-aged ladies and dignified balding gentlemen were having their lunches in plush chairs with soft armrests. Clockwork waiters fussed about the tables. I finally found a restaurant where the dining room seemed less posh and the customers younger and mustered courage to walk up across the carpet to a tall headwaiter with a perfectly groomed white mustache.

"How much do you want for the caviar, my friend?"

"One hundred shillings a tin." At the time a U.S. dollar equaled about ten shillings, and a tin of beluga caviar sold for four to five times what I asked.

The waiter smiled sympathetically and shook his head.

"No," he sighed. "Not interested. I don't even have caviar on the menu."

"But we could negotiate." I all but begged him to buy the caviar.

"I suppose, my friend, I could buy them for my wife. She likes caviar for breakfast. I'll give you one hundred fifty shillings for all three of them."

He counted out three crisp bills from his fat, oversized wallet, handed me the money, and with his muscular shoulder he nudged me to the exit.

I soon found a record store with posters of Whitney Houston in the display window. She wore a white tank top and smiled a big, lifeless smile. I spent half an hour lovingly picking up and putting back the records and tapes of The Beatles, a cult band among my Moscow friends. Finally I chose a cassette of *Abbey Road*.

The salesgirl was two heads taller than me, large-chested, with straight yellow hair. Her hair was kept from falling onto her face by daisy hairpins. In my head I called her "Gargamela." Her actual name turned out to be Steffi. Steffi the giantess listened politely to my account of the circumstances that had led to my family's emigration. She was the first non-Soviet my age I'd met in the West. I just couldn't stop talking to her. Two customers stood behind me, waiting for their turn.

"Steffi," I said in English, having by now brought her through customs at the Moscow airport. "What are you doing tomorrow? Would you like to meet?"

"Thank you, but I can't. My boyfriend and I are going to the beach." What beach in Vienna? I thought.

"Well, some other time," I said, and waved goodbye to Steffi.

I was getting tired of stores where I couldn't afford most things, and I decided to turn onto a small side street. Red neon signs sprang up from the buildings. *Sex Shop. Girls-Girls-Girls. X-Rated.* A porno movie. How many times had my Soviet peers and I imagined what it was like! I bought a ticket to one of the movie theaters and descended a littered staircase. Instead of a house with rows of seats there were tables and chairs, arranged like a café or a cabaret. A half-dozen men, some with drinks, were there watching. The film was almost halfway through. In the part I saw, a little man was being entertained by a host of ladies in a hotel room. The film was in German, but I did make out that the ladies referred to their client as "Kleine." They had Kleine tied to a bed. In turn, they took off their clothes and teased the little man. They finally left him on the brink of pleasure and drove off to some palace, where a marble Antaeus left his post at the fronton and in turn made love to each of the ladies. The lights were turned on, a few people walked out, a few came in. Several remained sitting at their tables in a stupor.

Soon the film began again, and I sat through the first half. When poor Kleine and the harlots appeared on the screen again, I got up and went to the washroom, where, in a stall strewn with cavemen's hieroglyphs and drawings, I hurriedly helped myself.

It was already well into the afternoon when I walked out of the dungeon, and I decided to turn toward Stephansplatz, Vienna's main square. Approaching the cathedral, I paused to touch the last remaining tree of the Vienna Woods within the confines of the city—actually not a tree but a disfigured trunk—for good luck. In front of St. Stephan's main gate there lay, sat, or stood, leaning upon their crutches, beggars of all ages and kinds. Several were playing musical instruments: a wheezy accordion, a recorder, a violin. Not too far from the cathedral, men in Peruvian costumes were prancing and playing. I also spotted ten or twelve punk rockers, whose upturned mohawks, in red, green, and purple, echoed the sharp spears of the cathedral's Gothic towers. The punks stood there peacefully, smoking and chatting. No one seemed to pay any attention to their presence. In the Soviet Union, they would've been picked up and driven away in a police van.

I examined the inside of St. Stephan's, and then added myself to a guided tour of the catacombs. There, I was told, in special copper urns, lie the intestines of the Hapsburg emperors. I wondered whether a secret link existed among digestion, faith, and dynastic power, but was afraid to ask the guide, a stern lady with the face of a precocious herring. I left the cathedral feeling pangs of hunger. I was standing in the middle of Stephansplatz surrounded by Asian tourists, hippies in rainbow T-shirts, punks, and just ordinary denizens of Vienna when suddenly. . . . It was Greta, Greta Schmidt, Greta from Chashnikovo. She was only a few steps away from me, studying the façade of St. Stephan's. Was it really her?

"Greta!" I shouted.

"Oh my God! What are you doing here?"

"We finally got out. We emigrated. This is my second day here."

"See, I always knew you had a secret of some sort."

"I couldn't tell you we were refuseniks. It was dangerous. Only my closest friends knew."

"We were pretty close."

"I know. I'm sorry. But wait, what are *you* doing in Vienna?"

"I'm here for a long weekend."

"A long weekend? Since when do girls travel from the Soviet countryside to Vienna for long weekends?"

"See, you couldn't tell me your family was trying to emigrate," Greta said. "I couldn't either. And then, two months after you and I had said goodbye, my family got permission to emigrate to Germany. We packed in three weeks and were gone."

"That's incredible! I would've never expected to see you abroad, in Vienna of all places."

"It's no different than Soviet Jews going to live in Israel."

"Or not going. I guess you're right." I paused, thinking about Greta's words. "So how's it been?"

"Fantastic! I'd just finished high school in Russia when we left, and in Germany I had to do my final year again. Classes were pretty hard, and I couldn't write well in German. But I studied a lot. They gave me credit for Russian as a foreign language, which helped me graduate. Last year I entered a university in Heidelberg. I want to be an art historian. I'm actually in Vienna to look at some paintings for a term paper."

"Do you miss Russia?" I asked.

"Not a bit. It's like I woke up one day in my new home, and it felt as though I'd always lived there. My parents, they feel different. But for me Germany is home now."

"Do you feel like you're forgetting Russian?" I asked. Greta and I were speaking Russian.

"I don't know. I rarely speak it outside of the family. Occasionally I write to my old girlfriends. We write in Russian, of course, but it's getting harder without practice. My life's so different now. I can't even explain certain things in Russian. So yes, I probably am losing my Russian. I don't really think about it. What's the point?"

"Greta, it's so good to see you," I said, glancing down at her yellow tennis shoes. "I still can't get over it, running into each other like this. And where? In the middle of Stephansplatz. No one would believe this!"

"I know."

"Listen, I'm starving. Is there a student cafeteria of some sort around here? Do you want to get something to eat?"

"I'd love to," Greta said, "but I'm meeting some friends from my university. And I'm already late."

"What about the day after tomorrow? I plan to be in Vienna again."

"That would be great."

"You want to meet here at eleven?"

"Eleven is perfect. See you soon."

She kissed me on the cheek and disappeared into the seething crowd. I slowly walked across the square back to Graben and found a quiet café. Quickly adding the prices in my head, I ordered a beer and a cheese sandwich and sat in the café's cool semidarkness, listening to Chet Baker sing and play trumpet. "Your looks are laughable, unphotographable . . . " Smoky clouds of recollections were rhythmically descending upon me the way morning fog falls on a lake's clear surface.

I met Greta Schmidt in June 1985. I'd just finished my first year at Moscow University, and I was spending the first two summer months in Chashnikovo, a small town some forty miles north of Moscow, in the direction of Leningrad. It was technically considered a town because it had a school and used to have a church, but it was really a village with geese strolling along the unpaved streets. In Chashnikovo, Moscow University had a summer campus and a research lab, and students in my department were required to spend a "field semester" there, studying botany and geology.

Greta and I met just a couple of days after I arrived in Chashnikovo. I was looking for a post office to mail a letter to my parents and asked her for directions. I had turned eighteen; Greta was seventeen and had just finished high school. She had liquid blue eyes and a solicitous smile. Her ash-blonde hair was arranged in two tight braids. The day I met her she had on a faded orange sun dress and a pair of tall black rubber boots. There was ankle-high mud on many streets of the village.

Greta, who had spent her entire life in Chashnikovo, came from a family of the so-called Volga Germans. The ancestors of the Volga Germans, thousands of them, moved to the Russian Empire under Catherine II and founded prosperous agricultural colonies along the Volga basin. They became part of Russia and regarded it as their true home, although they retained their language and traditions much the way the Amish have in the United States. When Hitler invaded the Soviet Union, about half a million Volga Germans were rounded up and exiled to Kazakhstan and Siberia, many of them dying en route. The Soviet textbooks said nothing about the mass deportation, whose American parallel was the internment of the Japanese Americans during World War II.

In the 1970s, the Volga Germans began to apply for exit visas to emigrate to West Germany. I found it fascinating that after almost two centuries of living in Russia, they would uproot themselves again to move to a country with which they had a largely symbolic connection. Was it the same as Jews who struggled to leave Russia, where they did not feel welcome? A Jewish refusenik and an internal émigré, I identified with the Volga Germans, which is probably one of the reasons I found myself drawn to Greta and her family history.

Greta's parents, who were children when the Nazis invaded the Soviet Union in 1941, were deported with their families to West Siberia, to the Kulunda Steppe, a remote area just east of the Kazakh border and northwest of the great Altai Mountains. Prior to the deportation, their families had been living in Engels, a city on the Volga. Greta's maternal grandfather had a job as an agronomist; one of her grandmothers taught history in a German-language school. In West Siberia, Greta's grandparents became collective farmers. Her mother had been orphaned at the end of the war and raised by relatives. In the late 1950s, after serving in the Soviet military, Greta's father was able to get into college in Moscow and study agronomy, like his own father. A stroke of luck had landed him a job at the university research facility in Chashnikovo. He wrote for his fiancée back in Kulunda, and she married him and moved from West Siberia. Greta's parents had two children and spoke German at home and Russian in the street. Greta's mother cooked German food and kept a decrepit Bible in a secret drawer. Greta's own knowledge of Germany and of the lost world of the Volga Germans came from reading whatever she could find in the miserable village library at Chashnikovo, but mainly it came from her parents' stories of their life prior to the deportation.

Greta and I saw each other every night, after I was done with my duties of digging holes and labeling samples of soil and rocks. We made love in haystacks under the open night sky. We lay in each other's arms, listening to a mare's anxious neighing, to freight trains hooting as they pulled out of a distant railway station. I told her about my favorite paintings at the Pushkin Museum in Moscow. She didn't know what impressionism meant, and at the time I thought I did. When I met her, Greta had only been to Moscow three times—this living only an hour away. Although German by origin, she was, in most of her ways, a Russian country girl.

However happy and nostalgic, this chance meeting in Stephansplatz left me befuddled. Back in Chashnikovo, I had found our summertime romance so alluring and delectable because it was framed by the Russian countryside. If Greta and I had met on my urban turf in Moscow, she would have seemed provincial, despite her natural intelligence and Boticellian looks. And here she was now, in smart Western clothes, fluent in German, comfortable in her skin and surroundings. And it was I who seemed so out of place amid the motley crowd of Stephansplatz; it was I who was now a Soviet provincial on the streets and squares of courtly Vienna. I sat in the café, sipped my blonde beer, ate my feeble cheese sandwich, and tried to make sense of such an unexpected change of fortune. A flock of Roma women with children flowed past the café in the direction of St. Stephan's. A teenage Roma girl gave me a quick biting look, reminding me it was time to return to Gablitz.

I got back to our hostel right before supper, cleansed of the memories of that morning's scandal in the dining room. But the next morning, as soon as my parents and I crossed the threshold of the dining room and saw Long Nose standing behind the counter and supervising the serving of breakfast, we turned around and left. We walked to the food market and bought instant coffee. We boiled water in my parents' room, using an electrical device called *kipyatil'nik,* which we had brought with us from Moscow. For the rest of our time in Gablitz we followed the same routine. We took long walks in Wienerwald. We picnicked on bread, cheese, and cured meats purchased from the ruddy-faced smiling fellow at the food market. We sat out by the communal pool in the company of Austrian children and their topless mothers. All the stress of the last weeks before leaving Russia, coupled with the aftershock of having emigrated, had finally bubbled up to the surface. We felt endlessly tired, and we relaxed—aimlessly, sweetly.

TWO DAYS AFTER BUMPING INTO HER at Stephansplatz, I saw Greta again. That morning I hitchhiked to Vienna and met her in front of St. Stephan's. She was wearing a cobalt blue sleeveless dress, which harmonized with her eyes.

"What do you want to do?" she asked.

"Perhaps we could go to a museum."

"Any preferences?"

"Well, I love Bosch. His *Last Judgment,* the triptych with all sorts of wonderful monsters, is supposed to be somewhere in Vienna."

"That's right," Greta instantly replied. "It's in the Academy of Fine Arts."

"Can we go?"

"I guess so, but wouldn't you rather see something modern?"

"Like what?"

"Like the Sezession."

"What's that in Russian?"

"That would be the Artists' Union. Haven't you heard of Jugendstil?" Greta looked at me with surprise, and I had a flashback of myself saying to her as we lay in a Russian haystack: "Greta, haven't you heard of Edgar Degas?"

"Not really," I answered.

"Klimt? Schiele?" Greta looked genuinely perplexed.

"Yes, I've heard of them. But I'd really like to see Bosch."

"We can go to both places. They're next to each other."

We walked down the broad Kärtner Strasse past the State Opera House. I remembered and told Greta a bittersweet anecdote about an elderly Jewish-Russian lady who was finally allowed to emigrate after a draining decade of applying and reapplying and losing her husband along the way. On her first night in Vienna, she went to the opera to see *Aïda* and died of a heart attack during the last act.

"I don't like Bosch," Greta said after we exited the academy. "Too depressing. And what kind of a Last Judgment is it anyhow if no one is being saved? They cannot all be sinners. At least some should deserve salvation."

"I like that a lot," I replied. "No one will be saved. That's great! Total punishment for humankind."

We walked silently for two blocks. What Greta called Sezession turned out to be a white stone building I would have taken for a synagogue or, perhaps, a mosque, except it was missing a minaret. The roof was crowned by a small dome covered in gold leaf. The faces of three muses adorned the façade. Two lines in gilded German lettering were written across the frieze. I recognized the word "Kunst."

"To time its art, to art its freedom," Greta translated for me. Her eyes brightened.

After touring the Sezession's collection, we looked for a place to have lunch.

"It's my treat," said Greta. "You'll take me out next time."

Whenever might that be? I thought to myself.

She suggested a fast-food place that smelled of fried oil. The menu was in German. Nothing seemed familiar.

"Why don't you get me whatever you're having?"

I sat down at a plastic table and watched Greta place the order and smile to the man working the counter. Then Greta brought a tray with two orders of fish, fried in light brown batter and flanked by fried potatoes, and two elongated bottles of an orange soda.

"This is called 'fish and chips' in English."

"When did you learn English?"

"I took it my senior year in high school, and I'm taking it now at the university."

"I like this name, fish and chips. Thanks."

"Could I ask you a question?" Greta said and took a long sip of orange soda. "How come you and your parents didn't go to Israel? Isn't that where your roots are?"

Oh, come on, Greta, not you. Don't do this to me! I thought before answering.

"That's a hard question. Well, I guess it's because we aren't convinced it's the right place for us. And we don't like half-measures. Going to Israel after the Soviet Union would be a half measure. We want to live in a vast country, where one could lose oneself. Without having to be a part of anything."

"That's so interesting. I don't think I could ever live in America. Or anywhere outside Germany for that matter. Not even in Austria. Germany took us back like her own prodigal children." Tears welled up in Greta's eyes, and I felt a little awkward being their witness. She wiped them dry, leaving black tire prints on her handkerchief. "We should probably get going," she added, folding the handkerchief and placing it back in her purse.

We didn't speak as we walked back to Stephansplatz. A juggler was in the middle of his performance when we arrived at the square. A tight ring of onlookers surrounded the juggler. An old monkey in a red shirt waddled along the inside of the human ring with a hat. She curtsied to everyone who gave her money.

"Look, there's Johann," Greta pulled me by the sleeve. She was beaming.

A tall, broad-chested fellow in a cotton sleeveless vest over a dark blue shirt approached us. Everything about him, including his small round glasses, seemed serious and benevolent.

"This is Johann, my fiancé. He knows all about you."

Johann shook my hand energetically and said in English: "Congratulations! Greta told me your family had it pretty tough."

"Thanks. Yeah. But we made it." I tried to hide my bewilderment at seeing Greta's fiancé. She hadn't said a word about him.

"Well," Johann put his arm around Greta, "I'm sure Greta told you that if you're ever in Germany our home is always open to you."

He shook my limp hand again. Greta brush-kissed me on the cheek, and they trotted off.

I can't vouch that everything happened precisely as I've described it here. A dense milky-blue fog envelops some of my Austrian memories as I recall those first days in the West. Remember, record, and, yes, reinvent them in English. It's been almost twenty years since I left Moscow and went to Vienna.

Imagine how I felt—as though I'd just been born. I remember slowly traversing Stephansplatz. I left behind smoking monsters with green horns and laughing dwarfs with blue beards. A bespectacled basilisk in a bumble bee bowtie waved me goodbye. A chorus of nymphs of Graben performed "The Vienna Woods" to a crowd of gleeful serpents. A black wild boar in a knitted vest offered his wares on a wooden tray: acorns, hazelnuts, and orange chanterelles. Two silver dragons patrolled the streets. A family of yellow snails each the size of a cat climbed a mossy gutter. A couple of toads with cowbells on their necks flitted by me, giggling and holding hands. A blind sphinx turned the handle of an ornate music box. The year was 1987. The Berlin Wall hadn't yet come down. I had a few shillings in my pocket and several shots left in my old Russian camera.

2

The Manchurian Trunk

The middle of June, 1987. We were leaving Vienna by the night express. The entire train had been chartered by JIAS to transport a group of about 150 Soviet refugees to Rome, the next station on our journey. Vienna had been our entrance to the West, a perfect place to experience a culture shock, especially if you were twenty, as I was at the time, and had spent an entire life behind what they used to call the "Iron Curtain." (I write this not without some embarrassment, but let the fat sheep of rhetoric graze the Alpine slopes I would cross on the way to Italy.) Although we had been in Vienna for about ten days, the time has been lengthened in my memory, every day's finite time multiplied by innumerable "firsts": first cappuccino, first porno film, first taste of Nazism, first ride in a Jaguar, first. . . .

The platform of the Süd-Bahnhof where we boarded the Italy-bound train was guarded by blond lads my age who held tommy guns like village bread loaves. Their guns looked like toys compared to the AK-47s that, at high school military training in Moscow, I had learned to disassemble and reassemble in some ridiculously short time—how short, I can no longer recall. All of us refugees had been warned to be careful and vigilant, although the JIAS officials weren't telling us exactly what to fear.

The refugees stood on the platform, vaguely anxious, the word *terrorist* dancing in our minds. The refugees discussed a possible terrorist attack at the Vienna train station. I remember my father talking with a bearded mathematician from Novosibirsk about the eleven Israeli athletes killed by Palestinian terrorists at the Munich Olympics of 1972, and about a 1981 bomb explosion in a square in Ostia outside Rome, where large groups of Soviet Jews would socialize in the evening. Palestinian terrorists, the Red Brigades, and Basque separatists were mentioned. On some perverse emotional level the word *terrorist* at the time possessed a romantic aura in my imagination. Even as I write this, the purple dusk of a Boston winter afternoon hanging outside my windows, I recall, with a rush of blood that accompanies a recognition of one's past self, reading in Soviet high school about the terrorists tossing bombs at the tsar's carriage.

None of us had tickets for the Vienna-Rome express. A JIAS official stood on the platform with a clipboard and list of typed names. This was the same self-absorbed official, a native of Bessarabia and a Holocaust survivor, who had earlier interviewed my family at the Vienna JIAS office while petting a Pekinese lapdog. Dressed in a colorful sport coat with a yellow tie, he was now reading names out loud and marking them off his list. His gold teeth sparkled in the gentle rays of the setting Central European sun. Everything was aglitter: the roofs of Vienna, the spire of Stephansplantz, the silver trays in the pastry shops. The nymphs of Graben, those Viennese ladies of the night, were combing their golden hair. I was thinking, would I ever see them again?

As we waited on the platform, Anatoly Shteynfeld, the former classics professor, came up and greeted us. We hadn't seen him since the day we'd all flown into Austria.

"Have you enjoyed your visit to Vienna?" he asked in phrasebook English.

"Thank you," father replied, also in English, unsure of what Shteynfeld had asked.

"I heard they'd put you up at some God-awful dormitory outside Vienna," Shteynfeld said, still in English, now addressing my mother. "In the Vienna Woods, wasn't it?"

"Yes, in the country," mother replied, voice soaring. "You're so lucky. I so wish we'd stayed in Vienna." Mother adored the English language and was eager to practice it.

"Well, I simply loved Vienna," Shteynfeld said, straightening a red paisley ascot that looked brand new.

"You've even managed to do some shopping, haven't you?" mother asked him, with a grammatical playfulness that struck me as oddly coquettish. Father stood there, looking none too pleased. He was quite insecure about his English, but he also didn't want to appear inane. Thus he chose not to speak at all, either in English or in Russian.

Then Shteynfeld's name was called, and he zipped up his beige denim coat and picked up two identical plaid suitcases. "Arrivederci, signora," he said to my mother. "See you in Rome. Ciao." And he glided toward his train car.

"Show-off," father grumbled.

"Don't be sore," mother shot back. "He's a very educated man. A true European, unlike many of the shtetl Jews on this transport," she added, under her breath.

The list of the refugees' names wasn't alphabetical, one of the many details that didn't make sense. The whole scene was perfect for a sentimental comedy, except it seemed far less comic to us back then. "What if they run out of seats?" my grandmother kept asking, but we ignored her questions while vaguely thinking the same thing. The chosen families, the lucky ones, who were named first, would step out of the crowd and proceed toward the train car to which they were assigned. Where were they taking us? No tickets, no seats. Vienna-Rome, that's all we knew. What was next? What lay ahead? Definitely a summer in Italy, perhaps even longer, depending on the speed at which our refugee papers were to be processed for American refugee visas.

A burly fellow with blazing red whiskers and mustache, flushed cheeks, and a beer belly stood under the platform clock. Every so often he barked something in German into his walkie-talkie. He smoked a fat cigar. "The Vienna police commissioner himself is here," someone whispered, and soon the entire crowd of refugees echoed with the words "police commissioner, police commissioner."

"Finally," my grandmother sighed when the JIAS official with gold teeth read our three last names—my parents' and mine, my aunt's and my little cousin's, and my grandmother's. Picking up our suitcases, we made our way to the middle of the train. And here memory tries to pull a trick and erase ten minutes of the departure scene, the ten minutes where my aunt's and grandmother's baggage is captured on film as it is being hauled to the train in slow motion, owing to its extreme weight and the inordinate number of individual pieces. I won't let those ten minutes of dragging and kicking my relatives' baggage along the platform spoil the scene of leaving Vienna. I'll speak about my aunt's pots and eiderdowns when we get to Rome—if we get to Rome. And especially about that old dark orange trunk of my aunt's that my father and I could barely lift off the ground. For now, follow me inside the train car where my parents and I shared a sleeper during our one-night journey across the Alps. For security reasons, so we were told, the refugees occupied not every compartment, but every other. In the case of my aunt, I hasten to add, this was also done to accommodate her extensive collection of baggage. I must have been so overcome with the sensation of leaving the city where the West had started for me—and also so focused on the anticipation of our journey, on Italy, on Rome—that I remember no faces or phrases, but only spectral images in sepia tones and the cascading voices of children. Goodbye, Vienna. *Auf Wiedersehen! Adieu!*

The platform had grown empty, except for the Austrian tin soldiers stationed near the front and back of every car. The man we believed to be the Vienna police commissioner had finished smoking his Havana, tossed it like a dart into a trash can, and motioned with his right hand. We heard a whistle, then a whistle's shrill echo. The train jerked and pushed off. "To Italy," my father said and kissed first my mother, then me. "Off we go."

My mother smiled feebly and began to unwrap our supper—caraway rye bread, cheese, hard-boiled eggs, tomatoes, cucumbers, and an assortment of Viennese pastries.

Why don't I remember reading any books—either on the train to Italy or later in Rome? We hadn't brought books with us from Moscow—the ones that the authorities had allowed us to take out of the country were traveling by land and sea to our friends' houses in New England. Still, I'm sure there were at least a few books with us on the train, as there had always been books in my parents' life and in mine; I just can't recall either their titles or even the experience of reading them. Later, in Italy, in the coastal Tyrrhenian town of Ladispoli where we would settle for the rest of the summer, we took out Russian books from the local Jewish refugee center. But on that half-full train taking us toward the foothills of the Alps? No books that I can recall, nor any newspapers or magazines. Only gazing. Peering out. Reading the landscape. Divining the future.

Miraculously, I slept through the night, missing the Alpine tunnels. In the morning, when I woke up, we were already approaching Rome. As it turned out, our train journey ended not at Termini, Rome's main train station, but at a smaller junction somewhere on the outskirts of the city. This arrangement seemed particularly outlandish because we knew that in Rome we were being put up in hotels and hostels right around Termini—a less-than-safe area, we had heard through the refugee grapevine. Disembarking the train at the little station was a last-minute security precaution, introduced, we were told, so as not to attract attention to such a large group of Jews. Outside the little station buses were already lined up awaiting our arrival. We were told to hurry onto the buses; by noon traffic was supposed to get hellish in Rome. Through the dusty windows of an old tour bus I caught my first glimpse of the Eternal City.

And here I've come to the unavoidable digression about my aunt and her baggage. At the time when we were refugees in Italy, my aunt was a divorcée, a tall brunette in her early forties. In Russia they might call a woman with my aunt's physique a "fierce brunette." Unlike my mother, who was conceived after the signing of the Molotov-Ribbentrop pact of 1939—during that brief prewar interlude of calm before the German invasion of 1941—my aunt definitely owed her conception to the jubilant Soviet summer of 1945 that followed the victory over Germany. As a child, my mother spent the war years in evacuation in Tashkent, the capital of Uzbekistan, whereas her younger sister spent her early childhood in postwar Moscow, never having tasted displacement and homelessness. In fact, my aunt had never lived away—or apart—from her mother, my maternal grandmother, who is almost ninety as I write these lines. My aunt was still a child when my grandparents divorced, and everyone in my family, my mother included, had always babied her, doted upon her, and tried to "spare" her. One of her favorite things as a teenager was to save up some pocket money and go

to Moscow's Central Farmer's Market, buy half a pound of the ambro-
sial farmer's cheese you can only find at farmers' markets in Russia,
and eat it whole for lunch. When she was in music conservatory, my
aunt had her heart broken by a popular stage actor of the Moscow
Taganka Theater, a man with a husky voice and not much in the way of
genuine talent. She ended up marrying a slender gold-rimmed young
man from a good family, son of an aerodynamics inventor. The father
of my aunt's ex-husband was a tall Jewish grandee; his mother was a
teacher at a vocational high school, a buxom Russian woman with Tar-
tar cheeks and eyes. My aunt's husband collected icons and had chronic
head colds. They had a daughter, my junior by almost nine years, and
divorced after my aunt told him she wanted to follow her sister "to
exile." At the time when we left Russia and came to Vienna and Rome,
my aunt dressed in tight-fitting, bright-colored clothes, usually wore
her long jet-black hair in a knotted ponytail, applied shaggy mascara to
her eyelashes, and exuded waves of exhausting liveliness.

There are things about my aunt I will never know or understand.
She had been unbelievably kind to me in my childhood and teens. The
first huge strain in our relationship dates back to that late morning
in Rome when the pukey Italian tour bus circled around Piazza della
Repubblica before pulling into a street east of Termini. The central
train station in Rome used to be flanked by a fiefdom of pickpockets
and pimps. The bus stopped at the corner of a narrow street, and the
driver signaled that we had arrived. On the bus with us was an official
from the large Rome office of JIAS. The official was a vampire of a
woman, heavily made-up, speaking Russian fluently but with a strange,
squeaky accent. She came to Italy with her parents after World War
II; they had spent the war hiding in the Transylvanian countryside.
She explained that we were being lodged in a hotel located "just a few
steps from here," in the sixth floor of an apartment building. "It's a
few houses down on the left, with large marble steps," she added after
going through a list of the refugees' names. "Take your belongings and
follow me," she said.

Among the three of us, my parents and I had five suitcases, four
heavy ones that my father and I would carry, and a lighter valise that

was my mother's responsibility. This way we could get around without having to leave behind any of our possessions. Imagine a whole life, my twenty and my parents' combined one hundred years, arranged in five suitcases! Plus there was my mother's purse, my father's briefcase, and his Olympia typewriter (the briefcase and typewriter would be belted to suitcases). Among the three of them, my aunt, grandmother, and little cousin had at least fifteen suitcases plus various smaller bags, sacks, and bundles. What was in most of these suitcases remains a mystery to this day. Sheets of music? Metronomes? Framed pictures of my aunt's favorite composers? During the three months we spent in Austria and Italy, I acquired an intimate knowledge of my aunt's baggage. I'm referring, mainly, to the shape and weight of the pieces, not to what was inside. But there was one item whose contents were revealed to me during that first, calamitous morning in Rome.

It was a trunk that my late grandfather, then a major in the corps of communications, had brought back from Manchuria in 1946. I imagine it had once belonged to the wife of a Scottish missionary. By the time we were leaving the Soviet Union, my grandfather's trunk had become as old as the century itself. It was badly scratched, and its bright orange leather had faded. But structurally it was still sound. What was inside the trunk? My aunt and grandmother had packed as though they were going not to America, the land of plenty, but to a remote and barely inhabited island in the Indian Ocean. They brought with them various household items, including dishes and pans, pillows and blankets, nails and tools, and even a cast-iron meat grinder.

My aunt evaded my questions about the contents of the orange Manchurian trunk. At first my questions were playful. Later they became blunt. "Some of my personal things," she would answer dreamily.

After we had checked into our hotel room, a dingy affair with cracked ceilings, cobwebs, and a folding cot that was to be my bed for about the next ten days, my father and I went downstairs to transport my aunt's baggage. My mother stayed behind in the room, exhausted after a sleepless night on the train, also ashamed of her sister's and mother's baggage, which was becoming the talk of our refugee community.

When my father and I had returned to the bus, we discovered my aunt, her eyes shining with revolutionary fervor, giving instructions to three immigrant males who had been on the bus with us. The Italian bus driver, who looked like a turn-of-the-century anarchist, stood in the shadow of a plane tree, smoking and observing us with lazy bemusement. Perhaps he was a cultural anthropologist who couldn't find professional employment? Again, I don't know. During that summer in Italy I encountered a number of Italian intellectuals working as porters, parking attendants, museum guards. In fact, the porter at the pitiful hotel where we stayed in Rome was one of those underemployed intellectuals.

The three men whom my aunt had recruited to help with the luggage had families waiting for them at the hotel. One of them was a chess master from Kharkov, a quiet, thin, ulcerial fellow who had had a hard time carrying his own bags. The other two were first cousins from Odessa, Misha and Grisha, both unshaven and glistening with steely beads of sweat. Soviet collectivism hadn't been washed out of their systems, and there they were, standing before my aunt's lined-up baggage, listening to her instructions.

"Very careful with these two," said my aunt in the voice of a Soviet Young Pioneer, forbidding of irony. "Extremely fragile contents."

By the time the five of us—my father, myself, and the three helpers—had reached the hotel, the two cousins were swearing like true grandsons of Odessa's legendary longshoremen (see Isaac Babel's gangster stories).

"You lucky guy," one of the interchangeable cousins said to my father. "Great family to be married into."

"I wasn't marrying my sister-in-law," my father replied.

"Yeah, right," said the other cousin, and spat on the ground.

What was my father supposed to do—stand there with two suitcases in hand and defend my aunt's—and his own—honor?

Here I come to the point where the story begins to spin out of control. After delivering my aunt's bags to the entrance of the neobaroque building where our hotel occupied the sixth floor, the two cousins had finally remembered they were now in the free world, where no one stuck his neck out for anybody.

"We're out of here! You fellows are on your own," they told me and my father. "Your family business."

The chess master was slowly approaching on his sandpiper legs, and I could see that he was about to collapse under the weight of the fiberglass suitcase he was carrying.

"Wait here, papa." I grabbed two suitcases and ran up the building's tall marble steps in order to call the elevator.

After pressing the call button many different ways, after banging on the doors, I gave up and began my ascent to the sixth floor by the stairs. Every flight of stairs seemed to be getting longer and longer, defying all norms of classical architecture. When I finally reached the hotel floor, my legs felt like two sacks of lead pellets.

"What's going on?" I asked the porter in English. "Why isn't the elevator working?"

"It's not working because I turned it off," the porter replied, also in English. He was a short man in his late thirties, dressed in black pants and a gray shirt. A thin black scarf was wrapped around his neck, although it was summertime. In his hands, clad in black beggar's gloves, he held a pocket volume. I glanced at the page and saw lines of verse printed on it.

"We have a ton more stuff downstairs. Please turn it on," I pleaded, catching my breath.

"Turn it on, turn it off," the porter burbled. "Turn it off, turn it on."

"What?" I asked, unsure whether he was mocking me.

"Nothing. You're a young man. I don't understand why you Soviets are leaving your country. You think it's better in the West? Look at me, I'm a medical doctor, graduate of the University of Bologna, and I can't find professional employment. Is that what you want?"

"What are you, a communist?" I asked the porter.

"Yes, that's right, a communist. A real communist, not a Soviet one, like some of you people. That's why I tell you this: Things aren't any better over here than in the Soviet Union. And forget America, that's a God-awful place. I have cousins there. But I'm a patriot and that's why I live here in Italy. And you should be living in the Soviet Union. Everyone has a job there. They've got great universities. Not everything's perfect over there, sure, I understand, but is it ever?"

Under other circumstances I would have probably gotten into an argument with this man. I would have told him about growing up Jewish in Russia, about the nine years that had been stolen from my parents when we were refuseniks, about all the anger and bitterness that I still carry in my heart after almost twenty years of living in the West. But my father was waiting downstairs, and my aunt at the bus, and instead of arguing about politics I asked again that the doctor-porter turn on the elevator. He got up from behind the counter, slowly walked to the elevator, put in a key and turned it. The elevator came alive with rattling and screeching.

It took my father and me about an hour to bring my aunt's things up the tall marble steps and load them into the elevator, and then transport them to the room where my grandmother was solemnly pacing, like Napoleon at Waterloo, and my eleven-year-old cousin peacefully sleeping amid the chaos her mother and grandmother had co-authored. By the time father and I had finished piling up the suitcases in the corner of their room and returned to the bus, where my aunt was still waiting with the last and heaviest piece of luggage, the sun had vanished and the sky had turned from clear blue to veiny purple.

"Boys," my aunt said to us, "I think it's going to rain."

"Yes, rain, hail, and snow. And I hope lightning hits this trunk," I replied, my mouth drying, my voice wilting as I spoke.

"Angelo has offered to help with the trunk," my aunt said cheerfully. "He's a wonderful boy. His father's a tuba player. In Verona." My aunt called all men between five and forty-five "boys." This subtlety, of course, was lost on the bus driver who spoke no Russian and little English beyond "okay" and "Chicago."

Why am I not describing Rome? The sweepingly changing colors of the sky, the percussions of thunder growing nearer and nearer? The gorgeous people embracing and kissing in the streets? The parti-colored fruit and flower stands? The fountains? First of all, the location of our hotel, just east of Termini, was less than desirable, the buildings run down and adorned with graffiti, the signs faded. And it wasn't until the following day, until my first walk around Rome, that my eyes would feel exhausted from taking in so much color and vivacity and splendor. But I remember clearly—no, wait, how can I remember anything clearly when all sensations had been dulled after the epic journey of my aunt's baggage from the bus to the hotel? So strike that: I remember ~~clearly~~ bluntedly how the three of us—my father, Angelo the bus driver, and myself—dragged the Manchurian trunk toward the day's impending denouement.

"What do you have in there?" my father asked through clenched teeth. "It feels much too heavy even for its size."

"Oh, some personal items," my aunt replied insouciantly. "Also a few of my favorite books from childhood. And some family albums."

"I'm not touching this coffin ever again," my father said, turning to me.

"Coffin is right, papa."

To get inside the lobby one had to go up four marble steps. And then up three more steps inside to reach the elevator. At the entrance, the three of us put the trunk down to rest before the final climb. Angelo took out a pack of Camel cigarettes and offered them to my father and me, but not to my aunt. Angelo lit a cigarette and inhaled deeply, staring straight at my aunt's legs and behind. I ran up the steps to make sure the communist doctor-porter hadn't turned off the elevator again.

"It's all set," I told my father. With my thumb I signaled to Angelo that we were good to go. "Hold the door," I told my aunt.

"You must be tired, boys," she said in her indefatigable voice. And she patted Angelo approvingly on the bicep of his left arm.

We picked up the trunk, which by now felt as heavy in our hands as a box with a shipment of wolfram ore. Angelo embraced a narrow side of the trunk from the front. My father and I each held it from the longer sides, he on the left, I on the right. Very slowly we made it up the marble steps. As the sole of my right sandal made contact with the porous gray marble of the last step, the ground began to slip, and my foot slid down. Losing my balance and trying not to fall, I unclasped my hands and let go of the trunk. Looking down at my feet, I saw a plum stone with some greenish-purplish flesh that had been left uneaten. I had stepped on a plum stone!

The Manchurian trunk, the cause of my forever-strained relations with my aunt, had ripped itself from both my father's angry grip and Angelo's bullish embrace and rattled down the dirty marble steps. Landing on the perspiring asphalt of a Roman summer afternoon, the trunk opened itself with such force that it became obvious it had tired of my aunt's shenanigans. But there's more.

As I sat down on the steps, facing the street and rubbing my right knee that I had bruised in the style of a soccer injury, I saw onlookers—mostly urchins and middle-aged men—flocking toward the trunk and toward us. And what I saw after that was perfectly phantasmagoric. A plaid throw that used to cover the old divan in my aunt and grandmother's living room in Moscow began to stir and quiver, and then a human hand jutted itself out of the corner of the trunk. A second hand, with a signet ring and a watch on a gold band, followed suit, and then both hands pulled the rest of the Scottish throw off. We saw a short man with a Chekhovian goatee sitting up in the trunk, apparently adjusting his eyes to sunlight.

The small crowd of Roman onlookers issued a powerful sigh. Angelo the bus driver stood motionless, his arms reaching out to the sky. A Gogolian silence (compare *The Inspector-General*) lasted for a minute or two.

"Who is this man?" my father finally asked my aunt. His voice was brittle like the yellowed pages of old newsprint. She was my mother's younger sister, after all. He was entitled to a dose of fatherly-brotherly scorn.

"I'm Evgeny," replied the man from the trunk.

"And she's Tatyana," my father said, nodding in the direction of my aunt. (He was referring to the love triangle in *Eugene Onegin*.) This reference wasn't lost on all the Italian onlookers, although we were speaking Russian.

"Ta-tya-na," an Italian gentleman in a white cotton cap sang out, smiling and using a folded newspaper to point to my aunt. "Ta-tya-na." He must have been a fan of Russian opera.

While my aunt rolled her eyes, trying to come up with an explanation, the short man stepped out of the trunk and came up to my father, extending his hand.

"Evgeny Katz," he said. "First violin. I know some of your writings." He was pale, his thick eyebrows tousled, his black trousers and white shirt all rumpled up.

"What are you doing in my sister-in-law's trunk?" my father asked.

"Well, I was just traveling there, inside," said the man with the most nonchalant intonation.

"For how long?"

"Since last night, since Vienna. Well, actually, since Moscow."

"Do you two know each other?" my father continued the interrogation.

"Oh yes, we went to music conservatory together," answered the man who called himself Evgeny Katz.

"So why were you in the trunk? You still haven't told me," my father pressed on.

"You haven't asked," the man answered, apparently pleased with his wit.

"Oh, don't be a wise guy."

"I was in the trunk because—"

"Evgeny," my aunt interrupted. Her voice implored.

"Why, it's over," the violinist said to my aunt. "I'm here, in Rome. We don't need to do this any longer." And then he turned toward my father again. "You see, your sister-in-law got me out. I mean, I left the Soviet Union in her trunk. She smuggled me out of the country. To Vienna! And now over here. I'm going to ask for political asylum in Rome."

"Asylum," father repeated in disbelief.

"Asylum, a Russian dissident, escaped," one of the Italians who apparently knew some Russian translated for the rest of the crowd.

"I can't take this any more," father pronounced dramatically, like an actor who appeals to the audience from the stage. "We spend nine years struggling to get out. We are persecuted. Galleys of my three books are destroyed. My writings are banned. And this . . . this fiddler leaves in a Manchurian coffin without being caught."

Father walked up the steps into the building. I stayed behind so one day I could finish telling the story.

The rainstorm had bypassed us. The sun came out of the puffy clouds, setting alight the contents of my aunt's trunk. I saw a pink woolen bundle tied with twine and, indeed, family albums and books of children's adventure stories. *The Library of Adventures.* As a young boy, I used to read these books at my grandparents' apartment where my aunt also lived. *Gulliver's Travels, Robinson Crusoe, Treasure Island* . . .

Evgeny Katz picked the bundle up, untied the twine, and unwrapped it, freeing a black violin case from the bosom warmth of a kid's pink blanket.

The story of the man from the Manchurian trunk has a happy ending. To this day I haven't found out the reason behind my aunt's risky enterprise. They weren't, my aunt insisted, lovers, and I'm inclined to believe her. What difference would it make anyhow? Several times, during family dinners—at Thanksgiving or Passover—I have asked my aunt what was in it for her, bringing with her this man (who had left a wife and two children in Russia) in a trunk. Wasn't she taking a huge chance, first at the Soviet customs and border control, later concealing him from the Austrian authorities and from her own family? She would only shrug her shoulders in a gesture of innocence. This much I do know: The violinist was granted political asylum and stayed in Italy. He started to perform. He changed his Jewish feline last name to a Russian aquiline name—a long one ending in "off" and hinting at refinement and nobility. Evgeny lives with his boyfriend, a former La Scala tenor. He runs his own music school in Rome, near Piazza Navona. He recently recorded the complete Brahms violin sonatas.

Last winter I heard Evgeny perform in Boston, now my home for more than ten years. He played glitteringly, impeccably, but not as passionately as the first time I heard him play. Imagine the steps of our hotel in one of Rome's shabbiest quarters, the steps of our hotel encircled by a crowd of idle Romans. Visualize if you can a seedy street lined with dilapidated hotels where whores brought customers for an hour of affordable bliss and foretaste of the other world, and where we Soviet refugees had drunk our first fill of Rome and the universe. The man from the trunk tuned his violin, wiped the dusty sweat off his forehead and temples, put a checkered handkerchief under his dimpled chin, and began to play. It must have been a piece of his own composition or else an improvisation. At least I didn't know the music he played. To me his violin sang about the half-empty express train carrying Jewish refugees through the Alpine tunnel at night, about coming to Rome for the first time after a whole Soviet life of longing to see Italy and the rest of Europe, about the thunder that was moving west over our heads, toward Piazza Spagna, Trastevere, and Vatican City. To me his violin sang about family baggage, about the inescapability of family ties and traps. It sang about my aunt's and mother's father, my late grandfather, returning to live and die as my grandmother's husband after a decade of being divorced from her and liberated, but never happy. How did the man with the violin know about my family past? He played about my late grandfather, a tired sixty-year-old, standing in the courtyard of his Moscow apartment building and feeding challah bread to pigeons; tall and still dapper in his long gray gabardine coat and his soft gray fedora, dapper although already blind from poorly treated diabetes and from loving life too much to give up its pleasures. I know I have it in me—in my gait, temperament, in trying to take people on their own terms—much of my mother's late father. It was he, my maternal grandfather, who had been for years pushing his daughters, my father, all of us, to emigrate. It was he who detested the Soviet system with all his might and yet knew how to survive in that twisted game of mutual deception, and my aunt had inherited from him but never quite mastered the fine art of ingenuity. The violin sang of Manchurian trunks that fall and break open on the steps of Roman hotels revealing runaway violinists who play about life's ardor and cruelty, about fate and its disguises, about my blind grandfather dying in agony, strapped to the hospital bed, screaming, "daughters mine, help me, those doctors are trying to poison me," dying and never seeing his children and grandchildren walk the streets of Rome.

As the man from my grandfather's trunk played on, two *carabinieri* came to collect him. They stood and listened, and when he finished, they politely applauded along with the rest of the street audience, then invited him to ride with them to the police station. Angelo the bus driver had telephoned the *carabinieri* and explained that a strange Soviet violinist had arrived in Rome in an beat-up orange trunk and wanted to ask for political asylum.

As the police car drove off and its siren's echo subsided, I consulted a pocket Italian dictionary, copies of which we had been given upon arrival in Rome. "Dove . . . si vendo vino?" I finally asked, addressing the gathering of Italian onlookers. "Where . . . do they sell wine?"

"Si vendo vino?" Several people in the small crowd laughed. Half a dozen hands pointed in several directions as their owners screamed: "Ecco. Qua. Qua."

I looked around.

I was in Rome.

I was free at last.

3

Rome, Open City

My parents and I sometimes laugh about it the way one laughs about surviving a shipwreck in trepid, alien waters. I still don't know for sure why they fought during our stay in Rome. It's been almost twenty years, and I'm still afraid to ask. Instead, I get up from my desk, walk across the striped carpet to my "Russian" bookcases, and pick up Isaac Babel's *Works*. I bought this two-volume set in Moscow during my first trip back, in the summer of 1993. Edited by Babel's Moscow wife Antonina Pirozhkova, it was published in 1992, the first post-Soviet year. The monumentalist cover design and flimsy binding are typical of the cheap newsprint editions of my childhood and youth. The set shows a print run of one hundred thousand copies. One of the simpler ironies: Babel, finally collected in the post-Soviet years, yet published after the fashion of Soviet-era mass editions.

I open the first volume to the section "Stories, 1925–1938." Here they are, my most cherished Babels. The childhood stories. On page three of "The Story of My Dovecote," I read this: "In our shop a peasant customer sat, full of doubt, scratching himself. When father saw me, he abandoned the peasant and instantly believed my story. He yelled to the assistant to close the shop and rushed to Cathedral Street to buy me a peaked cap with a badge. My poor mother was barely able to rip me away from that deranged man. Mother was pale in that moment and was testing fate. She stroked me while also pushing me away in disgust. She said the newspaper would print the list of names of those accepted to the *Gymnasium*, and that God would punish us and people would laugh at us, if we purchased the uniform too soon. Mother was pale, she was divining fate in my eyes and looking at me with morbid pity, as if I were a little cripple, because she alone knew how misfortunate our whole family was."

As I read this passage in my house in Chestnut Hill, just a few blocks from the Boston city line, I sob very quietly, holding back the tears—as if I were made of dry ice. It's springtime outside, and the workers digging an underground train station in my neighbors' back yard stare at me across the fence as they take their ten o'clock smoke break. My desk faces the windows, and the yard-diggers like to watch me at work. They probably assume I laugh at something I'm reading. But I'm not laughing.

If Isaac Emmanuilovich Babel were alive, I would tell him I think of him often as I write about leaving the Soviet Union and coming to the West. Actually, it would be better if I could just tell him this story . . .

IT WAS OUR FOURTH DAY IN ROME, our thirteenth in the West. And quite a day it turned out to be. It started with a pauper's breakfast that the refugees from the USSR took in a refectory run by a grinning proprietor in dark glasses who looked like a mafioso parody. The crowded refectory occupied an entire floor of a building adjacent to our hotel in a sordid neighborhood near Termini. Outside the refectory, from the middle of the stairwell and all the way up the stairs to the heavy double doors, a line of refugees was waiting to get in. While waiting in the line, the refugees told each other about scorching political events, such as an explosion at a train station in Paris, and shared information about apartment rentals in the coastal town of Ladispoli where the JIAS expected us to move after about a week in Rome. People talked about job and college prospects in America or Canada and argued with panache about the advantages of Boston over New York or San Diego over San Francisco.

My body exploding with hormones, I followed with hungry eyes the young Polish waitresses as they navigated through the narrow straits between the islands and archipelagoes of hastily breakfasting refugees. The waitresses, whom I would get to know by the end of our Roman holiday, were students from Kraków who had come to Italy as tourists and were working illegally. They spoke passable Russian, having been forced to study it in Poland, and the greedy Italian proprietor was underpaying them and making them work seven days a week, even on Sundays, when they were used to going to church. The Polish waitresses had pretty long legs, rough peasant hands, patient gray eyes.

When it came our turn to enter the refectory, we gave our meal tickets to a grizzly bear of a guard.

"Jeszcze Polska nie zginela!" My father greeted one of the waitresses after we were seated at a plastic table with wobbly legs ("Poland isn't yet gone!" from the Polish national anthem).

"No, not yet, still going strong," the waitress replied, smiling forlornly.

We, Jewish refugees from the Soviet Union, elicited a mixture of contempt and admiration in the Polish waitresses. We were stateless, penniless, we were being fed on public assistance—well, not public but private, on the money collected by Jewish philanthropic organizations. And yet, we were going to America as legal residents. To America!

That particular morning the breakfast menu consisted of large slices of white bread, peaches, and slabs of Swiss cheese that were placed in front of us on thin paper plates. No butter or milk was available.

"Well, my dears, I never," my father enunciated, "I never thought I'd see my family eating unripe peaches for breakfast. 'Hard are the peaches of exile,' says the poet."

My mother said she wasn't hungry and silently sipped coffee from a styrofoam cup.

"Bistro, bistro, tovarishch," the parody of a mafioso shouted as he walked between tables. The Russian word *bystro* means "quickly"; it's believed to have entered the European languages after the Russian troops came to Paris in 1815 and kept repeating it as they demanded service. Hence *bistro*(t), to designate a casual restaurant with simple, quickly prepared food. *Tovarishch* means "comrade."

After breakfast we had a meeting with a profiteer who bought goods from the Soviet refugees and sold them to souvenir shops or at his family's stall at the Round Market, as this large open-air bazaar was known in our midst. The man came to our hotel room at ten in the morning. He was a neckless giant with a small head and a sliver of a mustache. His name was Isak; he was a Bukharan Jew who had left the

Soviet Union in the early 1980s with his wife and kids and had settled down in Rome. He spoke Russian with a heavy Central Asian accent, like a person choking on a piece of gingerbread.

"Gorgeous city, Rome!" he said to my mother, pointing to the view outside our hotel window—rusty rooftops with an occasional pigeon but no cathedrals or palazzos in sight. "So, you're Muscovites? I was in Moscow in 1975. Bought some merchandise to take back to Samarkand. Also a very beautiful city. Impressive."

"Esteemed Isak," father said, imitating the ways of Central Asia. "Esteemed Isak, with your permission my junior will now show you what we have to offer."

I pulled a suitcase from under my cot and laid out the wares on my parents' bed. Mother stood by the window and smoked. I could see from the corner of my left eye that her lips were shaking. A tigress she had been back in Moscow, facing KGB thugs at demonstrations and protests. She used to organize hunger strikes of refusenik women and fearlessly gave interviews to foreign journalists. Now, in Rome, my mother looked despondent, powerless to confront her lot as a refugee.

"So, I see," said Isak, engirdling the bed with his cinnamon eyes. "Three amber brooches, four Palekh lacquer boxes, five tins of Chatka crab meat." (This tenderest of crab meats came from the Kamchatka peninsula in the Russian Far East.) "Also, three floral shawls, four pairs of opera glasses, a camera, a zoom lens. Anything else you got?"

"Russian vodka," my father said with hesitation.

"Keep it," replied Isak magnanimously. "A good gift. Americans are great suckers for Russian vodka."

From his trousers the profiteer removed a billfold. He counted out and tossed onto my parents' bed two hundred thousand lire, about two hundred dollars at the time. He and my father shook hands—to conclude the fire sale.

"Can I borrow your suitcase?" he asked. "I'll drop it off in a couple of days."

"Take it. One less for us to carry," my father replied with a grim smile.

Isak put the goods into the suitcase, closed it, and got up.

"You should pay a visit next door, to my sister-in-law and mother-in-law," father added when Isak turned the door knob. "They have a whole fleet—"

"Must you?" mother interjected. She knew my father was sick of moving their countless baggage, but in public she believed in maintaining family solidarity.

"Until next time." Like a flushing toilet, Isak exploded in laughter. "Good luck in the States." And he merrily slammed the door.

At noon we had to be at a medical clinic somewhere near Piazza dell'Esquilino, a short walk from our hotel. The appointment was for a medical examination, chest X-rays, and blood tests. This was required of all applicants for U.S. refugee visas. While we were waiting in a cold and scarcely lit corridor, my mother was overcome by a bout of nervous coughing. The harder she tried to stop, the louder and stronger she would cough. An overworked grim nurse came out of an office and called my mother's name. My father, whose Ph.D. dissertation had dealt with pulmonary TB, waved his hand. "No, no, no, she's fine, no TB," he said, and gestured to the nurse as she led my mother away. He was imagining a nightmarish scenario in which mother would fail her tests and not be allowed into America. But everything turned out well for us, and a few weeks later each of us received a medical examination form attesting that as applicants for United States visas, we had normal X-ray reports and showed no evidence of "dangerous contagious conditions" (chancroid, gonorrhea, granuloma inguinale, infectious leprosy, lymphogranuloma venereum, infectious stage syphilis, active tuberculosis) or of "mental conditions" (mental retardation, insanity, previous occurrence of one or more attacks of insanity, psychopathic personality, sexual deviation, mental defect, narcotic drug addiction, chronic alcoholism). The forms were signed by an Italian panel physician from the clinic, "Prof. Dott. V.P.C."

Inside the clinic we found a pay phone—there was no telephone in our desolate hotel room. Sometime in May 1987, right before leaving Moscow, we had met a young Italian journalist by the name of Claudia S. Stationed in Moscow, Claudia covered Russia for a leading left-wing Italian daily. She spoke clean, antiquated Russian that she had studied at the University of Naples and also privately with an elderly widow of a former White Army officer. Claudia was thin, long-haired, electrifying. When she heard that we would be passing through Rome and spending at least a couple of months in Italy on the way to America, she suggested that my father get in touch with the deputy editor at her paper. She said this man's name was Alessandro T., and he was a poet and a close friend of hers. "When you call him," Claudia told my father after scribbling the editor's name on the back of her card, "say you're from Carmen. He calls me 'Carmen.' Only he, no one else. He'll help you get your works published in Italian."

And so there we were, standing in the vestibule of an Italian clinic, telephoning an Italian poet-editor who was Claudia's "close friend." My father dialed the number; my mother and I stood waiting next to the open phone booth. Someone answered the phone. My father began to explain in his then-severely idiosyncratic English that he was "the Jewish-Russian writer" and "the medical scientist," "the Soviet refugee" staying in Rome for "the another week." That Claudia "the journalist" had given him the name and number of the Italian poet-editor. Then my father stopped talking, and we saw an expression of incomprehension take hold of his face. My father rolled his eyes and made a circling gesture with his left hand, a gesture that signified that he had no idea what to do.

"Carmen," my father said into the receiver. "Carmen, yes, Carmen. Your friend Carmen." And he smiled. "He doesn't speak a word of English," he whispered to us. "He's rattling off in Italian, and Carmen's the only word I understand. You try it," and he pressed the receiver into my hand.

"Buon giorno, Signore Alessandro," I said, and then I made an attempt at relating, in a better English, the story of meeting Carmen in Moscow and getting the poet-editor's phone number from her.

"Carmen, si, Carmen," said a throaty voice. "Si-si, Carmen. Non parlo Inglese. Francese?" asked the poet-editor.

At the time I knew no French and had barely picked up enough Italian to ask for directions and buy food and wine. "Grazie," I thanked the poet-editor. "Grazie. Arrivederci." And I politely hung up.

"What's he saying?" my father asked. My mother's face had acquired the expression of a captive firebird. I could tell she was finding the whole scene wretchedly absurd and depressing.

"He's saying 'Carmen' and 'I don't speak English.' He also speaks French. That's all I could understand for sure. But he must have repeated the name Carmen a dozen times. I think he was happy to say her name."

When we stepped outside the clinic, my mother said, "I feel very tired. I'd like to go back to the hotel."

"You're not sick, are you?" my father asked. "You were coughing before."

"Not sick, just mortally tired."

"I think I'll go for a walk," I said. I felt an urge to be alone, to split, to get away from it all.

AFTER LEAVING MY PARENTS in front of an obelisk in Piazza dell'Esquilino, I undertook an ambitious walking tour of Rome, one of the three day-long tours on which I would send myself during our stay in the city. I didn't own a Baedeker, and my only guides were memory and a simple street plan of Rome that every Soviet refugee would receive from JIAS officials. Although I remember the Roman sights I visited on that particular day, I have a harder time recalling my emotional state. But I do remember losing myself amid the walls of the Roman Forum and later having an attack of loneliness after I reached Piazza di Spagna and its famous steps.

Standing in front of Lapis Niger, a large piece of black marble under which lie the remains of Romulus, I experienced the same trepidation as I had once felt as a ten-year-old while hearing, in Soviet school, about the founding of Rome. And here's an oddity of memory: I remember coming up to and walking around Tempo di Vesta and thinking not only of the six patrician priestesses who in the ancient times would be selected to serve in the temple for thirty years, but of another priestess, my old Soviet history teacher, Valentina Sergeevna T. I can still remember her vividly, and back in 1987 the memories could only have been more virtual. She never changed the style of her clothes: gray and black woolen skirts, white laced blouses, knitted cardigans or woolen jackets to match her skirts. She never wore make-up or jewelry, only a round Lenin pin on the left side of her flat chest. She had silver-rimmed glasses, thin twinelike lips, short ashen hair. How old was she? Forty? Fifty? She never married and never spoke of her personal life. She had none, the Vestal Virgin of Soviet history. It was she, Valentina Sergeevna, Miss History, who for seven years, from 1978 until 1984, taught me about everything from Egypt, Greece, and Rome to fundamentals of Soviet law and state. It was to her that I owed much of what I knew of the ancient world, of Romulus, of the Colosseum, and all the ancient sights I was now visiting. She was a mesmerizing weaver of historical narratives. Had she been born in the USA, I'm sure she would have become a famous lecturer or narrated for PBS. She had made us experience a tangible reality of Jeanne d' Arc's burning at the stake while February hoar-frost enshackled bare branches outside the classroom. I can still visualize her scenes of the French Revolution: Danton's obesity and soiled clothes; the emaciated Marat stabbed in the bathtub; the spectacular execution of Marie-Antoinette. But with equal zeal Valentina Sergeevna told us about the "brotherly peoples of Eastern Europe" (in the early 1990s, when I was in Prague researching my first book, I wouldn't dare speak Russian) or Brezhnev's "remarkable reminiscences" (senilia he didn't even write), or else, which was even worse, how she passionately concealed any shades of dissent and turmoil in the Soviet past and present: the Gulag, Stalinism, Solzhenitsyn, and Sakharov, the dissident movement, refuseniks, anti-Semitism, Afghanistan. A recent escapee from the Soviet empire, an empire crumbling but still holding strong in 1987, I knew that all her talents notwithstanding, Miss History was an ideological cog in the machine of Soviet schooling. And yet, to lean on a comforting Dostoevskian conjunction, and *yet* I remember standing in front of the Temple of Vestal Virgins on that afternoon in June of 1987 and asking myself a question that I ask again today, some twenty years later: How did this woman manage to remain so sane? How did she not turn into a mental patient after decades of exhaling truths and lies in a single breath? Of course, this question concerns not only my Soviet history teacher but also myself and my Soviet childhood and youth.

How could I be both grateful to Miss History for brilliant lessons about the past and resent her for shameful lies about the present? For quite a number of years after leaving Russia and coming to America, probably until I had become a U.S. citizen and finally went back to visit my former homeland in 1993, my solution would be to despise and not to be grateful. It has taken me years of living in America as an immigrant to achieve enough distance necessary to appreciate parts of my Soviet education, or even to admit to thinking of my old history teacher amid the ruins of ancient Rome.

But enough sentimental politics, and on with the story of losing and finding myself in Rome. The sun was setting when I reached the Spanish steps from the top, from Trinita dei Monti, a French church with two symmetrical bell towers, which Napoleon had restored during his occupation of Rome. The area directly below the church was already very crowded. Visitors and young Romans were pouring into Piazza di Spagna and onto the steps from several directions. I hadn't had much to eat since that morning's breakfast of peaches, bread, and cheese. At the bottom of the steps, on the other side of a fountain, I saw stalls with postcards and souvenirs and carts with snack foods. Trying not to bump into anyone, I ran down the steps, many of which were cracked and dilapidated. After studying the wares and the prices—fairly high as the peddlers catered to the tourists—I bought a little sack of extra-large pale green olives, about six or seven of them. I'd never tried such divine-tasting olives before. They were overflowing with life and juices and the kind of vitality and sensuality that I associated with Italy and its people. I ate the olives slowly, relishing them in my mouth, sucking every bit of taste down to the pit, and wanting more. Instead of buying a can of soda, I ended up getting another little sack of those succulent olives. I ate them after sitting down on the steps.

Nodding my head to the music of street performers, I sat in the middle section of the steps, surrounded by a group of young American women. Many of them wore T-shirts or sweatshirts with names of colleges or universities. Those names—Oberlin, Washington & Lee, Boston College—meant very little to me at the time, a random assortment of names and geographical locations in my would-be country. Sitting

by myself on the Spanish Steps in the middle of Rome, I reflected on
how very little I still knew about America and its women. My previous
contacts with American females my age had been few. Over the nine
years my family had been refuseniks, we'd had visitors from America,
mainly Jews who came to the Soviet Union under the safe disguise
of an official Intourist trip. For the most part, they were middle-aged
or retired couples, and only on a few occasions we had had visits by
entire families with children. Once, I believe in the early spring of
1986, a family from Arizona rang our doorbell on a Friday night: a
dentist, his wife, and their son and daughter, both of them students at
distinguished colleges on the East Coast. All four were long-limbed,
tanned, bespectacled. We had a makeshift celebration of the Sabbath:
birthday cake candles, vodka, and a supper of matzo-meal pancakes
and herring that my mother had improvised (the visitors kept kosher,
so there wasn't much else they could eat). Then I took the brother
and sister to my room, and we talked for a long time, first about being
Jewish in Russia, but then, after the emissaries in them had yielded to
regular college kids and my peers, about being young in America. That
was the first time I heard about fraternities and sororities, and it struck
me as something rather Soviet and collectivist. "Why would someone
want to join?" I remember asking them. In the years 1982–87—when
I was in senior high school and later a student at Moscow University—
there'd been several visits of this kind, which one could never plan
or predict. I'd met two or three other college girls from the USA and
Canada. Serious and idealistic, they regarded me as some sort of young
martyr for the Jewish cause, and well do I remember our insatiable,
galloping conversations, during which I got a taste of the icing without
having the cake of campus life.

There was also Erica, a student from Boston University whom I
got to know a little better than the one-time visitors. Erica majored in
Russian and was spending a year in Moscow, at the Pushkin Institute.
I'd met her through my parents' friends at the American Embassy. She
was from Long Island, where her family ran a moving and storage
company. She had ginger hair which she pinned up. On the long escala-
tors of the Moscow metro's older stations, people going in the opposite

direction would always stare at her. She looked distinctly foreign, not necessarily Jewish, but foreign—her gestures and facial expressions, her small glasses, her yellow wool coat. For a period of two or three months—for some reason I remember Erica's winter coat—I took her around Moscow, to museums and some of my favorite haunts. Something had kept us from getting involved, not something, but actually a strangeness that we both felt, a tempting strangeness that finally kept us at a distance from one another. It was from Erica that I had learned the little concrete stuff I knew about American college life and American women before actually setting foot on American soil. It was a series of sporadic notes, much too little of an understanding.

Why am I thinking about all this? I guess because it helps me remember and relive the shock of my first weeks in the West. Much of the shock had to do with the realization of my inadequacy as a romantic subject. The sense of this new romantic inadequacy would become particularly acute after coming to America and plunging straight into college life. My habitually romantic behavior during the first year after coming to this country would cost me dearly on the campus of Brown University, at the height of political correctness, when ardor was considered aggressive and uncouth. In retrospect, as my present Americanized (or is it -iced?) self stares back at my former Russian self sitting on the Spanish Steps at the end of a long day of roving about Rome—alone, penniless, passionate—I'm faced with a predicament that one may or may not find bewildering. Consider for a moment that, notwithstanding my family's hardships in the Soviet Union, and despite feeling messed up and disoriented, I gazed at Rome now lying at my feet, I looked around Piazza di Spagna and the steps, and I yearned for sexual adventure. A young Jewish refugee from the Soviet Union I most certainly was. But I was also a young poet from Moscow, something of a cross between a knight who puts his Beautiful Ladies on an unearthly pedestal and a tomcat who undresses women with slinky looks.

Sitting next to me on the steps, a Nordic, blonde-haired, green-eyed girl was trading stories with her two girlfriends, who wore matching T-shirts. I believe the T-shirts said "George Washington." Listening to her innocent impressions of the "amazing" Colosseum and of the "breathtaking" San Pietro, I followed with my eyes the flutterings of the girl's legs, the glaring span of her short skirt, the silk straps of her mauve bra rolling over her tan shoulders as she moved her arms. I could feel my Adam's apple ready to burst. I was thirsty from eating so many olives and from so much gazing.

Down below, in the stagelike space between the fountain and the bottom of the Spanish Steps, singers took turns performing. One of them, a young thin fellow with a pallid face, wore black trousers and shirt and a Basque scarf. He and another performer, who had long hair and the standard looks and dress of a rock musician, stepped onto the stage with their guitars. Of the songs they played I recognized "Sunday, Bloody Sunday" (in Moscow I had inherited a U2 tape from Erica). As I earnestly twisted my body and nodded to the rhythm of the songs, the girl sitting on my immediate right, the green-eyed blonde with itinerant bra straps, turned and asked me,

"Where are you from?"

She must have taken me for an American, I thought, rehearsing the answer I would give her. My English at the time was grammatically accurate and vastly unidiomatic. It carried a patina of the Russian accent that to this day betrays the foreigner in me. Not just the accent, though.

"I'm from Russia," I replied. "From Moscow."

"Oh my God, that's so neat," she exclaimed. "Hey guys," she turned to her girlfriends, "he's from Russia." And to me she said, "You're the first Russian I've ever met."

My initial reaction was to explain that I was actually not a Russian—that is, ethnically not a Slav, but a Jew. In the Soviet Union this would make all the difference in the world, and back there I would never identify as a Russian. But seeing the amazement in the girl's eyes, I hesitated and said nothing. I became a Russian on the Spanish Steps in Rome.

"Where are you from?" I asked the girl.

"I'm from Oregon, outside Portland. But I go to school in D.C. A bunch of us are doing the Europass thing. We've been in Rome for three days now. Going to Florence tomorrow morning."

"Florence," I repeated after her.

"Are you traveling by yourself?"

"I'm on my way to America."

"Are you an exchange student or something?" asked one of the blonde's girlfriends, a stocky woman in jeans and a blue button-down shirt with a red polo player embroidered on the left side.

"No, my family and I are waiting for our U.S. visas."

"Did you like . . . defect or something?" asked the blonde's other girlfriend, who held a maroon backpack on her knees.

"No, we . . . ," and here I stumbled—and stumble I would countless times in the next year—upon the ordinary difficulty of explaining my status to an American who doesn't know about the Soviet Union and Jewish emigration and how my family had been able to get out. "We actually left for good," I finally finished the sentence, feeling embarrassed and looking down at my feet. "We're emigrants."

"Oh," the blonde girl said, losing interest. "Cool." The conversation flagged. A few minutes later the blonde and her two girlfriends got up from the steps.

"Nice to meet you," one of them said. And the others repeated, "Nice to meet you. Good luck with everything."

"Thank you!" I said and nervously laughed. "See you in America."

LESS THAN A YEAR LATER, I would have a chance to revisit this chance meeting in Piazza di Spagna when reading Henry James's *Daisy Miller: A Study* for George Monteiro's American lit class at Brown. How faithfully has James described the American Girl Abroad syndrome! I remember reclining in a chair at the Rockefeller Library, a copy of *Daisy Miller* in my lap, and reflecting on the artlessness of those American college girls, their provinciality, their exalted vision of Europe (and European men, I might add). A Russian on my way to America, in their minds I must have been "defecting" not only from the Soviet Union, but also from Europe. Were they wrong?

Henry James wrote *Daisy Miller* in 1878, after moving to London from Paris. In Paris he had met Zola and other French writers of the day, but he also met the Russian Ivan Turgenev. *Daisy Miller* starts in a tone characteristically un-American and almost Russian, as though not James but Turgenev, or else Bunin, who came in his footsteps, wrote it: "At the little town of Vevey, in Switzerland, there is a particularly comfortable hotel." Vevey, the place where Vladimir Nabokov is buried, is just above Montreux, where he lived from 1961 until his death. An émigré, Nabokov left Russia at the age of twenty, in 1919, never to see it again. He came to America in 1940 to write American novels about Russians and other Europeans in America and about Americans in Europe, *Lolita*, *Pnin*, and *Transparent Things* among them. In *Lolita*, Nabokov immortalized the perverse innocence of a teenage American girl by making her fatefully irresistible—both angelic and demonic—to a middle-aged European exile. *Lolita* was one of the first books I would read after coming to America. But on that warm Roman evening in June 1987, *Lolita* was only a distant and alluring name, echoing with the many sounds of the previously forbidden and still undiscovered.

As I walked back from Piazza Spagna to our hotel near Termini, I thought of another great Russian of the twentieth century, the Jewish-born poet Osip Mandelshtam. In a poem of 1913, Mandelshtam wrote of a nameless American girl, "amerikanka"—the American girl who sails across the Atlantic at twenty and then visits the Louvre and the Acropolis. "Not understanding anything," the American Girl Abroad reads *Faust* as she rides across Europe in a train car, disappointed that "Louis no longer holds the throne."

I RETURNED TO OUR HOTEL around eleven in the evening. My parents were arguing. From behind the door I heard a sarcastic melody in my mother's voice; her voice seemed to be rising without ever falling. My father's replies sounded like shots of a BB gun. My mother: "Tararà-rararà-rararà." My father: "Boom. Boom. Boom. Boom." I stood outside and listened for a minute before turning the heavy ornate knob.

When I entered our room, I saw my father sitting at the desk in front of the window. The window was open onto a narrow courtyard separating our building from the adjacent one. There was light in some of the windows opposite ours, and through their ochre curtains I saw spectral silhouettes that paced, raised arms, combed hair, undressed.

In a room one floor below and to the left, across the courtyard, a man and a woman were screaming, loudly, violently, and without pausing.

"Where were you all day?" mother asked. "I worried."

"Many places. I'm fine," I answered and recalled the ending of Babel's story "The Awakening," where the Jewish boy's father finds out he's been skipping violin lessons: "Father spoke more quietly and articulately than he had ever spoken in his life. 'I'm a military officer,' said my father. 'I have a country estate. I go hunting. The peasants pay me rent. I've placed my son in the military boarding school. I don't need to worry about my son. . . . '"

"So what's happening?" I asked as nonchalantly as I knew how.

"This is so like your father," my mother said to me from the corner where she stood, her arms interlocked in front of her. Her eyes were red and swollen. "This is classically, inimitably your father."

"What are you doing, papa?" I asked, accustomed since childhood to acting the role of a mediator in days and times of my parents' discord.

"I'm just writing a letter," my father answered, a quick half smile flickering across his face like a lizard's tail on a sun-heated rock.

"Okay, papa, I can see that. Now seriously, what are you two up to?"

"We don't even know where in America we're going," my mother said loudly. "Oh, for God's sake, we haven't even found a place to stay in Ladispoli. We're moving there in five days, and your father is sitting here like a cherub writing a letter to some Italian he's never met in a language he doesn't know. That's what's happening."

My mother lit a cigarette and turned to face the courtyard, from which the screaming came ever so loudly.

"Mamochka," I started the sentence but stopped, my voice trembling. "Mamochka, you know papa loves you. And you know I love you too."

I turned around and came up to the desk where my father was sitting.

"Papa, whom are you writing to?" I asked very quietly, in a tentative sort of way.

"I'm writing to the poet-editor, the one we tried calling this morning. Carmen's sugar daddy."

"How did you get his address?" I asked.

"I bought a copy of his newspaper. I'm sending the letter to the editorial office. Although I should probably have just walked there and introduced myself."

"But he doesn't speak English," I said, frustration bulging inside me. "Plus how would you get into the office?"

"I'm writing the letter in Italian," my father explained. "With a dictionary." He showed me a tiny navy-clad pocket dictionary, Italiano-Russo/Russo-Italiano, published by Antonio Vallardi Editore. We had received copies of it upon arrival in Rome.

"You see," my mother continued, "a letter to some . . . some poet-editor who probably couldn't care less about him. A letter consisting of greetings, opening phrases, and verb infinitives. Notes of a madman, that's what it is."

"Mama, you know he was busy," I said, quickly falling into my familiar role of a go-between during my parents' fights. "He didn't have time to study English, with two careers."

"He could have made time," mother replied, angrily. "We were refuseniks for nine years. Wasn't that enough time to learn at least the basics? He knew we were going to America!"

"That hadn't been decided," father said, tearing himself from his letter and pocket dictionary. "You know that."

"I was never going to Israel," mother screamed. "And besides, any educated person can speak English. Look at some of the people in our group. Look at Shteynfeld, for instance. He'll have no trouble adjusting."

"I've told you already," father said, in a paper-thin voice, "you can go on rendezvous with this pompous Marcus Aurelius and practice English all you want. I won't stand in your way. But I just want you to show some intellectual honesty: I always had misgivings about us not going to Israel. Always. And I still do today." And father slammed his pocket Russian-Italian/Italian-Russian dictionary against the scratched desk.

"Ah, I can't believe it," mother said to me, as if my father wasn't in the room. "And it's not just about Israel. It's about your father never wanting to do things he doesn't like—learning English, fixing things around the house—"

"—driving a gypsy cab at night with my myopia, when we were both without work and had no money to put food on the table," father interrupted. "Have you already forgotten that, my darling? Or has Mr. Shteynfeld totally clouded your judgment? God, why is it that Jewish women always feel like they must be the public defender for the entire world—excepting their own husbands?"

"And why is it that Jewish husbands are so antisemitic when it comes to their wives?" mother replied.

Across the courtyard, breaking of dishes had been added to screaming.

"Putana!" announced the man's indignant basso from behind the peach curtain.

"Bastardo," responded the woman's mocking soprano.

"Brava," another male voice emerged from a lower floor, followed by raucous laughter. "Bravissima!"

Undeterred, my father slowly copied several more lines from the pocket dictionary, folded the sheet in three, put it in a white envelope with red and green checkers along the edges, and sealed the letter.

"Remember, you two," he said turning to me and then to my mother. "I cannot and will not live in isolation. I'm a writer. I need contacts with other writers. And I will make them, Italian or no Italian, English or no English!"

Another round of operatic screaming and swearing erupted from across the courtyard, followed by more applause by the aficionado of domestic scandals living down below.

"I'm going to go insane in this mousehole," my mother said quietly and adamantly as she sat on the bed. "This flophouse. This outhouse. This bordello. This . . . ," she started bawling.

"Sweetie," my father dashed to her side. "It's just a horrible hotel. They put refugees here because it's cheap. It's only a few more days, and then we'll move to Ladispoli. We'll live by the water. We'll go to the beach. Eat sweet peaches, your favorite. Remember, I used to bring you the most amazing peaches in the Crimea, on our honeymoon? Please don't cry, my only one."

My mother smiled faintly. "Don't you two get it? It's not the comforts of our Moscow apartment that I'm missing," she said with tenderness, clinging to my father's chest and shoulder. "It's just that ever since we came to Rome, I've been feeling so . . . so lonely."

"Everything will be okay, my love. Just a few more days. "

IN THE MIDDLE OF THE NIGHT I woke up because I heard stirring and shuffling. My first thought was that a thief had gotten into our room. I sat up in my cot. In the room's inky darkness, I saw my father hunched over one of our suitcases.

"Papa, what's the matter?" I whispered.

"I can't sleep," my father replied.

"Sh-shh," I whispered. "Don't wake mama up." Ever since I remember, my father could never whisper. He was not made for hushed noises.

"I need a drink," said my father. He opened the suitcase and felt its contents with both his hands. "Here she is," he said after fumbling about for a minute. He removed a bottle of the vodka that Isak the Bukharan profiteer had suggested we keep and bring with us to America as a Russian souvenir. It was a special bottle, Posolskaya Vodka. Ambassadorial Reserve. My father unscrewed the top and took a long swig, then another one. Then he screwed the top back on and put the bottle on the desk. He pulled on a pair of pants, a plaid shirt, and sandals.

"Where are you going?" I whispered.

"I'm going for a walk," he replied. "To Villa Borghese." He took the vodka bottle and shuffled past me and out of the room.

WHEN MY MOTHER WOKE ME UP, it was ten o'clock in the morning.

"We missed breakfast," she said, "but I think I slept well." She looked rested and calm for the first time in over a week. "Where's papa?" she asked, pulling the curtain and letting orange sunlight into the room.

"He went out in the middle of the night," I replied. "And I think he had a bottle of vodka with him."

"And you let him go?!"

"Mama . . . but, he . . . "

Ten minutes later I was already traversing Piazza della Repubblica, running past government office buildings, racing in the direction of Villa Borghese. I knew the way from having walked there two days before. Running up Via Vittorio, stumbling on cracks in the asphalt, my head light after sleeping late and missing breakfast, I entered the grounds of Villa Borghese through Porta Pinciana. The racetrack, Galoppatoio, was on my left. Faint odors of hay and horseshit hit my nostrils as I veered right and ran toward Goethe's monument. Navigating my way amid dense groups of Asian tourists and young Roman mothers with prams, I ran east up a long park alley that leads to the Borghese Gallery. Halfway there, I turned left in the direction of the oblong Piazza di Sienna and passed a group of men who were playing soccer on the grass. Some uncanny familiar force, some genetic compass drove me and directed me to the monument to Byron. A few steps away from the monument to the clubfooted lord (whom many Russians love much more than they love the other English Romantics), under a blooming linden tree that emitted a sweet scent of oblivion, I saw my fifty-one-year-old father. He lay on the emerald grass of Villa Borghese, embracing the firmament with his open left hand, every finger pressed into the earth as though trying to hold on to it as it made its daily rotation. Father's head, its graying wavy hair fluttering about his bald spot like very tiny dragonflies, rested on the open palm of his right hand. His old tortoise-shell glasses had fallen off his nose and lay next to his left cheek, their handles jutting up like two bean stalks. An empty bottle of Ambassadorial Reserve lay near his feet, its neck woven into the stems of lush June grass like a wondrous squash or cucumber. His plaid shirt, known in Russian as *kovboika* (*kovboi* is "cowboy"), was unbuttoned and revealed the silver curls on his chest.

"Papa, papa," I shouted, getting down on my knees beside him and trying to hold back my tears. "Papa, it's me!"

My father opened his downsloping Chaldean eyes and turned onto his back. A blissful smile came onto his lips as if flowing in from another world.

"Papa, are you okay?" I asked, feeling his warm hand. "Papa . . . " A spasm of guilt clutched my throat.

"I had such fantastical dreams, incredible, with such colors!" said my father as he sat up and rubbed his eyes. Then he looked around and buttoned his cowboy shirt. Blades of grass had impressed a maze into his right cheek.

"Look, my dear," my father said, pointing to the right. There, not twenty steps away from us, a tall leggy woman was sailing up the park alley. She wore a short red skirt, high heels, and a low-cut blouse. She carried a small black leather purse in her right hand, and in her left hand she had a book with a soft matte cover. She was about thirty, perhaps a little older, with long wavy black hair. She resembled the Italian actress Sophia Loren who was very popular in the Soviet Union. She and also Marcello Mastroianni.

The Italian beauty sat down on a park bench directly opposite us and crossed her legs, sending her skirt on a hike up her swarthy thighs. She removed a shiny metal bookmark from the middle of her book and started reading.

"Incredible," I said to my father. "Like your dreams."

"She is. Go talk to her before I do. Go ahead." My father gently pushed me up from the ground where we were both sitting.

I walked up to the bench, trying to come up with an opening line.

"Excuse me," I said to her in English.

She lifted up her head and turned her eyes to me. Her lipstick was bright red and matched her blazing skirt.

"Excuse me. I was wondering if I could introduce myself."

The beauty smiled very naturally and invitingly, displaying no guardedness or irritation. "Non parlo inglese," she said, tilting her head just so slightly to the side and all the while continuing to smile.

Trying to muster up all the Italian I had managed to pick up in three days, I was able to produce this awkward locution: *"Io sono russo ebreo emigrante"* (I am Russian Jewish emigrant).

All the women in my Soviet past and in my American future probably felt my desire and inferiority as I stood before the Italian beauty, waiting for her to give me a signal.

"Ciao," said the beauty. She stopped smiling but continued to make eye contact with me. For about thirty seconds I swam in her eyes, silently and desperately. I drowned, and she shrugged her shoulders and lowered her gaze to her paperback.

I walked back to the lawn where my father was waiting.

"Let's go, papa," I said, patting my father on his back. "Mama's probably worried sick by now."

"Let's go, son," my father said and got up from the lawn.

I helped him brush blades of grass off his pants and shirt. We embraced and headed back to our hotel under the blue dome of Rome's midday sky.

PART TWO | Ladispoli

4

Notes from a Life in Transit

In *Etruscan Places,* first published in 1932, D. H. Lawrence briefly mentions Ladispoli in the chapter titled "Cerveteri": "We arrive at Palo, a station in nowhere, and ask if there is a bus to Cerveteri. No! An ancient sort of wagon with an ancient white horse stands outside. Where does that go? To Ladispoli. We know we don't want to go to Ladispoli, so we stare at the landscape. Could we get a carriage of any sort? It would be difficult. That is what they always say: difficult! Meaning impossible. At least, they won't lift a finger to help. Is there an hotel at Cerveteri? They don't know. They have none of them ever been, though it is only five miles away, and there are tombs."

Lawrence arrived from Rome at the Ladispoli-Cerveteri train station and rode, in some sort of an antiquated omnibus, to Cerveteri, known for its *tumoli,* the Etruscan entombments from the eighth century B.C.E. As far as I can tell, Lawrence never actually set foot in the town of Ladispoli, which shares a train station (Stazione di Palo Laziale) with its inland reliquary neighbor, Cervetori. Unlike Lawrence, who traveled around the area of Italy known as Lazio in search of vestiges of the Etruscan past buried under the ruins of a less distant Roman past, we, the Jewish refugees from the USSR, didn't have the choice of sidestepping Ladispoli. Like Lawrence, however, we had but a vague idea of how to find accommodations.

Back in the 1970s several seaside towns around Rome had been designated as holding sites for the Jewish refugees who preferred the mercantile prospects of the New World to the ancestral passion calls of the Promised Land. During the peak years of the middle to late 1970s, when tens of thousands were leaving the Soviet Union, and many of those thousands were going to America and Canada, Ostia and Ladispoli swelled up with the "Russians." I still wonder why Ostia, the seaport of ancient Rome, and Ladispoli, an innocuous seaside resort, had been identified as suitable points of transit for the Jewish immigrants knocking at the gates of the New World. Like the bored legions stationed outside Rome and ready either to sail off and conquer the world or to march into the Eternal City, we languished in the uncertainty of our futures. Ready for action, my parents and I had been thrust into two months of involuntary, anxious restfulness in the Russian fiefdom by the Tyrrhenian Sea.

IN THE SUMMER OF 1987, as the Soviet Union slouched in the back seat of the palliative reforms that eventually brought about its dissolution, the emigration numbers were just beginning to pick up. We were still a feeble creek as compared to the torrents of the 1970s—or to the massive outflow of the late 1980s–early 1990s. In the summer of 1987, most of which my family spent in Italy awaiting our American refugee visas, Ladispoli was the place where the JIAS officials expected us to move after a couple of weeks in the bowels of Rome. About twenty-five miles up the Tyrrhenian coast, Ladispoli was a sleepy seaside town where middle-class Romans owned weekend homes and condos. There the Jewish refugees would rent rooms and apartments and wait. Sometimes the waiting took three or four months, sometimes even longer.

We couldn't afford to purchase a guidebook, nor did we have access to libraries, so in addition to the bits of ancient history that I'd known prior to coming to Ladispoli, what I'd scraped together about the Etruscans came from Anatoly Shteynfeld. Shteynfeld deliberately stayed out of the sun, and his dominant color was that of dusty cobblestones. Depressive by natural inclination, Shteynfeld was disheartened that summer at his prospects for finding an academic job in America. From the first days in Rome, where we stayed at the same hotel, Shteynfeld had chosen me as a student in his open-air academy. During the first three weeks in Italy, in Rome and later in Ladispoli, he would lecture me, in bits and installments, under the porticoes, at shady street corners, under a beach umbrella.

I confess to being torn over Shteynfeld. I admired his vast knowledge, his rhetorical talent, and his flair for languages. I also felt both solidarity with my father, who at that point couldn't stand Shteynfeld, and jealousy of the sort a young man experiences when strange males show interest in his mother—and when the mother seems to reciprocate, however impalpably. And I should add to that tangle a certain unprincipled greed I felt for any new knowledge, a knowledge whose source was right there, free, at my fingertips, in the shape of Shteynfeld's moveable lectures.

At least initially, Shteynfeld wanted to ingratiate himself with me and thus please my mother. He was obsessed with the Etruscans. He lectured me, always impromptu, on the spot and about the spot. I still remember from his lectures that in the Etruscan Age the area near Ladispoli had a port that served the settlement of Caere, precursor of today's Cerveteri. The Romans called the port Alsium, and it was already known as a resort in the time of Republican Rome. Cicero mentions how Caesar contemplated landing in Alsium on his return from Africa. Classicists tend not to bother too much with the rest of history, and it was not from Shteynfeld but from some plaque or public map that I later learned that Ladispoli had not been incorporated until the 1880s. It received its name from its founder, Prince Ladislao of the Odescalchi family, originally from the north of Italy.

The Russian Ladispoli didn't extend beyond the town's central quarter. Its boundaries were: the Tyrrhenian sea to the south, train tracks to the north (and the ancient Via Aurelia just beyond the tracks), and two canals, one to the east and one to the west, both of them flowing into the sea. That seaside chunk of land—a strip of black sandy beach and a grid of boulevards running along the water and cross streets descending to it—altogether about three square miles in size—was our demesne. Some unspoken pact existed between the refugees and the local Italian authorities. They kept a vigilant eye on us, and we rarely ventured into the town's other quarters. An invisible demarcation line lay between the Russian Ladispoli and the rest of the area. There were bridges over the canals, and over the train tracks too, but most of us didn't venture over and beyond.

While Jewish refugees from other parts of the world also stayed in Ladispoli, the "Russians" dominated. Russian speech would be heard everywhere in the central quarter. How did the locals treat us? For the shopkeepers and owners of rental property we were a source of easy profit. For the town's fancy crowd of Romans who came for the weekend to laze on the beach and stroll the boulevards at sunset, we were a collective nuisance to their *borghese* sense of decorum. Do the Ladispolites still remember the wild Russians? Or have they forgotten us? How long did it take them to cleanse their memory of the guttural strangers? I can't get the half rhyme out of my head: Etruscans-Russians. Born out of sound, the parallel doesn't make much sense historically, as the Italians were there permanently, and it was the Russian refugees who just came and went, and yet I keep thinking of ourselves as the Etruscans whose civilization was wiped out by the Romans. Gibberish, I know, but sweet and melancholy gibberish.

Ladispoli's seedy Tyrrhenian beach with its fine black sand was our refugee parlor, library, and newsroom. Like the lives of hundreds of other refugees stuck there, our lives, mine and my parents', were centered on waiting for America. That summer was one of the few times, perhaps the only time in my life, when I completely surrendered to greater forces of being. There was nothing I could do to speed up the workings of the American consulate. I had but the faintest idea of where we were going in America. Having already been at university for almost three years before I left Russia, I knew that once in America I would try to transfer to some university. But that's about all I knew.

I've been to Italy twice since 1987, for extended stays, in 2002 and 2004. Both times I was working on books and faced deadlines, but I still carved out some time for travel. Many times I've thought of—and talked to my wife and my parents about—visiting Ladispoli, but something has kept me away from it, some force that dislikes closures and completed life journeys. When I think back to those summer months, I find it difficult to reconstruct many of them in linear order. During the first weeks there, our refugee time still lacked narrative vintage.

That summer I encountered colorful characters that many a fiction-ist would have snatched away for his story: Umberto Umberto, the So-loveitchiks, Bianca the Cowgirl, the Roubenis from Esfahan, and many others. Yet they refuse to bow to my designs. How am I to relate the memories of Ladispoli without overplotting? I must pause, at least for now, and resort to what rememberers often do when jammed in narra-tive grooves: tell anecdotes and weave vignettes, while waiting for the arrival of stories replete with heroic entanglements and confrontations. And so it will have to be until the narrative currents have picked me up again and carried me toward the end of summertime, toward America.

VIA FIUME

A Jewish refugee in Italy quickly escaped the calendary embraces in favor of a stretchable epic time. On a particular morning of a particu-lar day at the end of June, my father and I got off a regional train at the Ladispoli-Cervetori station at the very scene where D. H. Law-rence, the student of "vicious" Etruscans, once stood divining the landscape. I seem to recall this was on a Friday morning, and on the following Monday we were expected to be moving from Rome. A bus was supposed to take to Ladispoli a group of refugees and all our be-longings, including my aunt's Manchurian trunk, now emptied of its human cargo. The JIAS officials had told us that it was "imperative" that we find housing there, and that the hotel in Rome was only paid for through Sunday night. Back in Rome, mother was waiting for us at the hotel near Termini. "Please find something decent," she told father and me in the morning. Mother was now feeling a little less de-spondent, but she still couldn't face the prospect of spending a whole summer in another mousehole.

That morning on the commuter train, tubby Shteynfeld, who was dressed in a pajama-like striped shirt, knee-length shorts, and turquoise espadrilles, gave me a crash course on the ancient history of Palo, the location of Ladispoli. Meanwhile, my father perused a new issue of a Parisian émigré quarterly he had procured from a Russian ecumenical center near the Vatican.

When we first stepped out of the Ladispoli-Cervetori train station on that Friday, the sun was moving to its zenith, like a hot pebble from David's slingshot toward Goliath's whitish, bulging eye. In front of a news kiosk advertising an Italian-language biography of Lenin, we dropped Shteynfeld, deep in his Etruscan ruminations. We then traversed the train station square and headed south in the direction of the sea. After a couple of shabby blocks that not so rarely surround small-town train stations, father and I found ourselves walking down a wide avenue lined with shops—mainly selling jewelry, shoes, and flowers. Compared to the opulent store window displays in Rome, many of the Ladispoli vitrines looked as though they hadn't been changed since the 1950s, when the town boomed into a weekend beach resort.

Teeming with uncertainty, father and I had come to Ladispoli to find an apartment. For how long would we stay there? We didn't know for sure, and the JIAS bureaucrats weren't telling us. Perhaps they also didn't know, but at least a month, possibly two, even three.

A dark, photocopied map of Ladispoli's central quarter fluttered in my hands like a diagram of improbability. As father and I approached the sea and the seaside promenade, we went over our family's finances. From the proceeds of our recent rummage sale of imported goods to the Bukharan black marketer Isak we had about two hundred dollars. We also legally brought with us from the Soviet Union about three or four hundred dollars—I can no longer recall. And we had about eighty dollars left from the thousand shillings Günter W. had given us. Those sums, combined, were our total Western startup capital. The rest of our property consisted of things immaterial, such as manuscripts of my father's works that were being smuggled out of the USSR in diplomatic pouches (or had already been smuggled and deposited with friends in America). And also the collective baggage of our Soviet memories— my mother's, my father's, and mine—the baggage that at times felt so lofty and at other times would weigh us to the ground. We were supposed to be living off an allowance JIAS paid each refugee, plus an additional stipend per each family or household. During the weeks prior to leaving Moscow, and later at the refugee hostel in Austria, we had a number of calls from my parents' old friends who had gotten out in the 1970s. Several of them also sent us letters in Italy, and I remember one of them, from a former colleague of my mother's, a gifted linguist who made a stunning career working for a New York–based international agency. "Save every dollar, every penny," she preached on office stationery. "Every portion of gelato could later go toward a car, a house down payment."

The easiest way to save money in Ladispoli would have been on rent. Already in Rome we'd heard that in summer three hundred thousand lire (a thousand lire at the time equaled about one American dollar) would rent one a room, and six hundred thousand—a small apartment. My enterprising aunt, who had gone to Ladispoli two days before us, managed to find a room in a three-room cottage. She, my grandmother, and my cousin crammed in there all summer long, sharing a communal bathroom with the family of an astronomer, whose proverbial stinginess became the talk of refugee Ladispoli.

It was definitely the landlords' market; in the spring and summer of 1987, for the first time in years, the demand for smaller and cheaper accommodations had exceeded what Ladispoli had to offer. Much of the short-term rental market resembled Crimean resorts, where entire families of Soviet vacationers routinely shared one room or even a converted shed. When I was three, my parents took me to Sebastopol on the Crimean coast. We never went back, preferring the tepid Estonian summers to the Crimean heat and squalor. Year after year, in our beloved resort of Pärnu on Estonia's west coast, we rented the same lovely apartment by the sea and pretended we were living in a foreign, Western country—someplace in Scandinavia, perhaps. As father and I approached the sea—wet emerald flesh and black sandy curls visible through the chinks between the waterfront villas—we knew that a room without a view wasn't an option for our weary family.

The avenue linking the train station and the waterfront rested its dusty limbs on the main piazza. Despite the nearing hour of siesta, small groups of former Soviets stood on the chessboard of dark brown and pale pink stone squares: in the middle and around the flanks a few scrawny pawns in white or gray short-sleeved shirts; a couple of

taller officers in summer kepis; bearded and unshaven horses neighing Russian inflections. Who and where the refugee kings and queens
were, nobody knew. Father and I traversed the piazza along its shadowy edges. In about fifteen minutes we met up again, after shaking out
of our compatriots, most of them from Ukraine and parts of Belarus,
tidbits of information on what properties were available and who was
moving out that weekend. The pickings were slimmer than slim. There
was a possibility of a small apartment above a busy restaurant with live
music in the evening, and still only a maybe. There were vacancies in
what one elderly gentleman from Vitebsk (Marc Chagall's hometown)
had described to us as *"barskie pokoi"* (noblemen's quarters) but what
later turned out to be a ramshackle stucco villa with many missing roof
tiles, crumbling red brick gates, and a front door swinging back and
forth in the breeze. And there were a couple of other prospects, equally
lacking privacy and comfort.

By the time father and I had seen them all, it was almost three
in the afternoon. We had already eaten our apples and bananas and
didn't know what to undertake next. Images of rooms we would share
with apronly matrons from the former Pale, which my grandparents
left as young people to go to college in big Russian cities and never to
return; negatives of a littered courtyard with scabrous Odessan jokes
broadcast across the local earwaves from dawn to dusk; phantasmagoric communal bathroom scenarios. All these scenes danced in my head
as Father and I dragged ourselves up Via Ancona, one of the town's
main arteries running parallel to the sea.

"Bloodispoli." My father pressed the words out through his perfectly straight teeth. (In Russian, this variation on the town's name
sounded dirtier and slightly more ominous.) "What are we going to
do? We've got to find something decent for mama."

At this point an educated Russian voice overtook us, catching us
by surprise in an empty afternoon street of a strange Italian resort. The
voice materialized as a handsome man of about thirty, with nervously
twitching fingers and mercurial eyes. He was nicely dressed: a white
shirt, unbuttoned and revealing a small silver medallion with a star of
David on a thin chain; black cotton slacks; elegant sandals.

"Bloodispoli, that's a decent pun," was the man's opening remark. "I'm Daniil Vrezinsky," he said, ceremoniously extending his right hand. "You seem a little desperate, and I've already been here a month. Let me see if I can help you."

Daniil Vrezinsky was the son of a famous Soviet playwright and something of a writer himself. As we later found out, he was a former political dissident who had served a sentence in a Siberian labor camp for reading works by forbidden authors to his high school students in Moscow. Vrezinsky walked us to a modern apartment building on Via Fiume, five or six blocks north of the sea, and closer to the canal that served as the western boundary of Ladispoli's central quarter. He had heard there was an apartment for rent in the building.

"It's going to be pricy, I can tell you right now," he said to us.

He pressed one of the buzzers; a screechy Italian voice answered. Vrezinsky had picked up enough Italian to be able to communicate well with the screechy voice; a couple of minutes later we met its owner. It was an elderly signora, stooped, wearing loads of make up, dropping ashes from a cigarette in a cigarette-holder onto her ferric blue robe.

"She's not, strictly speaking, a concierge, but she's been in the building longer than anybody else and knows all the residents," Vrezinsky explained. "I've got to head back, but I told her you came to inquire after an apartment rental, and she understands how things stand with us refugees." He shook our hands, kissed the hand of the old signora that had forgotten about her cigarette and nearly burned a hole in her robe, and walked away. In our state of confusion, he struck us as the sort of person who jokes with death.

The signora, talking without let-up and lighting another long brown cigarette, took father and me inside the lobby, which—to us— looked like the interior of a luxury hotel. From her *recetativo* I gathered there was an apartment on the eighth floor available immediately, that it belonged to the parents of an unemployed engineer from Rome, and that the asking monthly rent was one million lire (about one thousand dollars), which was more than two-thirds of our combined monthly allowance. That was a great deal of money, and the thought of spending nearly all of it on the apartment was blasphemous.

We went up in the elevator. The signora removed a chain with dozens of keys from a deep sunken pocket of her robe, passed her dark, gouty fingers over the keys like a blind accordionist, found the right one, and unlocked the apartment door. The first thing we saw from an unlit hallway was the sea, sparkling, resplendent, and reassuring. It was like a promise of respite from refugee living. We entered a tastefully decorated one-bedroom with a seafront balcony the length of the whole apartment. The kitchen had an espresso maker, and the living room walls were lined with books. We liked it instantly, and we stood there on the balcony, airing our sweaty and dusty bodies in the breeze coming from the sea below. But one thousand dollars!?! The signora sensed our hesitation and picked up the phone. She dialed, as it turned out, the number of the apartment owners. After an exchange, of which I understood only the words *russi* and *simpatici,* the kindly signora turned to us, and said, beaming, *"novicento mille lire."* Father and I looked at each other, then both looked toward the sea outside the windows, and nodded as we both said our *"molto grazie, signora."*

The formalities were minimal, and the owner didn't even require a deposit. On Monday morning, exactly as the signora had explained to us as we said goodbye, the unemployed engineer met father and me in the apartment while mother waited at the piazza, where the bus had dropped off our group of refugees and the luggage. That afternoon, our first one in the beautiful apartment, after our first swim in the Tyrrhenian Sea and a long siesta, my mother and I walked to a local supermarket and brought back groceries. Cheered up, mother made a stew with turkey meat and zucchini, and we ate it with a bottle of cheap Chianti on our balcony overlooking the clement sea. We had regained a point of stability, a place we would call home for the next two months. The Russian refugees dubbed our street, Via Fiume, "Rechnaya Ulitsa" (in English I can roughly approximate it as River Street). The apartment on River Street brought back memories of my early childhood near the River Terminal area in the northwest of Moscow, where I spent the first four years of my life.

GLI STUDENTI

After the stormy days in Rome, when my parents fought over things they couldn't possibly change or control—the miserable hotel near Termini, the ridiculous amount of our relatives' luggage, or the gushing uncertainty of our future—the first weeks in Ladispoli were peaceful. All three of us rested, selfishly, greedily, feasting on the slowness of time and the somnolent atmosphere—just the way we used to rest from breakneck Moscow during our annual vacations in Estonia.

The Jewish-Russian refugees had claimed as their own a strip of public beach in the middle of Ladispoli's Lungomare Centro. Our beach was polluted and overpopulated, but it was still the same beach with Aphroditean foam on the waves and the same mirage of Sardinia on the horizon. All around us was the same fine black sand, sparkling like mounds of coal in a moving freight train, squeaking like a new bicycle tire on asphalt, and erupting like smoke from under our bare feet.

The Italians avoided our beach, going to the other sections, where umbrellas were lined up and chairs could be rented. They felt alienated among hundreds of foreigners lazing in the sun, arguing politics, feeding their children, and consuming their salami and tomato sandwiches on slabs of bread with crunchy radicchios, scallions, and cucumbers. There were no changing cabins on the Russian section of the beach, and those who changed in and out of their bathing suits would do it Soviet style, a towel wrapped around them. North African refreshment vendors would dash across the length of our beach, letting their voices rest from having to scream "Mama mia, mama mia, Coca-Cola fantasia"—and expecting few sales.

Meeting three Roman students on the third day in Ladispoli was pure luck for me. Returning after a swim, I found my parents struggling to communicate with Italians my age. One of them—his name was Leonardo, and he always added that he painted "like a cat" ("come gatto," which meant badly)—spoke enough English to be able to understand that we hailed from Moscow and were in Ladispoli at least for the summer. In fact, he and my father knew about the same amount of English. The other two young Italians spoke virtually no English. All three were university students, grew up in Rome, and had known each other for years. They had just gotten out of school and returned to Ladispoli for the summer, and curiosity brought them to the Russian section of the beach that morning. They had been in their early teens the last time there were so many Russians in Ladispoli, in the late 1970s.

At about five o'clock the next afternoon our doorbell rang, and Leonardo and the other two Italians, Tomasso and Sylvio, came to collect me. I'd told them our building number on Via Fiume, although I never expected they would actually turn up. But they did, and the old signora had helped my new friends find our apartment. Two years older than Tomasso and Sylvio, Leonardo was short and sanguine, with black wavy hair, small, brown eyes, a bumpy nose, and perfect white teeth. Tomasso was tall and lanky, green-eyed, with blonde and almost Nordic looks; his parents, I later learned, had come from Piedmont. And Sylvio was the sunniest of the three friends, and also the most stylish one, sporting fabulous short-sleeved shirts that he would wear unbuttoned down to the middle of his hairy chest. He always suede shoes, never sandals. ("Our Sylvio, he has a fixation with shoes," Leonardo later explained.) A half smile never left Sylvio's finely chiseled Roman face, and that afternoon when they appeared at our door, he charmed my parents by standing there and just smiling at them as though he'd known them his whole life.

For some reason my father was extremely excited when *gli studenti* showed up at our place, perhaps because they reminded him of his own youth and of reading Alberto Moravia's stories in Russian translation. "Go on, go with them," he said in his strident whisper, pushing me toward the door.

"We . . . meet other friends," Leonardo said, stumbling through the sentence. "At a café. We want that . . . that you come with us." And so it began.

Twice, sometimes three times a week for the next two months I would see my Italian friends. Leonardo, Tomasso, and Sylvio were part of a larger group of young men and women who either grew up spending summers in Ladispoli or lived there year-round. Leonardo had just graduated that year with a degree in agriculture, and the job prospects were grim.

"Why agriculture?" I remember asking him soon after we'd met.

"I want to live in Australia. For me it's the . . . the best country," he replied. "I want to practice English with you."

At the university Tomasso and Sylvio both took computer science. When Leonardo wasn't there, all communication between them and me had to be in Italian and in the not-always-universal language of facial expressions and gesticulations. On my first trip back to Rome (I would make weekly shopping trips to a big open-air market) I bought a short English-language Italian grammar book, by Olga Ragusa, that I still have with me today—one of the few material souvenirs of that Italian summer. I started looking things up and writing down Italian words in a small notebook. Certain words stuck to my ears, although I sometimes inferred their meaning quite incorrectly. By the end of our time in Italy I had learned (much of it incorrectly) enough grammar and picked up enough vocabulary to be able to communicate in more or less complete sentences. So jovially earned, much of my Italian quickly evaporated over the first few years in America, but some words and phrases haven't unlearned themselves and still come back with quick memories of Ladispoli.

Looking back at the Italian students (I call them "students" instead of "peers," although several in that extended group had already graduated and were looking for work) I can see that they were in some ways like Soviet students and in others like American students. And I related to them better than I would initially relate to the peers I would meet in America. Living in a free country, they were freer than the Soviet students, yet they were still given to both collectivism and camaraderie. Despite my shortage of spending money (about a dollar a day was my budget), I never felt like a poor refugee among them. At least looking back at my refugee self going to discos, pizzerias, and cafés, or simply hanging out in the streets with the Italians, I recognize that despite a communication barrier—and despite being penniless and stateless—I felt at ease with my Italian friends. Call it European, call it Socialist, call it flawed or whatever else you like; it won't alter my memories. Among the Italian students I felt different but not strange. During my first two years as a student at Brown, I felt both different and strange among my peers.

When I recall the Ladispoli months, I rarely see myself in the company of other young Soviet refugees, especially young men my age. I don't remember making any deliberate decision of the sort, but it was probably that I wanted to distance myself from my raw Soviet past. And also an urge to be a person of no identity, a citizen of the world. Running with the crowd of Italians accorded both a sense of anonymity (read: lack of difference) and an easy way to disguise my Sovietness. There were probably two more factors in place. One was a knowledge, which can be particularly acute when you've just left your whole world behind, that you will never again have such extraordinary friends—a kind of stubborn loyalty to the circle of my Moscow friends broken by my own departure. And there was also the sense that I didn't have enough in common (I'm not talking about political status) with the young men and women from Ukraine, Belarus, and Moldova, some of whom came from smaller towns where Jewish life of the Pale had not been completely erased after World War II and the Holocaust. To the outside world, oblivious to subtleties of our origin and cultural upbringing, we were the same—Soviets, Jews, but mainly "Russians." But in reality Russian was a lingua franca, not a language of shared culture that I had in common only with a few Soviet peers also waiting in Ladispoli that summer.

As I already mentioned, my Italian rescuers, Leonardo, Tomasso, and Sylvio, belonged to an extended group of students and recent university graduates who had known each other for years. They used to congregate at night in the main piazza or in a seaside café with red chairs designed for very skinny people. Several Italian young women I met during my first week in Ladispoli were studying to be school teachers. One of them, Bianca Marini, drove a mosquitoey postwar Citroen and had freckles brighter than the new moon. Bianca was small and slender, with muscular arms, breasts big for her frame, and a small, boyish behind. On the first night we stayed out well past midnight, kissing on a boulevard bench as the tired waiters collected and chained the outdoor chairs and tables. After that I didn't see Bianca for two days, and on the following day, in the late afternoon, I ventured into the territory beyond the canal—to the west of the central quarter. Bianca had given me the address and also said something about . . . cows. I crossed the canal and then followed the road for about a mile, as the houses became fewer and the landscape changed its face from a drowsy town to Mediterranean countryside.

It turned out that Bianca lived on a small dairy farm. There was the main house, barns, and sheds, a kitchen garden and fruit trees, and even a small olive grove in the far end of the property. I opened the gate and walked to the front steps of the house where I stood for a couple of minutes, stepping in place, hesitating to ring the bell. A blocky version of Bianca, also freckled and with toned arms, greeted me as she opened the door.

"*Voglio parlare con Bianca, per favore,*" I said.

"Bianca," she repeated, then delivered what felt like one very long sentence, of which I mainly understood the word gelato. And she (Bianca's elder sister, as it turned out) ran outside and disappeared into one of the barns, screaming out "Bianca, Bianca." In another minute I saw Bianca walking toward me, a floral apron tied around her waist, a cotton scarf hiding the wispy curls of her rusty-brown hair. Transformed this way, she looked more a Russian country girl.

"Well, this is where I live. We make our own ice cream," Bianca explained. "It's been a family business for two generations."

Sounds of mooing and smells of hay and manure—the overheated sounds and smells of a country afternoon—caught up with me on the porch, where Bianca brought out a large bowl of freshly made vanilla ice cream. Bianca's ice cream tasted not like gelato, whose novelty still hadn't worn off, but like *slivochnoe morozhenoe*—the Soviet buttery ice cream. Bianca herself had instantly lost her allure. I wasn't ready for dating Italian cowgirls and getting chubby on their sweet creams.

A FLAUTIST IN FLIGHT

At the Vienna airport, soon after we had landed, I briefly met a refugee my age, a musician. He was traveling with his parents, younger sister, and grandparents. They were from Baku, Mountain Jews. In Vienna their family and ours were put up in different refugee hostels. My father met the musician's father on our second day in Vienna in the JIAS offices. Their last name was Abramov and they were on their way to Florida, where they had family in Miami.

About two weeks after we had settled in Ladispoli, I decided to get a haircut and walked over to a barber shop located two blocks from our apartment building on Via Fiume. For the price of a dry haircut one could get four small gelatos, each with three different flavors. My mother then asked around on the beach and was told that one Abramov, a barber from Baku, was giving haircuts at his home for only about two dollars, the price of one gelato. The following afternoon, after what was becoming a customary siesta, I headed for the makeshift refugee barber shop.

It was in the eastern section of Ladispoli's central quarter, in a street of small villas, shady inner courtyards, crumbling stone walls, and overgrown orchards, where many Soviet refugee families rented rooms. One side of a green gate was slightly ajar, and I entered through it, crossing the courtyard of a decrepit villa, in the middle of which a *putto* pressed his ashen lips to a dead fountain. Outside the gate, shirtless children were kicking a deflated soccer ball and screaming in Russian. In the back of the courtyard, under the shadow of an old quince, I saw a hirsute man slouched in a chair and Abramov giving him a shave. Instead of the heavy woolen derby I'd seen him wear at the Vienna airport, Abramov was now wearing a taupe summer cap. Next to him, on a three-legged stool, was a basin of water. Abramov's daughter stood next to her father, smiling and holding a cup with foam and a towel. A few steps away, under a maze of undulating vines, an antediluvian couple sat on two chairs, just as they had on a suitcase at the Vienna airport, dressed in the same outfits, including the old man's astrakhan. A dagger was attached to the belt of the old man's fitted coat. Silent and motionless, the old couple observed their son's performance on the refugee, a piano tuner from Belarus whom I'd previously met in Vienna. Like cherry petals, the piano tuner's large curls rhythmically fell to the ground. "Like cherry blossoms in a Russian orchard," I thought to myself at the time. "Like cherry blossoms in D.C.," I edit myself now.

The barber from Baku sprayed his client with something that smelled like an air freshener, like in a real Soviet barber shop, then took the money and stuffed it in the pocket of his linen trousers. He then dangled a new cigarette out of the corner of his mouth and invited me to the chair. The girl wrapped a sheet around my neck and tied its corners in the back.

"What are we doing?" the barber from Baku asked quietly, like a singer sparing his voice.

"Just a trim," I answered.

"I met your father in Vienna," Abramov said in a deadpan voice. "A kind, educated man."

"Uh-huh."

"So what do you want to do in America?" asked the barber, scissors clacking.

"I'm not really sure."

"Not sure?" he cackled.

"Study," I replied, irritated by the man's intrusiveness. "Make something of myself."

"I'll tell you what." Abramov stopped cutting my hair and wiped his brow with a white handkerchief big enough to serve as an armistice flag. "Who lived well there will live well here."

What could I answer to such a maxim? Nothing, really. Abramov and I didn't speak for the rest of the haircut.

As I was getting up from the chair, having already refused the offer of being sprayed with air freshener, the old man in the astrakhan suddenly jumped up from his seat, like a Jack-in-the-box, and minced up to me on his crooked horseman's legs. He spoke in fearsome, heavily accented Russian, the words knocking against his teeth like rocks in a mountain stream.

"Have you heard the name Juhuro, son?" he asked.

"No," I answered.

"Figures. What do young men know these days? Juhuro, that's what we call ourselves in our language. We're Mountain Jews. You sometimes call us Tats, but we call ourselves Juhuro. You understand?"

"Yes, I understand. And I've heard of Mountain Jews—from my father."

The old man straightened the belt of his coat and made smacking noises with his lips.

"Do you know what an *aoul* is?" he then asked, disdainfully.

"Sure I do. Everyone knows that. *Aoul* is a Turkic word; it means 'mountain village.'"

"Well," the old man continued. "If you know that, you should also know that my ancestors had lived in the same *aoul* since the fifth century. And before that. . . . We are from the lost tribes of Israel, you see. We'd been in the Caucasus a long, long time. Long before the Azeris and various others. We were all warriors and winegrowers in my family, and I'm the last one." The old man looked me in the eye and violently shook his head, the top of the astrakhan striking me. It was warm, so warm that it felt like a ram nudging me on the temple.

"What did your grandfathers do during the war?" asked the old warrior.

"One commanded a tank unit and later a torpedo boat unit that stormed Königsberg. The other—"

"—and I," he interrupted, beating himself on the chest with his clenched fists, "and I cleansed the Caucasus of the collaborationist dogs. Don't believe anything they tell you. These dogs greeted the Germans like their liberators. We Juhuro fought against the bastards."

Saliva now sprayed from the old warrior's mouth. He grabbed me by the arm and held me, and I couldn't get away without pushing him—which would have been awfully rude, considering I was in the lap of this patriarchal family from the Caucasus. My captor saw that he could do anything with me, and he triumphantly switched the subject from family history to family woes. His son, the barber from Baku, stood under the shadow of the old quince, awaiting his next customer, smoking, and observing his father not without pleasure. The warrior's granddaughter stood beside her father, still holding a cup with lather and a towel, and still smiling like a village idiot. Smiling at what?

"My son moved to the city. You've heard of Baku, right? That's where they ship the oil from, so my son had a barber shop and did fine for himself, but he wanted to make more money and dragged us along."

What he was saying no longer made any sense to me, and I had trouble nodding to the old man's words. "All of you young people are a bunch of lazy good-for-nothings. Have you met my grandson Aleksandr?"

"Just briefly, at the airport. In Vienna, when we first arrived," I replied.

"My grandson's a sissy. I have two other grandsons—in the Israeli army. My older son went there in the seventies. They are warriors, like real men in our family. But my daughter is in Florida with her husband and kids. They've got a family business there, and that's where . . . Ah, it's no use." The old man bent over in a paroxysm of coughing and let go of my wrist and T-shirt.

I paid and turned around, preparing to make my exit, when I saw Aleksandr Abramov, the young musician with whom I'd briefly spoken at the Vienna airport. He was dressed in a rumpled white shirt and gray pinstriped slacks. He came up to me and put out his hand, small like a child's. I shook it.

"Let's take a walk together," he proposed, gently taking me by the wrist and leading me out of the courtyard and into the street. Sea-green rain clouds had gathered over Ladispoli by the time our walk brought us to a poorly lit establishment in the train station square, where a couple of drunks argued politics with a long-armed, sloppily peroxided woman who was tending the bar. I bought us each a Coca-Cola, and we sat there for about an hour, waiting for the summer downpour to subside and to release us.

"I'm sorry you had to deal with my family," he said. "Grandfather has somehow gotten an old blade through customs. What was he thinking, the old moron? And he now wears it attached to his stupid belted jacket. He says it's to defend the family honor. But I detest all that medieval barbarism and my grandfather's cruelty—he's killed men, you know—and also my father's crude barbershop jokes. I only love my mother and little sister . . . and . . . ," he paused, holding back the tears and fishing for a lighter in his pocket. "I just want to be left alone," he finally said, taking a long drag of smoke.

Aleksandr and I never became friends. Over the rest of the summer we would exchange an odd remark, trade a couple of words or a handshake, but not more. Our sole lengthy conversation occurred on that July afternoon, in a train station bar under pouring rain, after a haircut by his father and his grandfather's lecture on Mountain Jews. Aleksandr needed to unbottle himself, and I simply came along to serve as a chance confessor.

Aleksandr didn't ask me anything about myself and the Moscow world I'd left behind. He only asked one thing:

"What was it like for you, growing up Jewish?

"It was tough," I replied. "Especially in middle school." I didn't feel like getting further into the subject.

"I've heard about it from some other kids here in Ladispoli." The "it" referred to the taunting of Jewish children by their non-Jewish peers. "I personally have never felt discriminated against as a Jew," said Aleksandr. "In our yard in Baku all neighborhood kids played together." He held the Coca-Cola bottle by the neck between his thumb and middle finger, letting it sway and keep time with his words.

"We were like a family—Azeris, Armenians, Russians, Ukrainians, European Jews, Mountain Jews, you name it. Oh, you have no idea. It was such a happy life. I didn't want to leave, you know. I had everything there. I went to a special school for musically gifted children. At our Baku conservatory I had the best teachers. Oh, it was wonderful there. When we were leaving my whole neighborhood came to say goodbye. We all walked to the cabs, like brothers, arm in arm. I will never forget that, you see, never. And he was there, too."

"He who?" I asked automatically, without thinking.

"Just why did we have to leave?!" Aleksandr wailed, shifting his gaze toward one of the gesticulating drunks who was falling over the bar. "I just want to play my flute and be with him."

In my post-Soviet chivalry, I was quite innocent of anything that didn't concern liking girls.

"You understand, friend, don't you?" Aleksandr asked, and placed his limp hand on top of mine, prostrate on the table like a dead animal.

Ignoring my hypnotized stare, Aleksandr took the last gulp of his Coca-Cola and said, "To my simple parents he was an Azeri. To my fanatical grandfather he was a Muslim dog. But he was Adonis to me, you understand. Adonis."

The rain had stopped, and moisture quickly dried on Ladispoli's sparkly gills. We walked back to the sea without saying anything to each other.

THE ROUND MARKET

In its pre-Russian existence Ladispoli doubled as a weekend beach resort for the Romans and a commuting suburb. The refugees found the place decidedly unfit for food shopping. For some reason I don't recall any small grocery stores. Perhaps there weren't any in the area where we stayed, or perhaps we didn't feel comfortable stepping into a corner store and asking for something in English, or by gesture, or in rudimentary Italian, while being scrutinized by the wary storekeeper. There were fabulous supermarkets in Ladispoli—at least they seemed fabulous to us at the time. The anonymity and freedom of supermarket aisles appealed to us. We could touch and palpate various goods, admiring them as in a museum without having to buy them. We loved shopping in supermarkets and bought certain staples there, but on the whole they were too upscale for our narrow pockets. Occasionally farmers would bring boxes and crates of fruit and vegetables and sell them right on the main seaside boulevard, outside our apartment windows, but we couldn't depend on it.

Enter the "Round Market." At Mercato di Piazza Vittorio, located in Piazza Vittorio Emmanuelle II, refugees from the USSR bought their food supplies. Over the course of the summer I must have made seven or eight pilgrimages to the market. In the morning I would walk to the Ladispoli-Cervetori train station—Etruscans, Italian girls, and hazy plans for America all swirling in my head—and get on a commuter train, heavily graffitied and already sultry despite the early hour. The ride to Termini took about forty-five minutes. The train made a few stops in the suburbs and in several sections of Rome, of which I remember three: Roma Aurelia (because of a golden echo cocooning in its tunnel), Roma San Pietro (because of the Vatican), and Trastevere, which referred to what was on the other side of the Tevere, or the river Tiber.

The market opened early and operated Monday through Saturday until one or two in the afternoon, but the whole point was to get there an hour or so before closing, when the bargaining was unbridled and the merchants slashed the prices of the unsold fruit, vegetables, greens, and fresh meat. This is why I would leave Ladispoli in the morning and wander the streets of Rome before turning into a Roman housewife and heading for Piazza Vittorio. Two or three times I got off the train before Termini. I believe the Vatican museums were only free on the last Sunday of the month, so I couldn't combine a trip to the Round Market with a visit to the Sistine Chapel. But I didn't need tickets to stroll through the Trastevere, and I remember walking across an ancient bridge onto Isola Tiberina and then over another bridge to a nineteenth-century synagogue in the former Jewish ghetto where a sixteenth-century pope forced the Jews of Rome to reside as hostages of his own guilt. Walking the Roman streets and piazzas that summer, I thought a lot about a Jewish reformer by the name of Yehoshua, about leaving Russia, and about coming to Rome, as other Jews had done in the past centuries and millennia.

I remember leaving the Jewish ghetto and heading west toward Campo de Fiori. I preferred the main streets, which I could clearly make out on my small, poorly photocopied map of Rome: Corse Vittorio Emmanuelle II, then hopping a few blocks over the Roman Forum to Via Nazionale, where I ogled at the clothing stores and at the fashionable people, and then all the way into Piazza della Repubblica. I never took the metro in Rome, although it's just one stop on the direct line connecting Termini and Vittorio. There was also a trolley car that skirted the busy and squalid Piazza Vittorio, and there were buses from

Termini, but I always walked, there and back, to save on the fare. From Piazza della Repubblica I knew the way to Termini and beyond. The open-air market at Piazza Vittorio was less than a mile south of the train station. The first time I walked there from Termini, I ended up on Esquilino, one of the seven hills of Rome, reluctantly asking for directions to what I referred to, in Italian, as *marchetto tondo* (which means something like "round male whore") and getting only expressions of puzzlement in return for my earnest face. It was *market* in English, *Markt* in German, so why would it be *mercato* in Italian? I ended up in a vast park where Emperor Nero had built his Golden House and Emperor Trajan his baths, and where homeless plebeians now slept on benches and all the red poppies had already been harvested. From there I eventually made my way back to Piazza Esquilino, where, as realized, I'd been with my parents for a medical exam required for a U.S. visa. Of Santa Maria Maggiore I remember the long pistil of the belfry and rubbed-off dragonfly mosaics. Going into churches and cathedrals was free, and at the time, despite a certain Jewish militancy, I justified such visits as paying homage to Western art. In fact, at Moscow University I sat in on a course on Renaissance art, taught by the brilliant academician Nikolay Grashchenkov, who had at first encouraged me to switch to an art history major, but had a rapid change of heart after learning my last name—or whatever else he had learned about my refusenik family.

Ever since I was a small child in Russia, I've loved markets. This is my father's influence, no doubt, as my chic and metropolitan mother never cared for the experience of dealing with farmers in their stalls, of checking out the wares and negotiating prices. My father, however, probably because of the three wartime years he spent as an evacuee in a remote Uralian village, was his happy self amid pyramids of apples and barrels of salt cabbage. He had taught me the lexicon and grammar of shopping and bargaining at Russian farmers' markets, and I put it to good use in Rome. Mercato di Vittorio was a maze of circular aisles dotted with what looked like thousands of stalls, some of them covered and shadowy. The whole vast market was an octopus that spread its scorching, mottled tentacles around the central garden of this Baroque square, strangling its verdure and sucking life out of the customers. Being there gave me a different feeling, not the pulsating freedom and bravado of the Russian markets that I love and still miss today, but a combined sensation of being in a cramped and bustling Mediterranean fish market, an American flea market, and a roadside farm stand on a sweltering summer afternoon.

I read recently that the Round Market is to be closed as the city fathers believe it's an ugly blot on the face of Rome and Piazza Vittorio. I refuse to believe it. Without the market, the piazza will look so naked and sterile, so clean and cold. Although I've twice been back to Italy over the years, I haven't gone back to Rome. At times I wonder if this has anything to do with the bitterness that taints those otherwise thrilling memories of Rome—the bitterness I feel when I think of the tension between my parents. Or, perhaps I haven't revisited Rome and Ladispoli out of a fear of having to check and revise my memories. I know I'll visit Rome one day, but going back also means walking to Piazza Vittorio and stocking up for another week of waiting for America.

At the Round Market I bought turkey meat, vegetables, and fruit in volume; the supplies were supposed to last us a week. By the time I had finished the shopping, midday would have descended into the infernal Roman afternoon (Piazza Dante lay just beyond the south corner of the market square). I lugged back the provisions in a capacious extra-durable, East German–made plaid shopping bag that was part of a Soviet emigrant's list of objects that were supposed to become useful in transit. It had small wheels and a bottom reinforced with metal, but I couldn't very well roll it across the uneven cobblestones. The bag would be filled with layers of food arranged according to durability. Potatoes, carrots, apples, zucchinis, radishes, cucumbers, onions, garlic, and other crunchy fellows had to be bought first and arranged in the lower strata of the bag, followed by the more tender aubergines and pears, then by turkey meat and cheese, and finally toppled over with plums, peaches, apricots, cherries, delicate tomatoes, and bunches of greens. Since turkey breasts were more expensive, I mainly bought thighs, legs, and especially wings, which the refugees called "wings of the Soviet," after the name of the Soviet air force soccer team.

Every Thanksgiving I'm reminded of having overdosed on turkey while still in Italy. In Ladispoli turkey remained the foundation of our meat diet, which delighted us at first, but which we were totally sick of by the end of the first month. It initially delighted us because in Russia turkey meat was considered a delicacy and could only be found at farmers' markets, where it cost much more than beef. Turkey meat was believed by many to be extremely nutritious, and in the fall of my freshman year at Moscow University, when my mother spent several weeks fighting for her life in one of Moscow's hospitals, my father went to our favorite Leningradsky farmers' market to buy fresh turkey. Every two days he made a turkey stew and brought it to my mother's ward. That was back in 1984, and now it was I who did the marketing for our family. From the trips to Rome I always brought back with me not only descriptions of the sites I'd visited in Rome, but also tales of bargaining.

I had to do the bargaining in Italian, which meant that half the time I wasn't sure that I understood the responses. "Fresco?" I would ask, pointing to a counter plastered with mauve pieces of turkey. The responses varied from the cheery "Of course it's fresh, my friend," to the tenser "You haven't seen fresher," to the downright aggressive "Wipe your eyes," which I knew was still not true hostility. A couple of times, and this was at closing, an exhausted, tousled fellow behind the tomato counter gave me bruised tomatoes for free. And it didn't particularly bother me at the time that this was a form of almsgiving. I had my juicy tomatoes in the bag, and nobody needed to know how I had procured them. I also didn't tell my parents that I passed the stall where Isak the Bukharan speculator sold Russian-made opera glasses, nesting dolls, and other goods that he bought cheaply from the Jewish refugees in their wretched hotel rooms near Termini. Instead I described vivid scenes of the market, the colors and smells of the wares, and the feeling of oneness with a crowd of Roman shoppers.

UMBERTO UMBERTO

He had skin of the sort that many Mediterranean men and also some men in Southern California possess—not a true suntan but a golden facial mask. About sixty-five, medium height, muscular. His thinning hair, combed forward over his shining forehead and his angular temples, was dyed blond. His jade green eyes looked at you a bit off center, as if their owner had made a lot of use of his peripheral vision. A commanding, square lower jaw hinted at his willpower and stamina. This suave Italian spoke excellent Russian, taking his time with the mouthing of the multisyllabic words and displaying a fine sense of the verb aspect. What more could you ask for? He would appear out of a Tyrrhenian breeze, position himself beside a group of refugees, and observe political debates about the country we had all just left and the countries we were going to. Rarely did he say more than *"interesno"* or a similar Russian word or expression, equally weighty and uncommitted. When someone asked for his name, he said, "Umberto," emphasizing the syllable *um,* which in Russian means "intelligence." And he would grin, revealing gold crowns. Since none of us knew his last name, he became known as "Umberto Umberto." "Which Umberto?" the new arrivals would ask. "What do you mean, 'Which Umberto?'" the Ladispoli old-timers replied, as though the question was "What do you mean, 'Which Round Market?'" or "What do you mean, 'Which Ladispoli?'" "The Umberto Umberto." At the time associations with Italian neorealist cinema or with a character in a famous novel by a Russian exile didn't enter my mind, and, like most other refugees, I took Umberto Umberto to be another local landmark, like a gelato stand by the main piazza or a moped-riding rabbi in black and white. There are many things a refugee doesn't question in a strange country. Umberto Umberto was one of them.

After a month in Ladispoli I had found out a bit more about Umberto Umberto. My source was Lyonya Soloveitchik, a former refusenik from Lvov and a doting paterfamilias who exuded such an air of gentleness and harmlessness that, despite his heavy frame, he appeared to walk on water. Out of pure innocence Soloveitchik once came up to Umberto Umberto in the middle of his usual morning at the beach and asked him where he had learned his excellent Russian. Umberto Umberto, who was standing on the stone parapet, periscope eyes scanning the public beach and the refugees, shook his hand and offered him a cigarette from a pack he kept in a chest pocket of his crispy white shirt. Umberto Umberto was about to turn around and walk away when he stopped, half a step in flight, and suggested they take a stroll along the water. Soloveitchik told us that he felt entirely in Umberto Umberto's powers and, unable to stop and turn back, followed along just as he was, in swimming trunks, with his youngest son's yellow sand bucket in hand. By the time Umberto Umberto had returned and released Lyonya Soloveitchik, about half an hour later, at the very spot on the parapet where he had stood observing the refugees on the beach, Soloveitchik had become convinced that Umberto Umberto was a secret agent. And so he worried for the remaining weeks in Ladispoli—until the summons came for his family to appear at the American Consulate for an interview—that by engaging Umberto Umberto, he had ruined his family's chance for happiness in America.

"You wouldn't believe it, but this man hypnotized me," Soloveitchik told us over a cup of tea on our balcony.

"How do you mean?" asked my mother, who doesn't much believe in practical magic.

"Well, he told me this story, which logically makes no sense, about being taken prisoner by Soviet troops. And I listened and nodded and felt absolutely convinced. The guy was probably trained by the CIA or the KGB or the Mossad or some other service to watch over us and file reports."

"So what exactly did he tell you?" my father asked, beginning to smell out delightful threads of fiction in our friend's account.

"He claimed he was captured at the 'Valley of Death' on the Don, after a bayonet charge, in 1943. He said he was wounded in the charge. And that he and thousands of Italian men from the Eighth Army were taken to a Russian POW camp. And that's where he says he learned Russian."

"So what's so unusual about this?" I asked Soloveitchik. "Weren't there Italian and Romanian troops who fought in the south of Russia—not very well, but still?"

"Sure there were. And, in fact, there's an old man here in Ladispoli, going to his daughter's in Detroit. I knew him back in Lvov. He was a political officer during the war, and he vaguely recalls doing propaganda work among Italian POWs in 1945–46. You know, trying to make Communists and Soviet sympathizers out of them. That sort of thing.

"I just can't see his type as a former POW, that's all," Soloveitchik added. "Plus there's something creepy about him. I have a twelve-year-old daughter, you know."

We accepted Umberto Umberto's daily rotation on the orbits of our refugee living the way we accepted the black sand, the sweltering Ladispolian afternoons, and the screams of the Moroccan beach vendors. My aunt tried to befriend him, but it didn't work. A forty-something-year-old woman from Moscow wasn't Umberto Umberto's thing. In the odd spy dream I have every now and again, I see Umberto Umberto speaking through his teeth, by walkie-talkie, to Colonel Ivanov or Lt. Commander McNab or Major Ben-Ami about the next "deployment of rabbits." Umberto Umberto stands there on the Ladispoli promenade, like a pineapple god, smoking his cigarette and smiling a perfect James Bond smile.

APTEKMAN AT FARMACIA

Every story, including this refugee romance of mine, needs its moments of banal beauty.

Back in Gablitz, at the refugee hostel outside Vienna, we had met Mrs. Perelman, a pudgy widow from Moscow. She was headed for Calgary where her son, who had emigrated in the late 1970s, was living with a Canadian wife and two Canadian-born children whom Mrs. Perelman had never seen. She was the inveterate gossip who first told us about a Jewish refugee from the Transcarpathian town of Uzhgorod, who was having an affair with Charlotte, the Austrian owner of the hostel, the one I'd dubbed "Long Nose."

"His name's Aptekman. Such a nothing, a provincial from some God-forsaken town in Western Ukraine," Mrs. Perelman indignantly whispered at the table we shared in the dining room of the Gablitz hostel. "He can't even speak Russian properly. One of those wheeler-dealer types with vulgar mustaches."

In Gablitz we never got to see the Carpathian gigolo, who left before we had arrived from Moscow. And now in Ladispoli we ran smack into Mrs. Perelman at the refugee piazza, a bronzed and rested Mrs. Perelman sporting a straw hat with pink silk flowers. One of the first things she shared with mother and me, after the trivially polite questions about housing and health (father had stayed home to finish writing a story about a Jewish boy traveling to Rome with his young mother), was that "the gigolo had done it again."

"Done what again, Mrs. Perelman?" mother asked.

"Dearie, what else could this type have done?" Mrs. Perelman clasped my mother's wrist, as though trying to infuse the gossip juices into her veins. "He's found himself another foreign victim. This one's an Italian girl from that beautiful pharmacy over by the fountain. It didn't take him long. How does he entice them? I don't understand. Oh, if I only knew the language. I swear I'd reveal to the poor Italian girl what a swindler she's dealing with." Mrs. Perelman pronounced the word *reveal* with much affectation.

Of Ladispoli's many pharmacies, the one to which Mrs. Perelman referred was the nicest one. We had all visited it on separate occasions: My father asked for fishing worms and was offered leeches, my mother had bought some divinely overpriced aspirin, and I had requested, with a lump in my throat, a box of protection. The sales clerk who worked at the *farmacia* looked like an Italian model well past her prime, fittingly so for that aging resort and its local inhabitants. At work she wore her dyed yellow hair up, and her white robe lived a fervent life of its own, apart from the lace and the body it concealed.

I should explain that in Russian, the last name Aptekman immediately brings to mind the word *apteka* (pharmacy, drugstore, apothecary). An ancestor of this Aptekman must have been a pharmacist or owned a pharmacy and thus received his name. A name is a destiny, and it was Aptekman's destiny to win the heart of the Italian woman from the *farmacia*.

Based on Mrs. Perelman's verbal portrait (eyes like prunes, a gangster's shuffling gait, an obnoxious jaw), I pictured Aptekman as a muscular, handsomely crass fellow. Imagine my surprise when I first saw him up close at the beach. That is to say, I recognized the Italian lady from the *farmacia* and assumed that the man in her arms was Aptekman. Except that the real Aptekman turned out to be a stereotypical Soviet Jewish intellectual, nothing like the type Mrs. Perelman had described. A Russian working man would have labeled him an *ochkarik* (from *ochki,* "spectacles"), a bespectacled geek of the sort that shuns physical work and fills the platoons of chess players. Aptekman was tall and skinny, and his unathletic, bony body seemed to repel sun rays. With his thinning wavy hair, big drooping ears, and square plastic-frame glasses, Aptekman from afar conjured up the image of a much older man, but he couldn't have been more than thirty.

They were lying, intertwined, on a large turquoise towel in the thick of the public beach the refugees had colonized. She was wearing a black bikini with sequins. Her stomach was flat like the black Tyrrhenian beach, on which the bodies of thousands of refugees left their daily imprints. Her waist was thin like the tip of a gelato cone. Her tanned body was a lesson in the geometry of desire. They were the most unlikely couple, this timid, myopic Jewish man from Western Ukraine and his Italian lover, all aglow with sensual confidence.

In retrospect I can see why Mrs. Perelman and our whole refugee enclave were so taken with the affair of Aptekman and the bombshell from the *farmacia.* It wasn't just because life in Ladispoli was fairly uneventful. Stealing glances over their shoulders or shamelessly staring at the Italian woman as she kissed and transformed Aptekman, other Soviet refugees imagined themselves in her arms. They, too, were ready to be caressed and seduced by Italy as they waited at her plenteous shores.

5

Rafaella's Rusty Mustang

The narrative currents are gathering on the coast of Ladispoli, and I can feel the winds of storytelling in my sails. I'm ready to describe my adventures with Rafaella. She belonged to the group of Italian students I met in Ladispoli that summer—Leonardo, Sylvio, Tomasso, Bianca Marini, and others. Behind her back, the Italians, men especially, called her "Sarda," and in their attitude toward Rafaella I sensed admiration for her strikingly good looks, an admiration that was laced with prejudice. Rafaella's family had moved from Sardinia when she was eight, and she had grown up in Ladispoli. Yet, even to me, a Soviet refugee uninitiated into the nuances of Italian national identity, Rafaella seemed different—in appearance, in temperament, in style. She stood out from that bunch of Italian friends.

Rafaella's parents owned a flower shop on Ladispoli's main commercial street, which ran from the train station to the sea. She had a younger sister, still in high school, and also an older one, who was married to a navy man and living near Brindisi. Rafaella was studying psychology at Urbino, and for the summer she was back home working at the family shop, where her younger sister also helped out. Her family lived a couple of kilometers west of Ladispoli's central quarter; they grew most of the flowers they sold at the shop. Although I knew her for about two of the two and a half months we stayed in Ladispoli, I was never introduced to her family and only saw them through the windows of the shop as I passed it on the way to and from the train station. Like Rafaella herself, her father, mother, and younger sister had dark complexions and expressive, dolorous faces. Once, and this was after we started dating, I broke a promise to Rafaella and went inside her flower shop to say "hello." It was a late morning in July, and I rode from the beach on a bicycle Tomasso had lent me for a couple of weeks, a trusty old Velossinant to assist me on my quixotic pursuits. I was taking a chance. Luckily, her younger sister wasn't there; Rafaella's father must still have been out making morning deliveries, and her mother was fussing over a flower arrangement in the back of the store. I swaggered in, pretending never to have met Rafaella, and asked for a red rose. A tall one, I indicated with the span of my arms, knowing by the furious flashing of her Moorish eyes that she had no choice but to play along and pretend we weren't acquainted. I waited for her to wrap the thorny flower, then paid for the rose, uttered an unconcerned *"Grazie, buona giornata,"* and motioned toward the door, but then I quickly turned around and handed the rose to Rafaella. *"Per lei, signora,"* I said, using the formal pronoun, and ran out of the store before she could say or do anything. For about a week after that she missed our late-night secret rendezvous, although that same evening I saw her among a group of friends, wearing a red rose in her long, loose hair.

Something stylized and overwrought in Rafaella's appearance now bleeds through the sheets of memory, but I certainly didn't make much of it when I knew her in Ladispoli that summer. Light sandals with straps woven up and around her slender ankles and calves, long billowy skirts, and low-cut blouses with long, drooping sleeves. That was her fashion. There was a muddy creaminess to her face, a dark glow that enhanced the coral whiteness of her perfect teeth. Like myself, Rafaella was a true Gemini, with two conflicting personalities. She was pensive and subdued, even sulky, or else almost mad with sensual energy. And I have no idea why, for almost a month, she kept me as her nighttime companion. I certainly would have chosen her—who wouldn't? Rafaella was the most dazzling girl I met that whole summer in Italy. But why did she choose me? Was it because she, too, felt like something of a foreigner?

Her English was the best of all the Italians in the group, better than that of Bianca Marini, who was studying to be an English teacher, and with Rafaella I felt I could express myself more adequately. I didn't find myself alone with her until the end of June, two weeks into our

Ladispoli stay, and our first date was an American movie, a Wednesday-night screening at the local American Center run by a proselytizing pastor and his wife. The movie was called *Breaking Away*. It was set in Bloomington, Indiana, where three years later I was to teach Russian during a summer session. In the movie a local boy, the son of a used-car dealer, pretends to be an Italian exchange student as he romances an American college girl. When I saw the movie with Rafaella, I had a hard time relating to the conflict between the frat boys at Indiana U. and the "cutters," the local Bloomington kids who didn't go to college.

After the movie we walked to the beach. Rafaella couldn't move at a steady pace and was now running ahead of me and hopping across the breaking waves, screaming and lifting up the bottom of her skirt, then slowing down to pick up and study a shell or a sliver of polished glass or a bleached chunk of wood. It was already past eleven, the beach having grown empty. Under a glowering moon we settled in the cooling sand near the edge of the water and sat for a while, talking, groping for something we both shared. She told me after university she wanted to move to Rome and get a studio apartment in Trastevere. "And live life," as she put it. Unlike the other Italians my age, Rafaella was completely indifferent to politics and didn't ask me about my Soviet past. She was a lot more interested in my American future, yet there wasn't much I could tell her about it beyond my family's vague plans to settle on the East Coast.

"When I was little my parents considered going to America," Rafaella said dreamily. "But we moved here instead. So I could've been an American girl if things had been different."

"Cold sand," I said, snaking my arm around her waist. It was a come-on line worthy of eternal damnation.

Without shaking off my hand, she turned to me and said: "You're like the others, aren't you?"

"Like who?" I asked.

"Like the Italian boys."

"No, I'm not," I replied, both trembling and laughing a nervous laugh. "I'm not like the Italian boys."

"If you're not," Rafaella said, changing her tone to playful and jumping on to her feet, "if you're not, then I'll take you someplace else."

"Where?" I got up to follow her.

"A special place. Come."

We walked silently to the parapet, where we'd left her sandals and my espadrilles. I followed Rafaella through the nighttime streets of Ladispoli, illuminated by thirsty streetlights. A neon rose flickered in the vitrine of a flower shop on Via Ancona. A rotund, balding man in a long apron was pulling a chain through the gilded backs of chairs in front of a café-gelateria that was too upscale for Soviet refugees.

"*Ciao,* Rafaella," his lethargic voice greeted my companion.

"*Ciao,* Giuseppe, *buono notte,*" she replied, speeding along, two steps ahead of me.

"Rafaella, where are we going?" I asked as we approached the train station.

"We're almost there, you'll see," she answered, singing out her vowels.

We traversed the empty square in front of the train station, our own slack shadows rising over the walls and falling onto dusty cobblestones. I caught a glimpse of a monument to some Italian dignitary of yore—a duke, perhaps a general, or the fearless Garibaldi himself. To the left of the train station, abutting the ivy-strangled fence that separated the train tracks from the town's underbelly, there was a parking lot where commuters left their cars in the morning. Now only three or four strays remained, their owners caught up in their daily chores or nightly revelries. Only two streetlamps lit the parking lot, and myriad moths celebrated their nightly nuptials under the lamps' greasy halos. The lot, it seemed, hadn't been repaved in years, and gigantic cracks in the surface made it look like an abandoned Etruscan dig.

Rafaella took my hand and tugged at it, sensing my hesitation. We now stood in the center of the parking lot, under an ancient streetlamp with a cast-iron post, its black leaf rendered even more ornate by noble streaks of rust.

"You're going to America," Rafaella said, releasing my left hand to powers of gravity. "Right?"

"Right," I answered, bewildered by her question and her tone.

"So you've got to experience a real American car."

Rafaella sprang around, gave me a look of triumph, and pointed her right hand to one of the cars I thought had been abandoned for the night.

"Just look at it, Russian boy," she said, speaking with some artificial, chewing-gum accent meant to sound American. "Ain't this sumptn'."

It was a yellow sedan, the sort of canary yellow that looked mustardy when bathed in the empty lot's dusky air. I peered closer. From the front the car looked like a living creature with glassy eyes set widely apart, a black mustache on its upper lip, a narrow mouth of badly corroded metallic teeth, and a brace on the lower jaw. Plastered onto the front teeth was a rearing horse.

"A real beauty, isn't it?" Rafaella said, stroking the car.

I said nothing. I didn't know what to say, how to react. The rusty old thing didn't mean much to me.

"It's a Ford Mustang. The real deal," Rafaella impatiently explained. "Have you heard of Mustangs?"

"Only the horses," I said, studying the inside of the car through the passenger's side window. The car had a red interior and red seats. And a black and red steering wheel.

"All vintage 1965," said Rafaella, her fingers sliding like raindrops down the roof and the driver's-side window. On the driver's side I noticed a couple of rusty wounds from assassin's blades and the long deep scratches of jealous lovers' nails.

"It has a personality, a temper," Rafaella said, as if reading my mind. "And a soul."

"An American soul?" I asked, catching on and now playing along.

"Of course. What else?" Rafaella said, laughing and pulling back her long hair.

"How long have you had it?" I asked.

"Two years. It belongs to my mother's older sister. She's great, and very, very beautiful. She married a man from Milan—that was before I was born. And she used to drive this car herself."

I reflected, in passing, that in the Soviet Union, getting one's first private automobile amounted to such a life event that people gave them personal names and treated them as family members. Our first car, a Zhiguli—a Fiat-lookalike manufactured in the town of Togliatti on the Volga—was bright red, and my father named her "Corrida." As in bullfights.

"Is it a boy or a girl?" I asked.

"It's a . . . both," Rafaella answered, pulling the door open.

"Don't you lock it?"

"I do, but the lock's broken, and I just push down the lever, and it looks like it's locked. It's an old baby, you know," she said, getting into the car and starting the engine. The stations kept changing on the broken radio, songs flowing in and out of each other.

"Sometimes it doesn't start, and I just sit inside and listen to the music—when the radio's working—or the rain. My father keeps telling me not to leave it here. One day it's probably going to get stolen. We live outside the town center, and I like to ride to town alone. To town and back home, as late as I want. I like the freedom."

I walked around to the other side and pulled on the lock, but the door didn't yield.

"Sorry, mister," Rafaella said. "It only opens from my side. Your side's jammed."

She jumped out of the car and lowered the seat. "Welcome to America," she said.

I crouched into the back seat and slid over to the window; Rafaella climbed in and sat close to me.

"Do you know what a lover's lane is?" she asked, slipping her hand into mine. "They have them in small towns in America." And she bit my lower lip.

"Uh-huh," I uttered, no longer capable of speaking English.

"Do you have?" Rafaella asked.

I understood what she asked and said "yes," reaching for my wallet and remembering a recent visit to the *farmacia* where an Italian bombshell reigned over the counter. "Yes, I have it," I said, ripping open the small checker.

"Good boy," Rafaella said. "Come here."

And so it was on the back seat of a rusty Mustang that I let out my first Italian scream of passion. It lasted so long that, it seemed, several trains had rushed by, up the coast to Pisa and Genoa and Milan and down to Naples and further south, to Sicily.

"So loud, so wild," Rafaella finally said, pulling down her long skirt. "The temperance police will come and arrest you."

"You still have temperance police?" I asked, imagining a scene from a neorealist film.

"Of course not, silly." She kissed me on the nose and got out of the car—something she had to do in order to move to the front seat. "Now let me give you a ride back."

We pulled out of the lover's lane, and a few minutes later I was back in our apartment, where my parents were already sleeping. Where America was both a remote dream and a near future.

Now I've come inescapably close to a nostalgic digression. It's about Lana Bernshteyn, whom I had dated my freshman year at Moscow University. Lana Bernshteyn was almost five years my senior, and our parents knew each other through the Jewish refusenik circuit. A classic ingénue she was, a worrywart, a great lover of ballet. She was in her last semester at the Moscow Institute of Communications when we became close, and she spent most of her time at home, where she was supposed to be working on a senior thesis. Twice a week I would cut my midmorning lectures and hide in Lana's apartment a few blocks from the student dormitory of the Moscow Conservatory of Music. Her parents were at work and her younger brother at school. She pampered me with homemade Jewish delicacies; I brought her stems of fluffy mimosa, bunches of waxen tulips, and crumpled daffodils. She read and critiqued my first poems, focusing almost exclusively on what she deemed "lyrical truth." She had small pointy breasts and symmetrical birthmarks on her clavicles. After we first made love, Lana leaned back on the pillow of her pull-out sofa, reached for a cigarette, and lit up, staring at the ceiling. "Don't worry, darling," she whispered tenderly and then exhaled, letting a stream of cigarette smoke circle above her head.

Prior to becoming a refusenik, losing his professional job, and joining the stalwart lines of Soviet appliance repairmen, Lana's father had been an ordinary *Pravda*-reading radio engineer, one of those good family men who, at the sunset of their lives, begin to resemble old ladies. Her mother, who had been pushing the family to emigrate, was remarkable. She was an art appraiser in an antique store on Arbat Street in the center of old Moscow, and she possessed a phenomenal knowledge of art and poetry. She radiated intelligence and charm; all of Lana's friends adored her mother and often sought her counsel on subjects ranging from fashion to finding a gynecologist with a clandestine private practice. Lana's mother was also manic-depressive. About once a year, usually around November or December, when her melancholy became the color of Moscow's winter dusk, Lana's mother would disappear. When it first happened, Lana was still in middle school and her brother was little. On the morning of the third day, Lana's father found his wife in one of the waiting areas of the Kievsky Railroad Station, sleeping on a wooden seat surrounded by bundles and boxes, Roma women with small children, and visitors from Ukraine and southern Russia awaiting their delayed trains. She was hospitalized for several weeks, then resumed her everyday life. Or did she? Lana told me that the hardest part was that her mother knew painfully well what was happening to her. In her days of darkness, she was overcome by the urge to run away, and a huge railway station with tracks going to many different places was a perfect place to disappear.

If Turgenev were to tell this story, he might have called it "First Love," probably thinking of the singer Pauline Viardot and also fictionalizing some other young woman—Russian or French—into a heroine. But Lana Bernshteyn wasn't my first love. In fact, as a true admirer of Victor Shklovsky's novel *Zoo, or Letters Not About Love,* she insisted on using an antiromantic code, according to which it was considered tasteless to speak of love, even if you were overcome with love. Instead, we spoke of "desire" and anatomized lovemaking. If Ivan Bunin were to entrust this tale to a first-person rememberer, he would have let Lana call herself my "secret wife"— that in contrast to my "mistress visible to the whole world." The aging, broken-hearted Bunin had a historical woman in mind, his last love Galina Kuznetsova, when he worked on *Dark Avenues* during the late 1930s and early 1940s at his villa in Grasse, the European perfume capital in the Maritime Alps. When I think of Lana Bernshteyn—and of our Moscow closeness—Chekhov's "my affectionate and tender beast" leaps to mind. The expression "tender beast" used to be something of a private phrase between Lana and me when we were lovers. Who started it—me or her? I believe I once told Lana that next to her former fiancé, who was her elder by ten years, she looked like the sixteen-year-old Olenka, the gameskeeper's daughter in Chekhov's story. But it could have been the other way around, Lana calling me her "tender beast" after we made love.

By the time Lana and I became close friends, her father—who loved his wife unconditionally, in fact, more unconditionally than I've known anyone to love another person—had the search down to a science. There were more than half a dozen major railway stations in the Soviet capital, and it usually took him a day, sometimes two, to locate Lana's mother. He never let his children help him with the search. He would bring his wife home, dreadfully exhausted as she was, draw a bath and wash her, carry her to their bedroom, and make her a cup of raspberry tea with cognac. Lana's little brother would crawl into bed with his mother and fall asleep clutching her arm with both hands. For the next week or so Lana and her father would take turns staying up at night to watch her. Then things assumed their everyday course and thus continued until the next disappearance.

Lana and I broke up by the end of the spring of 1985, although we remained friends. Pretty quickly she got back together with Matvey Grubman, her former fiancé, a gifted sculptor. About forty at the time and from Kiev originally, Matvey sculpted scenes of the destroyed Jewish life in the Pale of Settlement as he knew it from his grandparents and as he imagined it to have been. He had trouble exhibiting his work, so he worked at a foundry outside Moscow. Once, before Lana and I became a secret couple, I'd visited Matvey's studio with three other friends Lana and I had in common, and I remember his olive-brown eyes, his muscular, bearded face, and blackened, thick fingers.

I was away most of the summer that came after our break-up, and Lana and I saw each other only once the next fall, at an art exhibit she attended with Matvey, who resolutely didn't care for me. I remember so clearly the day when the phone rang in December 1985, my mother answering it and calling me, and Lana telling me her mother had walked out of the window, falling onto the pavement from the eleventh floor. It was before seven in the morning, and, half awake, all I could say was: "I understand, Lana." Memories of that funeral—hoar frost on the naked branches, despondent friends crowding the smallish apartment, and, instead of a *shiva,* a Jewish-Russian wake with vodka and pickled mushrooms and tears and sobs—will stay with me always. This was the first death of a close person that I faced as an adult. And to know that this beautiful, loving woman literally escaped her life, flinging open the living-room window and stepping out—that to me was most unbearable. The story of Lana's mother has become a lasting antidote: Feeling low, I remember her death, and my own passing mood seems like a flutter of spring wind compared to a hurricane. Although I've lived in America for a long time now, I still question the bourgeois nonchalance with which some people here use the word "depression," as if it were an accoutrement of our civilization, a luxury car, a work of art, or a bottle of aged wine.

Soon after her mother's funeral, Lana moved in with Matvey, and we were barely in touch for over a year. She knew of my peripatetic amorous pursuits, which included her former classmate Masha Vishnevskaya. Lana called me in May 1987 to say she'd heard we were leaving the country and that she, too, was emigrating with her father, brother, and grandmother. She and Matvey had broken up, this time for good, she told me. I didn't ask what happened. To my farewell party Lana brought as a gift a book that I'd always coveted, *Images of Italy* by Pavel Muratov, a 1924 Berlin edition. I was its happy owner for less than a week; it disappeared in a package of other rare books that a profligate American journalist had promised my parents to smuggle out the country and conveniently lost.

Lana and her family left Moscow two weeks after my family had, catching up with us in Ladispoli. I bumped into them one evening at the main piazza, which the refugees had appropriated as their open-air salon. They were standing there eating gelato: Lana, her father with Lana's Yiddish-mumbling grandmother on his arm, and Lana's younger brother.

With shorter hair, in a turquoise sundress showing a lot of back and chest, Lana looked younger, college-age, and she was then twenty-five. I was happy to see her; in Ladispoli she was a present link to my past Moscow life and friends. Yet I was embarrassed about running into her in front of our families and the whole piazza full of bored and gossip-thirsty refugees. It felt like someone had staged this reunion with my old flame. The fourth act was only beginning, complete with jealousy, confessions, mutual estrangement, and tears of despair, and Chekhov's double-barrel had yet to shoot our love dead at the corner table of a seaside trattoria.

Lana and I left our family members at the piazza and walked in the direction of the Odeschalchi-Palo castle built on the Roman ramparts. We stopped at a concession stand on the way, and I got each of us a curvy bottle of Coca-Cola, still a novelty to us both. Lana took out a cigarette and asked the fellow behind the counter for a light, pronouncing *"per favore"* with a stress on the *a,* sounding like somebody imitating a Boston accent in Italian. As Lana leaned over to the concessionist's fist with the lighter in it, I felt a pang of irritation. Why can't she pronounce it right?

We sat on the rocks near the ruins of the castle, finishing our Coca-Colas and filling in the various blanks we hadn't had time to complete before leaving Moscow.

"So tell me about you and Matvey," I asked, overly cheerful.

"What do you want to know?"

"Weren't you two living together? I actually thought you'd get married this time."

"He thought so as well."

On the other side of the rocks, a man in a Panama hat with a long telescopic fishing pole was yelling something against the wind to a boy who was fishing farther away from us, off another group of jagged rocks. Maybe he wasn't yelling but just had a trumpeting Italian voice.

"What can I tell you?" Lana said. "I wasn't even surprised when Matvey told me he wouldn't hear of not making *aliya*. For a year he'd been wearing a knit white and blue *kipa* and talking about 'shooting the fuck out of the Palestinians.'"

"At different times we all have our urges." I found myself defending my ex-girlfriend's ex-fiancé.

"And then there was my own darling papochka," Lana continued. "My own darling papochka, who would go berserk every time I mentioned going to Israel with Matvey. After my mother's death, you know how tough it's been for him. So I felt guilty leaving him and my little brother. Do you know how much I hate feeling guilty?"

"How much?"

Spent waves were depositing foam on the rocks. Nothing had happened yet, we were just talking, catching up, and already I could feel tedium rolling over and enveloping me. Like starchy evening fog. Like a romance with the past.

Lana grew silent. For awhile we sat without saying anything to each other. "An angel of quiet has flown by," someone might have said in a Russian classical novel. But we weren't living a classical novel. Ours was a modern refugee story set in Italy.

"Can you get me a light?" Lana asked.

She put a cigarette onto my open palm, and I walked up to an Italian couple descending, arm in arm, from the ancient ramparts. He had long matted hair and a grand Roman nose, she a mousy but attractive face. Both seemed oblivious to the world outside their new love; the man didn't look at me as he flicked his lighter, and the woman said *"Ciao"* and giggled.

In the setting gloom Lana couldn't make out the faces of the light-givers, and when I came back with her smoldering cigarette, I described how they barely acknowledged me and how I felt like a beggar. I don't know why both Lana and I found it so amusing, in the sense that when we were still living in Moscow, neither of us could have imagined sitting together at sunset on the shores of Italy as refugees bound for America, and having to borrow a lighter from some aloof Italian couple. The episode with the lighter had dispelled an awkwardness that Lana and I both had felt, and we started chattering at random about seeing Rome, about the Vatican museums, about Italian fashion. And also about the funny habits of many of our fellow refugees stuck in Ladispoli.

"And hear this, the whole time in Rome my grandmother was afraid to leave our hotel room," Lana said. "When we were going to see the Vatican, she asked: 'Is it allowed?'"

"Well, my grandmother was the opposite," I took over. "She kept talking about signing up for an audience with the pope. Imagine, the old Soviet enthusiast now wants to visit with the pope. She even remembered some Polish from her youth."

"How are your parents doing?" Lana asked.

"Mama almost went crazy in Rome. She's better now. Papa's writing, but I think he's very anxious about America. About his English. And being able to publish and practice medicine there."

"God, we both sound so old, so mature," Lana said, and we exploded with laugher. It felt like we were back in Moscow, New Year's Eve, and we were heading over to my friend Misha Zaychik's all-night bash and stopped at a famous old bakery on Arbat Street, just a couple of blocks from where Lana's mother worked, and bought two dozen *bubliki,* Russian poppy seed bagels that came on a string. Lana wore them like a necklace over the collar of her short white sheepskin coat, and people on the subway stared at us. We didn't care. We were so happy and in love even though we never called it love at the time.

"Are you seeing someone?" Lana asked point-blank, surprising me.

"Why? No, not really," I answered, thinking of what had happened two days before at the parking lot outside the train station, of Rafaella's Mustang and the night trains roaring by.

"Because I want to get back together," Lana said in the same voice as when she used to critique my poems. "I want to be your girlfriend."

We got up from the rocks and walked back along the water. Lana's cool fingers tickled the small of my elbow before enmeshing themselves in mine. We were still some distance away from the Russian section of the beach when Lana stopped. Except for a couple of cigarette embers glowing above the parapet, we were alone on the beach.

"I'd like to go in the water," Lana said.

"How will you dry yourself off?" I asked.

"With my sundress. You coming?"

"No, I'll wait here."

She dropped her sundress and underwear into the sand and ran into the water. I waited, her dress in my hands, her panties in my pocket, as Lana splashed near the shore.

"It's warm, like milk from under the cow," she yelled. "Are you coming?"

When she finally stepped out of the water, lithe and moonlit, a strip of white dividing her in two, I stood behind her and dried her off with the sundress. My hands cupped her breasts and held them.

"I've missed you," Lana said, placing her hands on top of mine. "Don't stop."

I pulled my hands from under hers, and the wet sundress fell into the sand like a drunk reveler.

"What's wrong?" asked Lana.

"I don't know."

Lana stepped aside to shake the sand out of her dress, then put it on crooked.

"It's that provincial belle Irena, isn't it?" she asked. "I've heard about her and you."

Irena came from a family of former refuseniks from Riga. I met her at the beach, and for weeks we maintained an aimless and public flirtation.

"No, it's not Irena, believe me," I answered.

"Why then don't you want to get back together?"

"This just doesn't feel right, Lanochka. I'm sorry."

"I guess you're just more honest," Lana said, caustically, and ran off into the brackish darkness.

On the way home I remembered her clumped panties in my pocket and slipped them into a trash bin.

FOR THE NEXT THREE WEEKS, when Lana and I met at the beach and the other Russian hangouts, we acted as though the walk and her night swimming never happened. Finally, one sunset, I saw her on the boulevard in the company of a gangly fellow from Leningrad, the son of a famous astronomer whose family shared accommodations with my aunt, grandmother, and cousin. I heard through the Russian grapevine that Lana's new friend was a "mathematical genius." Lana and the genius were dripping gelato on the red gravel path and arguing about something, a poem, perhaps, or a painting. I muttered *"Buono notte"* and waved feebly as I passed them by. I was hurrying to meet my Italian friends.

During the early part of the day I would usually spend time at the beach, where Irena, with her soft pale curls, large freckles, and submissive smile, was my regular flirt-du-campe. Occurring under the gaze of her parents and her elder brother, the whole thing couldn't have been much more Victorian. The early parts of many evenings passed in the company of Italians, and seeing Rafaella only sharpened the anticipation of what, I hoped, was to come later at night. In public Rafaella and I continued to pretend we were just friends. Oddly enough, throughout the whole month of our late-night rendezvous, only Leonardo—the short Leonardo—had an idea of what went on between Rafaella and me. He'd been secretly fantasizing about her since high school, he later told me, convinced that he didn't stand a chance with the leggy Sarda.

Usually between eleven and midnight, I would walk to the lover's lane behind the Ladispoli train station, hoping to find Rafaella's Mustang. Sometimes it would be there, grazing in one of the lot's murkier corners. I'd get in and climb into the back seat, and on a few occasions she was already there expecting me. At other times I'd sprawl out and listen to the crickets chirruping, to tiny cracking noises under the dome of the yellow street lamp, and wait, fretfully, for her arrival. *"Ciao,* Russian boy," Rafaella would say in a voice that parodied itself. "I haven't seen you in soooo long."

"I was here yesterday, and the night before yesterday," I would reply.

"I'm sorry, honey," she would drawl out, stroking my forearm with her fingertips and puckering her lips, "I had to go to Trenton with my mom and dad to visit my aunt who's very sick. But I'm here now, aren't I? Aren't I?"

We would rest on the back seat, my arms locked around her shoulders and chest, listening for the approach of the furious trains bound for great cities and telling each other about the American lives we had never had.

Without setting the terms in advance, Rafaella and I played a waiting love game, whose main suspension of reality consisted in pretending we were lovers in a small American coastal town, perhaps somewhere in Maine or Connecticut or New Jersey. I barely knew the difference. Nor did she, for that matter. Neither of us had been to America; everything we knew about it was from movies, from reading, from what we had heard from others. In retrospect it seems that to render it more authentic, the game might have been better served by a bigger car—like the silver Chevy Malibu Classic that would become my first car in America. But in Ladispoli Rafaella's trusty Mustang more than did the trick.

For about a month my secret trysts with Rafaella followed their own pattern of furtive desire, until one night at the end of July, when Lana did a number on me. And I didn't even see it coming. There had been a rainstorm earlier that afternoon, at the time the closest thing I'd experienced to a tropical downpour. It had started during lunch, and my parents and I observed it from our apartment's balcony: sheaths of dark water ripping leaves and young branches off the chestnut trees on the boulevard, the tin fruitier piling up his wooden crates under an asparagus-green umbrella and running for cover to his rickety truck. When it had finally cleared up at sunset, the air felt pristine, cleansed of the usual smells—culinary and charry—of a southern resort.

Later that evening, as I climbed into the back seat of the rusty Mustang, a familiar scent filtered into my nostrils. The scent brought with it the spring of 1985, the old subway station across the street from the old Moscow Zoo, shrieks of fowl from the pond where grayish panes of ice still floated in the middle. Instead of sitting through a double orgo lecture by Madame Gudkova, I was walking to Lana's apartment at a late-morning hour in spring. Lana was standing in the door, wearing her mother's bathrobe. From the staircase I could smell her perfume, flowery with a whiff of spice. Like all good Soviet perfumes it was French, with the word *mystère* in its short, iambic name. "I'd have to change my personality if they ever stopped making this perfume," Lana told me soon after we started seeing each other.

I imagined Rafaella when Lana and I made love on the back seat of the Mustang—recklessly, just as we had in Russia. I thought not of Lana, to whom I used to know how to make love, but of Rafaella, who made me nervous. But as Lana and I made love on the back seat of the car, I was picturing Lana's cluttered old Moscow apartment: the heavy chocolate-brown drapes, the herniated radiators overheating the rooms, a framed spectral photo of her parents on their Crimean honeymoon, and the swelling but still naked limes and birches outside the windows, also a decrepit bench with a row of elderly ladies warming their bones in the feeble April sun. "*Oy mamochka*," Lana said, just as she used to back in Moscow when she crossed over, the familiar "*Oy mamochka*" instead of Rafaella's cinematic "*Mamma mia*," which was hard to believe even as it transported me across the Tyrrhenian Sea all the way to Tunisia or Libya. Our lovemaking was rougher than it had ever been in Moscow, less tender and comforting, and it arced over my whole youth. If it's possible to relieve oneself of romantic attachments to a shared past, Lana and I accomplished it on the back seat of Rafaella's tatty automobile.

The lost chemistry was returned to us—not the chemistry of love but the chemistry of a dear old friendship—and we saw each other effortlessly for the rest of the Ladispoli summer. In America Lana and I have stayed friends, although we don't see each other very much, especially since she switched coasts. She is living in La Jolla, California, with her husband—the mathematical genius whom she met in Ladispoli—and their two girls. And I'm here in Boston, tap-tapping these lines in my office overlooking a neo-Gothic college quadrangle. It's a hazy morning in August, the salty breeze is licking the blinds, and

I have no other choice but to give Lana a fictional name, a made-up haircut, and to sweeten for posterity the scent of her perfume.*

And now back to Rafaella and the conclusion. Two days after finding Lana in the Mustang, I overheard Rafaella talking to a friend about her car. We were standing among a group of Italian friends and I understood—more or less—that before she went to Urbino for the autumn semester, she would be taking the car to the shop to be refurbished. Rafaella's father had apparently agreed to give her money for the repairs after reading an article about the Mustang Club of Rome and inquiring about the value of this model. "Well," I thought to myself, "that marks the end of the affair."

Another week went by, and I saw Rafaella cruising down Via Ancona in her Mustang. Next to her, grinning like a gangster on holiday, his hairy right arm dangling outside the window like a braided Cossack whip, was a fellow my age, an immigrant from Odessa. They were sailing through sunset, all gusty with pleasure, "Hotel California" blasting at the top of the Mustang's wheezy lungs. The radio must have been fixed, or a tape deck installed. "Lucky dog," I remember thinking about my Odessan rival, "out on a joy ride with Rafaella."

THE LAST THREE WEEKS IN LADISPOLI sped by like Italian motorcyclists on a cliff road. My mother and I took a jaunt to the south of Italy, a trip which almost ended badly for us, and then it was finally time to be packing our suitcases again. Thus ends my story with

---

*Running slightly ahead of myself, I should add a footnote to this story. My father's eighty-one-year-old Uncle Pinya, a left-wing socialist from Tel Aviv, stayed with us in Ladispoli during the first week in August. He, my parents, and I were having dinner on our balcony, and Uncle Pinya, who was given to bouts of propagandizing, declared to us in his slightly outmoded Russian:

"You, my dears, are prudes. You don't share intimate details with one another. That's a serious problem."

And Uncle Pinya told us about his seventy-eight-year-old girlfriend and their unsure love life. Inspired by Uncle Pinya's spirit of utopian openness, I told him and my parents about finding Lana on the back seat of Rafaella's car.

"What's so surprising?" Uncle Pinya exclaimed. "She was hungry."

Rafaella, Lana, and the rusty Mustang as protagonists. Three days before my parents and I took a transatlantic flight from Rome to New York, my Italian friends threw a dinner party in my honor. It was in a tavern on the northern outskirts of town, off Via Aurelia, in an olive grove. A long table had been set under a canopy of sun-filled branches. The fare was inauspicious, paid for by students with slim pockets: pizza, salad, watery red wine out of sweating carafes. The group toasted my departure and new American life.

"Good luck in America," said Sylvio, who offered the toast. "Come back to us if you don't like it. We'll all be here."

"I may be in Australia, if I'm lucky," Leonardo said, taking a gulp of wine.

"Ask Sylvio to send you some suede shoes," Tomasso added. "They probably don't have such nice ones in America!"

"I will, I definitely will," I said.

"You know, don't you, that you'll never find such good ice cream there," said Bianca Marini, and we all started laughing.

After dinner, when it came time to say goodbye and exchange addresses ("exchange" doesn't describe it, as I didn't have an address, only the name of the New England city my parents and I had picked), Rafaella scribbled something on a napkin and passed it to me, folded.

"You can always write care of the flower shop," she said.

At home, as I copied the addresses into a notebook, on Rafaella's folded napkin I found this note:

Tomorrow

7 o'clock

R.

I went early, of course, but she was already there, sitting in the driver's seat and humming along with a tune on the radio.

"Can you drive, Russian boy?" she asked, pulling at a button of my short-sleeved shirt.

"Of course I can," I answered, taken aback by the question. In Moscow my father had taught me to drive our pared-down version of a Fiat, although I never did get a Soviet driver's license.

"Get in, take it out for a spin," Rafaella said, and she moved over to the passenger side, straightening the lap of her long black skirt.

"Right now?" I asked.

"Yes, right now," Rafaella shouted back, dialing up the volume. "Come on, Russian boy. Let's go. What are you waiting for? America?"

The Roubenis of Esfahan

There was also a small number of Iranian Jews waiting in Ladispoli that summer. Less than two weeks after we'd arrived, my father—amateur ethnographer that he was—made the acquaintance of a Jewish family from Esfahan. One evening on the main promenade he separated himself from us and walked up to a group consisting of three men and four women. Despite the warm night, the men were dressed in black suits of fine light cloth, and the women wore heavy long skirts and long-sleeved blouses. The oldest woman in the group was wearing dark clothes, loose and drooping, and a heavy head shawl similar to the one worn by the grandmother of Aleksandr Abramov, the flautist from Baku. The other three women were dressed with conservative chic, the oldest of the three covering her lustrous black hair with a silk scarf. Her hair was not so much covered as adorned, since the scarf was very slender. Red gold sparkled in the woman's ears, around her neck, and on several of her fingers. The remaining two women, girls really, wore similar cream-colored outfits, and from afar their heads looked like gorgeous black pearls. I remember pointing this out to my mother as we stood waiting for my father, who had struck up a polite conversation with the family. Mother languorously responded that I hadn't written any poetry since we had left Moscow. This was true; that whole summer in Italy I would write only two or three poems and a short story about Vienna. Poetry just wasn't writing itself that summer. There was too much to observe and store up in memory, too much to take in.

Picture a balmy summer night in Ladispoli, my mother and I waiting, my father doing field research for his fictions, speaking to the three men in black suits (the four women lingering beside them) about the great Nizami and his Leyli and Majnun or the immortal Hafiz or another Persian poet, or else about the Jews of Bukhara and Samarkand who speak Hebrew-Farsi.

My father emerged victoriously from the initial encounter. He found out that the family had been in Ladispoli for two months, "waiting and waiting." The older, dignified gentleman, "Mr. Roubeni," as father referred to him, had been in the rug business. With him were his wife (the lady in dark heavy clothes) and two sons. The married older son, whose name was Vida, had also been in the family rug business. He had a wife and two unmarried daughters a bit younger than me. The younger, unmarried son, Babak (and father especially liked the name Babak), was a dentist and, as it later turned out, a passionate Communist. Over the next week my father ran into the Roubenis a few times, taking pleasure in having brief ethnographic conversations with the soft-spoken Mr. Roubeni. Then followed an invitation for afternoon tea at the Roubenis'.

They were renting a villa—palatial by refugee standards—a few blocks north of our apartment building and away from the sea. A second-floor open terrace, where the table was set for tea, faced a broken fountain with a headless cupid aiming his bow at the upstairs windows.

Mr. Roubeni welcomed us at the gate. "This could've been a lovely garden," he said, leading us to the house along a red gravel path, "but the owners don't seem to care. And now it's so overgrown, and the fruit trees have gone for so long without proper cultivation, that it would be most difficult to turn it around."

To my ear Mr. Roubeni sounded like an Englishman. Perhaps like an old Englishman who was chewing molasses candy.

"Well, no use complaining," he added after a momentary onset of pensiveness. "We're fortunate to have such privacy in this town of refugees."

Both of Mr. Roubeni's sons were waiting on the terrace, and after we all sat down the women brought out tea on a tray, a plate with desserts, and a platter with fruit. They whispered "good evening," arranged the afternoon tea treats on the table, and went back inside. It was probably a good thing mother didn't come with us and instead went to see *Terms of Endearment* at the American Center, which ran a Wednesday-night program of English-language films for refugees from the USSR. The tea was bright amber, strong, and aromatic. I hadn't had such good tea since leaving Moscow. The cookies were baked with honey and nuts; they released into the air the sensuous aroma of rose petals. On the platter were peaches, apricots, pears, and slices of an oblong melon. The color of the melon skin, a dark yellow, harmonized with the pale linen short-sleeved shirts that all three Roubeni men wore around their house. All three were the same height and looked alike. Their finely chiseled features suggested ancient pedigree, nobility, centuries of family traditions. To me the Roubeni men, with their wavy dark hair, opulent brown eyes, and beaked noses, looked simultaneously Georgian and Tadjik. Mr. Roubeni spoke slowly and never said a superfluous word throughout the whole conversation. He would sometimes pause, as though smiling inwardly to a trusted double, and we could see his dimpling cheeks through the silver filigree of his flawlessly trimmed beard. His older son, Vida, was about forty, broader in the chest and stockier than either his father or brother. He said little, sipping tea in measured gulps. He was very unhappy about leaving Iran and distressed at being stuck in Ladispoli without a business to run. Babak had the face of a dreamer, a thin moustache instead of a beard, and John Lennon eyeglasses. Babak chain-smoked and talked in a rapid staccato. Too shy to look at the people he addressed, he gazed downward at the headless cupid. Mr. Roubeni projected wisdom, his older son, sheer anger, and the younger son, vulnerability.

"You've been in Iran a long time," my father remarked. "Since the end of the Babylonian captivity, right?" He found these Iranian Jews intriguing, very different from us. And yet he felt an affinity for them. And father also liked to show his knowledge of ancient history and the Bible.

"We're one of the oldest Jewish communities in the whole world," Mr. Roubeni answered. "And what good has it done us? We're enemies again, and at the mercy of those fanatics. We're—imagine, to them we're impure," he said, taking a bite of a honey cookie as if to sweeten the thought.

"But there are still lots of Jews in Iran, aren't there?" father asked.

"Oh yes, still about fifty thousand, perhaps more. Some have been passing themselves off as Muslims. Mainly in Teheran, but also in Shiraz, Kashan, our beautiful Esfahan. Our home. And about as many must have left since the founding of the state of Israel. At least Iran didn't expel us like the other Muslim countries around. Still a lot left. Most Jews in Iran have relatives in Israel. We also do, but we . . . ," and Mr. Roubeni stopped himself short and made a gesture with his right hand, as if waving off the thought of going to Israel. His older son gave him a piercing look.

"But wasn't the last shah pretty good to the Jews?" father asked. "I've always thought so."

"Oh sure," and the older gentleman's eyes lit up. "All of us Iranian Jews liked Reza Shah. When he came to visit Esfahan he prayed in our temple and paid respect to the Torah. And my father was among the elders of the community who greeted him. Under Reza Shah Jews felt safe. Now they say—"

"—stop it, father," Babak interrupted. "Our Soviet guests should know better than that." It was peculiar that Mr. Roubeni's younger son, the dentist-Communist, called us "Soviet." "He was an imperialist puppet and a bloody murderer, that's what he was, your beloved shah. And he only showed tolerance because he knew the West would reward him for it. Same old story."

"So when did you first start thinking of leaving?" I asked the Roubeni men.

"Thinking?" Mr. Roubeni raised the perfect crescents of his eyebrows toward the sky. "Oh, my late father and I were already talking about it in the early fifties, soon after Israel became a reality. But we waited, like many others. How long have you been in Russia—two, three hundred years? And we've been in Persia for more than two and a half thousand years. Try leaving after that."

"We were here, I mean there, long before the Muslims," Vida said, his voice dry with vexation, his left hand twisting the neck of a cigarette against the edge of a heavy marble ashtray.

"Yes, my son is quite correct," continued Mr. Roubeni. "Thus we waited. And hesitated."

"This is just like many refuseniks in Russia!" my father spoke. "This is why we hadn't applied for permission to emigrate until 1979. We, too, wavered. And we missed the boat."

"My esteemed friend," Mr. Roubeni turned his gaze to my father. "Our story is similar, but also very different. After the revolution I knew things were going to be very bad. And still I wavered. Then in 1982 I finally decided to get my family out. But I wanted to take it slow." Mr. Roubeni picked up half of the oblong yellow melon and sliced it into even servings.

"I didn't want to cause suspicion and make trouble for my family. I found a partner, a Turkish Jew in Istanbul, also in the fine rugs trade, and I slowly started transferring funds to him. It took four years. And then I liquidated my property, also slowly, but left some assets with a partner in Esfahan who isn't Jewish. But his family and mine have done business for several generations."

"Didn't the officials see any signs and suspect something?" I asked.

"Young man, you're from Russia. I don't have to tell you how to make the officials look the other way," Mr. Roubeni answered, with a dolorous smile and a nod. "So I shall spare you the tedious details."

"And then?" I asked again. In this decorous home I probably came across as too forward with my questions. "What happened then?"

"And then I took my whole family on vacation to Turkey, seven people and some luggage in an old Cadillac. A big American car. You'll see plenty of such soon. We first went to Tabriz, and then crossed at Bazargan into Turkey. And the pockets of customs and border officials were equally wide on both sides of the border. And then a long journey to Istanbul. But I got them out—my sons, my granddaughters. And then we flew to Vienna, just like yourselves. Like the other Jewish refugees. And here we are, all of us. Waiting."

This was the only moment during the whole tea party at the Roubenis' that I felt that despite the huge differences—they people of the Orient, we stepchildren of the Occident—we shared a fundamental Jewish destiny. I even had a quick fantasy of living in the same city in America and befriending Mr. Roubeni's elder granddaughter Farideh, going to American bars and movies with her. I didn't know what I was thinking about. I absolutely assumed the Roubenis, like my family and most of the refugees waiting in transit in Ladispoli, were headed for America. And I imagine so did my father, since he asked my very question: "Where in America are you planning to live?"

An awkward pause hung in the air.

"We're not going to America," Mr. Roubeni finally answered, speaking so slowly that it seemed he was a calligrapher writing out on air every loop of each letter.

"We've decided to go to Australia, perhaps New Zealand," Babak took over from his father. "We don't know yet. Either one is fine. I've persuaded my family to get as far away as possible from political confrontation. All the other Iranians here are going to America or Canada. But that whole continent is unsafe, you know. Just like Europe. Too much tension both here and in North America."

I thought immediately of my Ladispolian friend Leonardo whose dream it was to immigrate to Australia because he found Europe and especially Italy so suffocating and overcrowded. Now as I write this, I cannot restrain myself from thinking of 9/11 and the Madrid and London train bombings and. . . .

"The trouble is that Jewish communities over there mainly want skilled menial workers," Babak said. "Isn't that odd? And for us to go there, they're supposed to invite—to sponsor us. So we wait here in Ladispoli. We wait by the sea."

"Why don't you want to go to America?" my father asked Mr. Roubeni, who sat silently in his wicker armchair, hands stoically folded on his stomach. Vida sprung up from his chair and went inside the house.

"Things are bad in America," Babak answered. "Just a different kind of bad than in the Soviet Union. A different exploitation, that's all. But you wouldn't understand. You Soviet Jews, because you've suffered there, you think you should be so right wing. What, you think Reagan will protect you if there's a pogrom in America?" Babak laughed bitterly.

"Reagan helped Soviet Jews," I countered.

"Reagan? The actor?" Babak choked on his own acerbic laughter. "Only because it suited his scripted political agenda. His Hollywood movie. Believe me, you're trading one dictatorship for another, that's all."

Father and I felt it was time we should be going and started shuffling in our chairs. Babak offered to walk us to the gate. Mr. Roubeni stayed on the terrace, and as we looked up from the path across the lush, uncultivated garden, we saw him leaning against a marble post and waving goodbye. He suddenly looked old and frail, like the Diaspora itself.

A few days later, on the way to the beach, I ran into the two Roubeni sisters strolling on the sun-striated boulevard, nimble like two gazelles. With them was another Jewish-Iranian girl, with layers of makeup over her puffy face. All three were wearing long sleeves and ankle-length skirts. I stopped to greet them and then I don't know what came over me—I invited the girls to walk with me to the canal and sunbathe on the rocks, where I sometimes went to read and be alone. The girls giggled nervously, and the older of the Roubeni sisters, Farideh, whispered something to the other two in Farsi. Walking on the boulevard in the company of the three girls, I felt like a master of a harem. And also a little bit like a trespasser.

"Do you like the beach?" I asked when we reached our destination. Of the two Roubeni sisters, I thought Farideh more beautiful, with a velvety birthmark above her upper lip, the glowing pallor of her face framed by her foamy black hair.

We sat on the rocks, and without giving it much thought, I pulled off my T-shirt. The Iranian girls stared while trying not to look. What did I care about shame and propriety? Guilelessly I thought: There, I'm helping these three young women set themselves free. Of course, as usually happens in stories that have nowhere else to go but to their own abrupt endings, just as I was about to sit next to Farideh on a rock, her grandmother stepped out of the past like a dark sentry. She yelled something in Farsi and led the girls away.

Passing each other on the promenade for the rest of the summer, Mr. Roubeni and my father exchanged a perfunctory nod while Vida cast vengeful looks in my direction. One time I ran into Babak at the train station, and we rode all the way to Rome without saying a word to one another. When my parents and I left Ladispoli, the Roubenis were still there, waiting for a visa to New Zealand.

6

The Rabbi and the Pastor

Two faiths—and two missions—competed for the hearts and souls of the Jewish refugees from the Soviet Union, many of whom had not been exposed to religious practice. Upon arrival in Ladispoli my parents and I immediately heard of the American Center and the Wednesday night movie screenings. We were only getting our bearings. It was perfectly logical, if you were a refugee bound for America, to assume the center had some official connection to the American Embassy in Rome or, perhaps, to JIAS, our sponsor. It was also logical for us to draw a parallel between the center and the cultural events at the American and British embassies in Moscow, to which my parents were invited along with other refuseniks and dissidents. Perhaps in our state we weren't even capable of logical reasoning. Or, perhaps it just sounded so calming, Il Centro Americano. The American Center. Like an oasis of peace. Like a promise that once we get to America, our lives will unfold according to somebody's permanent if unwritten plan for happiness.

The center occupied a stately villa on the main boulevard, just a couple of blocks from the Russian section of the beach—a prime location. Added to the site of the villa was a modern auditorium, where screenings and lectures took place, with a reception area where punch and cookies were served. Whoever funded the center certainly had deep pockets, and the contrast with the dingy offices of the Jewish refugee center was immediate—and negative.

The munificent Italian sun was arching northward over Ladispoli when we walked up the marble steps of the villa, which were dotted with buckwheat marks of age like the hands of an old preacher. Almost symmetrical lion cubs slept on either side of the front door, resting

heavy chins on their cracked paws. Entering the villa, we saw a car-
peted marble staircase and wild flowers in a gaudy green vase. The
villa must have been repainted after its wealthy Italian owners sold it
to the American Center, but one could still see square, circular, and
rectangular shadows where paintings used to hang on the walls. In the
foyer we were greeted by a tall, lean man with an oval face shaved to a
shine, fleshy ears and lips, tobacco green eyes, and a distinguished nose,
which had the trappings of future bulbousness. Parted perfectly to the
right, the strings of his hair fell low onto his forehead, and he sometimes shook his head or waved a balletic hand across his brow. The
thick lenses of his wire-rimmed glasses reflected the world like a hall
of mirrors. When he smiled or frowned, his face quickly creased into
frog skin. In retrospect, the director of the American Center makes me
think of both publisher Steve Forbes and a ruthless Harvard lawyer in
a TV series long taken off the air.

"Welcome to the American Center," the American greeted us,
both in English and in Russian. "Menia zovut Dzhoshua Friman" (My
name's Joshua Freeman). In Russian, he sounded like a Latvian or an
Estonian.

Dressed in beige khakis, a candy-cane red shirt, and a brown car-
digan, Joshua Freeman first struck me as supremely American, a professor at a small college or a country doctor. Standing next to him in
the foyer and directing the stream of refugees into the auditorium was
his wife, Sarah, a horsy woman in her mid-forties, attractive in a Mid-
western sort of way. Unlike her husband, she spoke very little Russian
beyond "hello" and "thank you," which she repeated diligently, with
an energetic nod; much of the commerce between her and the refugees
who didn't speak English consisted of shaking hands, smiling, and
more smiling. Sarah Freeman had thin, wavy red hair and a mole on
her chin. On her freckled neck dangled a string of creamy pearls; she
was wearing a white blouse with long sleeves and a plain navy skirt that
covered her knobby knees. Her tanless skin had a scarlet flush of mod-
esty, and her long, colorless eyelashes fluttered above her eyes like pale
butterflies over wilting cornflowers. There was something strained in
her whole frame and demeanor, and, unlike her suave husband, Sarah

Freeman didn't look at ease in our midst. Or was it only my hyper-alert imagination?

By eight o'clock the auditorium was filled with the refugees, about a hundred altogether. Joshua Freeman came onto the stage, accompanied by none other than Anatoly Shteynfeld, whom he introduced, in English, as "Anatoly, my new brother." From the stage, standing six feet tall and speaking slowly, Joshua Freeman greeted the audience. He spoke in English, pausing professionally and allowing Shteynfeld to translate his words into Russian.

"Good evening and welcome to the American Center," he said. "My name is Joshua. My wife Sarah, our daughters Rebecca and Rachel, and I come from Chicago, the Windy City, as we call it back home." Joshua Freeman smiled all the way through his opening remarks. He avoided contractions and moved his lips like someone using sign language.

"We have been here in Ladispoli for almost ten years, and we are delighted to see so many of you on your way to America. On your way to freedom." He paused, as though expecting applause, and indeed some people in the audience, especially those without much English, started clapping upon hearing the words *America* and *freedom*.

"This is a very exciting time for us," he continued. "All through the spring and early summer your numbers have been rising, which is just fantastic. For those of you who are here for the first time, I should explain that because there are so many ex-Soviets again here in Ladispoli, we have reinstated our weekly Wednesday night movie screenings. Through the movies we want to help you not only practice your English but also learn about American life, our history, our family values."

He paused and reached into his pocket for a folded sheet of paper.

"We want to help you get acquainted with our American values and traditions," he continued. "This is why we also offer English classes, which my wife and I teach, every Tuesday and Thursday afternoon. Finally, we invite you to join us here at the center every Saturday morning, at ten, to celebrate the Lord."

Barely consulting his sheet of paper, Joshua Freeman spoke for a little while about the movie they were showing that evening. His final words before the screening were: "After the movie please join us for a little reception. And once again, welcome. Shalom!"

The refugees, my parents and I included, applauded as the curtain opened. The clapping quieted down. As the lights went out and the bobbing black hieroglyphs scraped the brightening screen, I could hear people to my left and my right whispering: "He said 'shalom'? Did he say 'shalom'?" "That's right, 'shalom.' He said 'shalom,' now you be quiet."

After the movie Joshua Freeman's teenage daughters served us cookies so sweet they made your teeth hurt and a soapy pink punch out of a plastic bowl. They looked more like their father but dressed like their mother, even though they were too young for such a fashion sacrifice, especially in Italy. It was a crush in the reception area; we didn't stay very long. Outside the villa, in the center of the boulevard, refugees stood in concentric circles, discussing the event.

"They all have Jewish names—Joshua, Sarah, Rebecca," a short wiry man was intoning when we walked up to the group. "And 'Free-man' could have been 'Friedman.'"

"In America those aren't necessarily Jewish first names," my mother threw in a comment. "They are biblical names."

"That may be," bassoed a dignified gentleman we'd met on the bus from Rome to Ladispoli, a retired architect. "But he also said 'shalom.' Did you hear him say 'shalom'? That's positively Jewish."

"You're absolutely right, my dear friend," said Shteynfeld. He was wearing a chocolate-brown ascot with a yellow shirt. The combination made his face look even pastier. "Mr. Freeman regards all Jews as his brothers, and, therefore, his coreligionists."

"But that's total nonsense and also a sham," my father exploded. "And you, Shteynfeld, of all people, sullying yourself this way. You were a refusenik. Remember, you suffered as a Jew."

"I find it absolutely and utterly pointless to argue with such people as you," Shteynfeld replied to my father. "At least I take pleasure in the fact that your wife and son don't seem to share your blind tribal loyalties. Well, I should be going. *Buona sera,*" and he vanished out of sight before my father had a chance to say or do anything.

We walked back to our apartment with a vague sense of having been manipulated into some untruth. There was something sterile and prudish in the atmosphere of the American Center, and also something that in my heart of Jewish-American hearts I would now call goyish. And on top of it, there was Shteynfeld as Joshua Freeman's personal interpreter, Shteynfeld with his elegant rhetoric that smacked of perfidy. But then again they were so welcoming, our American hosts, the Freemans, and the movie, *Alice Doesn't Live Here Anymore*, was excellent.

"It's good English practice for all three of us," my mother said as we sat down to our evening tea on the balcony.

"Zeros cannot practice," my father replied. "Zeros just fill the room with gaping mouths and with smoke. But you two should go."

Mother and I looked at each other but didn't say anything. My father's English was a dogged subject in our family.

This was on our first Wednesday in Ladispoli, and two days later, on the way to the beach, we ran into Daniil Vrezinsky. He was hurrying to the post office, he told us, to make a collect call to America.

"The American Center?" Vrezinsky crowed. "Ha ha ha! A damned racket. Preying on our innocence. And a pay raise for every ten Jews the good pastor converts. Stay away. Especially now, when he's got this Shteynfeld fellow as his sidekick. I have no time for those turncoats from the Moscow Jewish intelligentsia."

"Is it true?" I asked Vrezinsky.

"Is what true?"

"That it's all about trying to convert the Jews?"

"What are you—naïve? See for yourself if you don't believe me," the answer came flying, and Vrezinsky walked away.

A sense of curiosity had now been added to one of vague alarm, and mother and I decided to check out the Saturday morning "celebration of the Lord" at the center. I think both of us refused to believe that something so obviously deceptive could be coming from Americans. After all, many wonderful American families had visited us when we were refuseniks in Moscow, and they even included an Episcopalian minister from New York and a Catholic couple of German descent from Minnesota. We had had friends and supporters at the American Embassy in Moscow, both Christians and Jews, both observant and not. And never once had we felt "preyed upon." We didn't know what to believe. We hadn't shed our illusions about Americans, so we had to see for ourselves.

This time rows of plastic chairs had been lined up in the lobby. When mother and I arrived, about twenty people were already there, and about ten or fifteen more trickled in before ten o'clock, when Joshua Freeman stepped in front of the gathering and began to speak. A table along one of the walls was set with soft drinks and pastries covered with plastic wrap. In a bookcase mother and I discovered, in addition to vinyl-bound pocket-size Bibles—one shelf in Russian, the other in English—beautifully illustrated Russian translations of books by C. S. Lewis, published in Chicago.

Waiting for the event to start, mother and I kept looking around to see if we knew anyone. We didn't. And for some reason the refugees appeared anxious, as if they were caught cheating and now sat in the school office, waiting for the headmaster's reprisal. Among the participants there were three or four who didn't look like Soviet refugees; they must have been local Italians or American expats.

Several refugee couples came with children. Not allowed to leaf through the colorful books, the children fidgeted in their chairs and yawned while Joshua Freeman spoke. Once again, gloating Shteynfeld was introduced as "my brother Anatoly" and served as his interpreter.

"Dear brothers and sisters," Joshua Freeman began. This time he spoke only in English, although the leaflets we received at the entrance had text and prayers both in English and in Russian. "We are gathered here on the Lord's Sabbath to celebrate our Hashem Yeshua and his love for humankind. Most of you have just escaped from an atheist, godless country, and I want to tell you that you are now free to open your hearts to the Lord. You are now free."

He paused, clasping pink hands at his chest and then unclasping and rising them, palms up, as though to take a deep breath. A few people took that to be an invitation to get up and applaud, but most remained in their seats.

I heard the woman behind me whisper, "What's 'Hashem Yeshua'?"

"Shhhh, Lida." Her husband in heavy metal frames admonished her.

"I just wanted to—," she said sulkily.

"—just shut up." He cut her off as Joshua Freeman gathered his face into an unctuous smile.

"In the Lord's home there's room for all of you," declared Joshua Freeman, stepping closer to the front row of chairs. "We celebrate both your new freedom and the Sabbath. Millions of our brothers and sisters in America and the world over are all celebrating with us. I want to remind you that Hashem Yeshua lived and died a Jewish man. Jews are truly blessed to be the favorite children of the Lord. And Jews who chose to embrace Hashem Yeshua are doubly blessed. You will always remain Jewish—and this is why I want you to open your hearts to the Lord. By embracing Hashem Yeshua, our Lord Jesus, you fulfill your nation's promise of millennia."

The last flourish of Joshua Freeman's inspired speech must have been lost on quite a few of the refugees in the audience. He made a gesture with his right hand, which was meant to say, "Okay, let me explain," and started speaking very, very slowly, pausing after his every clause and making eye contact with the bald man in heavy metal frames whom he had chosen as a privileged audience member.

"You are preparing to enter a new life of freedom in America, and I hope, in fact I am confident, that in this new life you will dwell in the house of the Lord. I know that in the Soviet Union some of you already sought to find the Lord. Here in the American Center, and here in this house of the Lord, you will find that whether or not we were born to a Jewish mother, we are all spiritual Semites."

"As long as they aren't spiritual anti-Semites," mother said in my ear. Her sharp wit was returning to her after a three-week absence. In our family mother has always been the one most acutely sensitive to deception, falsity, and poor taste.

"Let's sit until the end of the speech and get out," I whispered, but loud enough for the man in the heavy metal frames to cough with disapproval.

"And now," said Joshua Freeman, "I would like to invite you to join us in singing some of the American songs we like to sing in praise of our Lord. My wife Sarah will lead us, and on your sheets you can find the words."

When everybody got up, mother and I made for the exit.

"How rude. Typical Muscovites," someone whispered. We didn't look back, afraid of turning to pillars of saccharine. Only outside, already standing on the boulevard's red gravel path under the shadows of chestnut and plane trees, did we glance back at the villa with its terra cotta tile roof and dozing lion cubs on the front steps. We saw a family of refugees, parents and two boys in matching yellow caps, scurry out of the villa and turn the corner, aiming in the direction of the sea.

Mother and I stopped by the apartment to collect father and head over to the beach. He was reading on the balcony, Russian émigré magazines published in Israel and Germany scattered around him on the tiled floor. Sipping coffee from a heavy mug, dressed in a white shirt and faded shorts, father looked relaxed like a Roman writer or an academic down in Ladispoli for the weekend, and not a refugee with dim prospects for the future.

"How was it?" father asked tepidly, without getting up from his chair to greet us.

Mother went over and embraced him from behind, pressing her head to his right shoulder and kissing his earlobe.

"I'm sorry. I should have said it right away." Mother's voice was tender, fragile.

"Said what?" father asked, dreamily, although I think he understood what she meant.

"You were completely and totally right about Shteynfeld, and I was wrong. I apologize."

"Mama, you apologize? That's incredible!" I interjected.

Father got up from his chair and kissed mother, then me. "I have an inner sensor for these shteynfelds," he said. "When I was a kid, we used to beat the living crap out of such traitors," he added triumphantly, thrusting mother into one of those happy dances to no music my parents would perform in moments of nascent harmony.

OVER THE NEXT TWO WEEKS we heard on the local refugee news service that during the Tuesday and Thursday English classes at the American Center, Pastor Joshua and his wife read passages from the Gospels in English and explained them in "simple" terms. There were no vocabulary quizzes or grammar drills.

Mother and I never went back to the Saturday celebrations at the center, but it was harder to forgo the Wednesday night film screenings. We tried to slip in without making contact with the pastor and his wife, and we never stayed for the sweet and soapy treats. And we even tried to drag my father with us when the movie promised to be particularly good. He resisted, saying that former refuseniks and prisoners of Zion should not be lending moral support to converters of the Jews. And to their collaborators from our midst.

Two or three times in June and July my father let himself be talked into coming along to the screenings.

"If only I could treat patients or publish my work here," father would say. "My darlings, I would take you to the movies as often as you like."

With our apartment already putting us over the top, there was no money for entertainment in our budget. I think otherwise we would have gone to a local movie theater, even though the American films playing were all dubbed. Besides the occasional dance and social in a rented hall, the JIAS officials didn't offer much of a cultural program, and nothing in the way of Jewish entertainment or spiritual activities. Which brings me to Reb Motorcycle and his film series.

Blue laurels of exhaust fumes carried his fame around Ladispoli. This passionate, tongue-twisting rabbi actually rode on a scooter, an ancient precursor of today's fashionable Vespa; the refugees gave him the nickname "Reb Motorcycle." He was short, all sinew and bones, with a quintangular stubbly face and disproportionately large eyes burning with fires of hell and paradise. The neorealist in me wished

I had a movie camera every time I saw Reb Motorcycle tearing up the boulevard in his 1840s black-and-white clothes, right hand on the bar, left holding his black hat to his head, cigarette pressed into his mouth almost like a flute, the white fringes of his undershirt—the *tsitsit*—and black flaps of his coat flying in the wind like the wings and tails of a kite. Traditional though it was, his garb was not devoid of a certain rumpled elegance, the coat fitting him perfectly, the pants never baggy, too short, or too long. And he did—perhaps in violation of some of his movement's tenets—sport two items of luxury: driving gloves and suede shoes with buckles. There was another touch of style in the rabbi's appearance: yarmulkes made of the richest velvet, smooth and shiny like a mole's pelt. He was actually a handsome fellow, the way small, dark, Mediterranean men can appear handsome to willowy neuras- thenic blondes whom they sometimes marry. It was even rumored that a refugee widow in black visited him at the ramshackle cottage on the eastern fringe of Ladispoli's central quarter, which he occupied with his tall, skinny wife and their three boys. But it's quite possible that the refugee rumormongers had actually gotten it all wrong.

The rabbi's real name was Boruch T., and as destiny should have it, not only did he come from Kamenets-Podolsk, the ancestral home of both my grandfathers in southwest Ukraine, but his mother was born in Zhvanets, the small Podolian town where my father's grandmother was born. So who knows, perhaps Reb Motorcycle and my family are related just a little more closely than most Ashkenazi Jews. Certain things we'd better leave unprobed.

Reb Motorcycle was in his mid-thirties when we met him. He'd been in senior high school when he left Ukraine with his parents. They settled in Brooklyn, and he soon fell in with the Lubavitch Hasids. He had spent five years working at a Chabad center somewhere in Brazil, and by the time we arrived in Ladispoli, Reb Motorcycle had only been there about eight months. He came with the mandate to relaunch the activities of the local Chabad House. It had been dormant since 1984, when the annual numbers of Soviet emigrants had dropped to under a thousand people—as compared to tens of thousands at the peak of the Jewish exodus in the 1970s. As the wave started to rise again in the spring of 1987 (it would reach eight thousand by the end of the year), his predecessor was recalled to Brooklyn, and Reb Motorcycle was dispatched to Ladispoli.

"The Rebbe sent me here," Reb Motorcycle liked to say, with great reverence in his voice, when somebody asked him about his employer. "The Rebbe" meant the Lubavitcher Rebbe, leader of the Lubavitch Hasids, based in Brooklyn's Crown Heights. As far as I could tell, Reb Motorcycle spoke Russian with a double accent: a Jewish-Ukrainian one and a Brooklyn one. Emerging from his mouth, the words *"predstavitel' lyubavicheskogo Rebbe"* ("representative of the Lubavitcher Rebbe") sounded mysterious, alluring, like the name of a folk tale.

Although the rabbi's cottage technically functioned as the local Chabad House, with a room for services and another one for hosting meals, during the week Reb Motorcycle preferred to conduct his activities outdoors, receiving visitors at home only under special circumstances.

I remember a late morning at the end of June, my father leading me through the streets of Ladispoli. The sun is so violent that I close my eyes and walk like a blind Jewish boy, holding my fearless father by the elbow and stumbling on the cracks in the pavement. The light changes—I can feel it through the chinks of my eyelashes—from a blazing orange to a lush emerald, and I lift my eyes and see sun rays twining themselves into the tree crowns. We're in a green park on a red gravel path. We approach a green gazebo. Reb Motorcycle stands at the entrance to the gazebo, staring me straight in the eyes. His gaze incinerates.

"Reb Boruch," father says, pushing me up the gazebo stairs as the rabbi steps back and opens his arms to engulf me. "This is my son. Could you say the prayers with him?"

For the first time in my life, Reb Motorcycle lays the *tfillin*—wellworn leather straps with black boxes containing divine words on parchment—on my head and hand. I recite Hebrew words I don't know. As I repeat after Reb Motorcycle, I see his eyes smile in their full daily orbits, and I feel a shiver of something beyond my own life. What is that? I wonder. I still do, almost twenty American years hence when I sometimes sit in synagogue.

The gazebo in the public park served as Reb Motorcycle's daily office and rabbinical court. Fathers brought their young and grown sons to recite the prayers. If a refugee boy looked particularly young to be a bar mitzva—a grown man at thirteen according to Judaic law—the rabbi would squint and ask his father, "Let's see now, how old is your boy?" If a father hesitated with his answer, scraping his cheeks and pouting, the rabbi would pat the boy on his shoulder and tell him, "You'll have to wait, my good friend." But if he was told that "the boy just turned thirteen a week before we left Russia," Reb Motorcycle didn't ask for further proof and proceeded with the laying of the phylacteries.

At the gazebo the refugees came to seek Reb Motorcycle's advice, to complain against JIAS paper-pushers or Italian landlords, or to ask his opinion about a particular American or Canadian city where they planned to immigrate. "Providence, oh sure, good place," he told my father. "I know the rabbi there. Nice Chabad House on Hope Street." By "the rabbi" he always meant a local Lubavitch rabbi.

Reb Motorcycle had his inner circle and his groupies. Of the rabbi's closest associates that summer in Ladispoli, we had known Savely (Savva) Niterman since his days as a bard and songwriter in the Moscow refusenik underground. A grasshopper of a man with albino hair and skin, in Moscow Savva rarely parted with his guitar. People joked he was married to his guitar and not his second wife, a bespectacled, straw-haired biochemist who, after they became refuseniks, supported him by working as a phlebotomist. In refuseniks' apartments, or at unofficial concerts in the woods (when it was still warm outdoors), Savva performed an endless repertoire of Odessan, Yiddish, and Russian émigré songs. He also performed songs of his own composition. We had already been in Ladispoli about a week when Savva arrived with his wife, two small children, and guitar. He told people he was on his way to Philadelphia, where his first wife and teenage son had been living since 1979. In Ladispoli Savva quickly transformed himself into a veritable shtetl boy, dressed in black pants, a black vest over a white shirt, and a black yarmulke. Instead of strumming his guitar and philosophizing about the strangulation of Yiddish culture by Stalin's henchmen, Savva now ran errands for Reb Motorcycle. "Reb Boruch sent me . . ." or "Reb Boruch asked me to tell you . . . ," he would blurt out, hop back on the scooter, and be gone. Reb Motorcycle's highest sign of trust was to let his followers ride his bike, and Savva and a few other zealous messengers now made themselves busy with the affairs of the House of Chabad. They kept Reb Motorcycle abreast of all the developments in the refugee community. I suspect it was through the efforts of Savva Niterman and the rabbi's other partisans that a Thursday night film series was started in Ladispoli—to counter the Wednesday night screenings at the American Center.

It was always by word of mouth. There was no schedule, no printed program. Reb Motorcycle despised flyers and believed in the power of conversation. At best, he would allow his underlings to put up an announcement at the JIAS office. "FILM. TONIGHT. USUAL TIME AND PLACE," an announcement would read. The rabbi's movies weren't shown every Thursday and rarely started on time. They took place in the social hall of the local Boating and Fishing Club where JIAS also rented space for its occasional functions. It was a musty, poorly lit space with long wooden benches for seats, with dusty regalia and faded pictures on the walls. The floors and walls smelled of seaweed, burned anise, and old fishermen's breath. The projection equipment was poor; the sound would implode and go out in moments of high drama. Some of the prints were so scratched they made you feel like you had cataracts in both eyes. Compared to Reb Motorcycle's events, the screenings at the air-conditioned American Center with its soft chairs and new equipment felt like being at an American movie theater—even though at that point we hadn't been to an American movie theater.

What about the films themselves? At first it seemed Pastor Joshua was just showing American—or sometimes British—movies: family and historical dramas, love stories. They weren't in-your-face Christian movies. They were popular, some of them wildly famous films. At the American Center we saw, for the first time, *Terms of Endearment* with Debra Winger and Shirley MacLane. It was in the company of my Sardinian flame Rafaella that I saw *Breaking Away*, in which I swear I didn't detect Christian subtexts. And while one visit to the Saturday morning "celebrations" at the American Center was enough to convince us what that was all about, it wasn't for a while that we began to see subversive logic to the pastor's film series.

Pastor Joshua chose some of the movies in such a way that they showed Jew and Christian side by side, often contrasting one with the other. Such was the screening of *Chariots of Fire,* where the two protagonists are Harold Abrahams, a Jewish student at Cambridge University whose father came from Lithuania, and Eric Liddell, a Scottish missionary. They couldn't be more different, Abrahams and Liddell, but both have a gift. Both are great runners. And both represent Britain at the 1924 Olympics in Paris. The "flying Scotsman" Liddell, a devout Christian, refuses to take part in a one-hundred-meter race, in which he is considered a favorite, because it falls on a Sunday. In the movie Liddell doesn't yield to the request of the Prince of Wales to run for his king. He says he cannot and will not run on the "Lord's Sabbath" and goes to church as he does every Sunday. Abrahams ends up winning the race. Liddell later runs in the four-hundred-meter race and takes first place. The movie's portrayal of Abrahams as an arrogant and ambitious Jewish neophyte—and of Liddell as a martyr for his Christian faith—was not apparent to me when I first saw it at the American Center. But I did wonder, as did some other refugees in the audience, about the use of the word "sabbath." It sounded so much like "shabbat," the Hebrew word. This conflation of Jewish and Christian meaning is, I believe, what Pastor Joshua was hoping to impress upon the Soviet refugees. Some of the pastor's movies were Jewish stories and myths wrapped in Christian blankets, like *The Ten Commandments,* which a few refugees later referred to as a "great Jewish film." In retrospect it becomes apparent that Pastor Joshua was after the souls of the confused Jewish refugees. The film series, the Saturday morning celebrations of the Lord, and the English classes were all part of a plan to lure us with familiar Jewish symbols and signs.

By the middle of July the rivalry between the pastor's and the rabbi's film series was escalating into an open war. Reb Motorcycle was responding to the pastor's choices of films, at first not always successfully. Unlike Pastor Joshua, the rabbi himself never appeared at the screenings or introduced the films. Perhaps the idea of a film series struck the rabbi as something quite un-Jewish, something ostentatious. But what about his driving gloves, stylish shoes, and designer yarmulkes?

The week following the screening of *Chariots of Fire,* Reb Motorcycle showed *Exodus* with the young and handsome Paul Newman. When it first came out in 1960, Otto Preminger's film, based on Leon Uris's bestseller, was a landmark in popularizing Jewish history in America. But in the summer of 1987 *Exodus* wasn't a great hit with the Soviet refugees. Many in the audience had conflicted feelings about Israel; many experienced guilt over not going there. People complained. Reb Motorcycle learned a lesson, and the films became subtler. The pastor showed *The Goodbye Girl* with Marsha Mason and Richard Dreyfuss, and a week later the rabbi gave us *Funny Girl,* where Barbra Streisand plays Fanny Brice, the Jewish comedienne who rises from the pits of the Lower East Side to Broadway's stardom. There were shades of mockery in Reb Motorcycle's choice of film, and also notes of his sardonic commentary on Pastor Joshua's series. Yet Reb Motorcycle's series still lagged behind, and people complained that his films were too bland and old-fashioned. For several more weeks Pastor Joshua had the upper hand in their rivalry. Then the pastor decided to show something totally mainstream. Something recent, with appeal to the younger refugees. It was *Flashdance,* a film by Adrian Lyne, who would go on to make *9½ Weeks* and *Lolita.* Reb Motorcycle responded with *The Jazz Singer,* not the original movie but the 1980 flick starring Neil Diamond, with Lawrence Olivier as the old cantor Rabinovitch. Some refugees liked the rabbi's wry sense of humor, but others were less pleased. After the screening a group of older men stood outside the Boating and Fishing Club, smoking and grumbling.

"What, is he warning us or something?"

"Ah, a Jewish boy going after a *shiksa*—what's new?"

"And the old cantor Rabinovitch ripping his clothes? Come on now."

On the way back to our apartment I remembered an old joke about an author who brings poems to the editorial office of a Moscow monthly. The editor looks over the poems, then says to the author: "Very nice. We'd like to print those, but there's just one thing." "What's that?" the author queries.

"Well, you see, it's your last name, Rabinovitch. Why don't you take a Russian pen name instead." The author looks at the editor indignantly and says: "Rabinovitch *is* my pen name. My real last name is Chaimovitch." My memory still swarms with such anecdotes from the Soviet past, but I have little use for them now in America, except when I recall those Ladispoli days of dallying on the brink of an American future.

As July started to turn its dusty tail around the corner where at night the band played "Arrivederci Roma" at a restaurant with lanterns and empty cane chairs, the films in the pastor's series only got better and better, and even Reb Motorcycle's ardent groupies privately admitted that "things weren't looking very good." I remember the screening of *Children of a Lesser God*. On the way to the American Center, mother and I almost got into an argument right in the middle of the boulevard over the fact that my parents still hadn't made up their minds about our final destination in the New World. At the time, Washington, D.C., and Philadelphia were still in the running along with Providence, Rhode Island, which I visualized as a fishing village surrounded by water and miles of marshland. My father felt we would be better off in a smaller American city, while my mother abhorred in advance the prospect of living in the provinces. Despite the anxiety over the future, after seven or eight outwardly tranquil weeks of daily sunning and swimming, mother looked rested. She tanned very darkly, and under the sun her hair grew shades lighter. I remember walking on the boulevard with a swarthy Mediterranean version of my mother dressed in a white blouse and a new Italian skirt she and my father had bought at a going-out-of-business sale in Rome. I remember arguing about the future on the way to the screening and then settling in the soft chairs in the cool auditorium to hear the pastor's long-winded introduction about life in America, where as we were soon to find out, "all different folks" live together. Pastor Joshua seemed especially pleased with himself that evening, and he mentioned twice what a "special treat" he had in store for us, a movie just released a year ago. The copy came directly from the American Embassy in Rome, he announced. Several people in the audience applauded. Before making his exit off the stage, Pastor Joshua said:

"When Sarah and I worked on putting together this series, we didn't plan on showing the film you are about to see. And in fact some of you may wonder if a film that shows sexuality even belongs in this House of the Lord. I believe it does belong here, for Hashem Yeshua judges not, nor does he cast away any of his children. Welcome, once again, to the American Center."

Children of a Lesser God was a hit with the refugees, especially the scene where William Hurt's character, a teacher at a school for the deaf, joins a naked young woman in the swimming pool. Our misgivings about going to the pastor's screening had not dissipated. But it would have been hypocritical for me not to admit that I wondered whether it's better to be entertained like apostates than bored like faithful Jews.

Two weeks went by after the screening of *Children of a Lesser God,* and Reb Motorcycle still hadn't responded.

"Has he surrendered?" refugees asked at the beach and the piazza.

"Conceded defeat?"

"Probably not enough funding," others speculated.

"The pastor, he's got government connections," the refugees mused. And then Reb Motorcycle's foot-and-wheel soldiers spread the word that a screening was going to happen on Thursday.

"It's going to be something special," Savva Niterman told me, blowing out the word *special* like a soap bubble. "The rabbi himself will be there this time."

It was the end of the first week in August, when my father's Uncle Pinya came from Tel Aviv to stay with us. My parents and I were emotionally drained by the end of his visit, of which I'll have more to say in the pages that follow. On the afternoon of the screening my father and Uncle Pinya had returned from a two-day trip to the south of Italy, and the eighty-one-year-old Uncle Pinya was all abuzz with impressions of Pompeii and its magnificent lupanaria. This is the other reason I remember that particular screening so well: In my memory, the film Reb Motorcycle showed us that night has strangely merged with Uncle Pinya's descriptions of Pompeii's erotic frescoes.

When we walked up to the Boating and Fishing Club—mother and father, and Uncle Pinya in Boy Scout–type shorts over his old man's earthen legs—we saw Reb Motorcycle standing near the entrance in a tight circle of followers. Smoking like a man who had just spent his family's last few bucks at the racetrack, he greeted the arriving refugees with brusque nods of his burdened head.

When the social hall had filled up like a Moscow trolleybus during rush hour, Savva Niterman went outside to summon the rabbi. Reb Motorcycle entered the room and positioned himself in front of the first row of refugees. Unlike the American Center, the rented space of the Boating and Fishing Club had no stage. For two minutes Reb Motorcycle stood there, smoking and not saying anything, scanning the audience with his squinted eyes. Then he exploded into a wrathful oration.

"Word has reached me," Reb Motorcycle began, in his doubly ac-cented but exacting Russian. "Word has reached me that you complain about the pictures we've been showing here. I was told some of you say the rabbi's pictures are not too exciting. 'Too bland,' some of you say. Not too exciting? Too bland?" The rabbi pulled his right hand out of the front pocket of his trousers and brandished it furiously. "So the Jewish pictures aren't too exciting for you, and the pictures they show on the boulevard you find exciting—is that what I'm hearing?

"Well, I've got news for you, dear Jews. Or have you forgotten who you are since you've been going to their goyish shows? In case you've forgotten who you are, and also in case you're too blind to see what goes on in that villa, let me remind you: They're after your souls. The pastor, he may talk a slightly different talk than those evangelists in America, but he walks the same walk. Believe me, they all want the same thing. I've seen this before, under different disguises. In Russia it was Orthodox priests who talked about the doubly chosen Jews—a whole bunch of garbage. Then there's the Jews-for-Jesus tomfoolery. And now the sweet-talking weasel of a pastor. It's all tricks, deception, and spiritual holocaust. Like they haven't killed enough of our people, they wouldn't leave us alone. So I'm warning you, Jews, they all want the same thing. They want a piece of you. And some are getting caught in their snares. I'm warning you again, it's not just about the pictures, here or over in America."

The rabbi paused to wipe his brow and light another cigarette. Those in the audience, about one hundred fifty of us, sat without stirring. Only my father's Uncle Pinya loudly blew his nose and giddily whispered in my ear: "All servants of the cult are crazy fanatics."

Reb Motorcycle moved one step closer to the front row and continued with his oration.

"I hear from my sources that some of you say the rabbi's a hypocrite. He doesn't want to show you anything racy, anything with naked people in bed. Is that what you think?

"I said a little earlier it's not just about the pictures, but let me correct myself. If it's to be about movies, I don't have any problem with it. 'Cause remember, Jews, everything the goyim have, we Jews also have. In fact, we had it first. So, as the pastor says, enjoy the show. Let's go." Reb Motorcycle clapped his hands and signaled to the projectionist.

The lights went out, and with the first notes of the soundtrack my breath grew shorter. My heart started pounding with triumph. The film opened with a sequence on a half-empty plane flying to Bangkok. During the brief opening scene, the protagonist, a young married French woman, has sex with two different men—with one in the restroom, the other right in the cabin, under a flimsy blanket. I'd never before seen this film, based on the novel by Emmanuelle Arsan, but I knew the music. I had the entire soundtrack in my head. Back in Moscow I used to play it on tape. Many times my friends and I imagined being in the West, going into a movie theater, and experiencing the film's footage together with the soundtrack. That was one of the fantasies that I was the first in my Moscow circle of friends to match up with reality. Incredible as it sounds, Reb Motorcycle showed us the original 1974 *Emmanuelle,* a gem of plotless erotic cinema.

Just picture the whole scene. The print was old, and it was not always easy to hear the dialogue. In fact, come to think of it, I don't remember if the film was dubbed in English or shown in French with English subtitles that were difficult to read. Darkness entered the social hall through the open windows, bringing no relief to our overheated lungs. There were children and elderly people in our packed audience of refugees. Some of the women started pulling at their husbands to leave, but the husbands wouldn't budge. They were glued to their seats and to the screen where the still-unsated Emmanuelle explored herself with men, women, in couples, and in groups, in Bangkok, and in the country, beside turbulent waterfalls and in roadless Thai hamlets. And all the while I kept thinking about the soundtrack, with its whispering and prattle. Back in Moscow my father used to call it *"okhi-vzdokhi"* (moans-groans). I kept thinking of eighteen-, nineteen-, twenty-year-old Soviet boys and girls dancing in small crowded apartments with the lights turned off and making out to the sounds of "dá-da-da-dadáda-da-da-dá-Emmanu-élle, dá-dadá-dadá-dadá." The sentimental often becomes ludicrous in retrospect, so let me stop right there.

On the way back to our apartment, Uncle Pinya seemed very pleased with the rabbi's choice.

"He's a stinking clerical," he said of Reb Motorcycle. "But at least he's no prude. That's the first step away from organized religion."

Our dear Uncle Pinya left the next morning, and for the next few days Ladispoli was a-tremble with discussions of the debacle at the rabbi's screening.

"He's gone mad, your black-hat rabbi," objected some refugees.

"Mad? No, quite the opposite. He did the right thing," others countered.

"The right thing? You call this smut 'the right thing'?"

"Of course I do. Our Reb Motorcycle's a gutsy fellow. He really gave them hell. Outgoyed the goyim. The pastor couldn't beat that, could he?"

"The pastor's a pleasant, educated person, not a shtetl brute like your rabbi," said some members of the refined Moscow intelligentsia. Their small faction was headed by the depressed classicist Anatoly Shteynfeld.

Reb Motorcycle had won a decisive victory in our refugee court of public opinion. Perhaps that's saying too much, but at least he'd won in my family court. After the screening of *Emmanuelle*, mother and I never went back to the American Center.

How many of the lost souls got caught in Pastor Joshua's "snares" (Reb Motorcycle's word) that summer? How many continued in America as the new brothers in Christ? I imagine only a few, which may or may not have been the success of Reb Motorcycle's pugilistic efforts at protecting us. Or perhaps it was the pastor himself who had miscalculated, putting too much stock in mere attendance of the refugees who practiced their English any way they could as they prepared themselves for America. As they attended the screenings and drank the soapy punch, as they practiced their English by reading Gospel passages during the Tuesday and Thursday classes, the vast majority just went about their ex-Soviet lives. Not very discerning in what they watched, read, and ate, the refugees remained distrustful of ideology, authority, and preaching.

In the final analysis I'm tempted to say it was Emmanuelle and her rolling sighs of love that defeated the pastor's evangelizing efforts. Now, almost twenty years later, when I see a Hasidic man crossing down Beacon Street in Brookline, hurrying to save Jews from extinction, I smile, remembering the duel of Reb Motorcycle and Pastor Joshua. I do smile, and these lyrics play in my head when I remember myself as I was during that long Ladispoli summer:

> Melody of love your singing heart, Emmanuelle
> Your heart beats, you fall apart,
> Melody of love your singing heart, Emmanuelle
> You've discovered your body's heart,
> Your are alone,
> Only a child,
> You've only known
> One lover's charm,
> Twenty years of age. . . .

PART THREE | Baggage

7

Napoleon at San Marino

The summer when we first came to the West from the Soviet Union, we were poor and thirsty to see the world. And we were not living according to our means. In Ladispoli my parents and I were renting a perfectly middle-class apartment with a view of the sea while entire refugee families shared tiny airless rooms that opened onto dusty courtyards. And we weren't saving a penny when many others, our own relatives included, economized. What could they have saved up in two or three months of living in Italy like misers? A thousand dollars, two thousand—perhaps a down-payment on their first American car? A beat-up Oldsmobile Cutlass Sierra instead of their own daily Tyrrhenian Sea rising and falling outside the windows?

It was impossible to be living in Ladispoli, where even a suntan had a shade of refugee anxiety, without being reminded of how little had survived of the tangibles of our Russian past. And conversations like the one my father and I had with the Roubenis on the terrace of their rented villa didn't help either, unearthing some of my father's old fears about living in America.

By the very end of July we had finally made up our minds about moving to Providence, where we had Jewish-Russian friends who had emigrated in the 1970s, before the Soviet exit doors slammed shut. The knowledge that with the assistance of our friends the Rhode Island Jewish community was making arrangements to welcome us, that an apartment was being rented for us on the first floor of a frame house on a quiet residential street, that we now had a bit more than the vaguest idea of the whereabouts of our American future—all of this calmed us down. I should rather say it calmed us down only for two or three days, until my mother announced that her sister, niece, and my grandmother were all coming with us to Rhode Island. Once before, when we had received permission to emigrate, my mother had put her foot down and told a KGB officer she wasn't leaving without her sister and her family; this time she said it to father and me. If the KGB officer had acquiesced, how could we not?

"But tell them to get rid of the trunk," my father said. "I'm not touching it again. Lord knows what will be in it this time."

Mother called father a heartless egoist and me an ungrateful grandson and nephew, but accepted the condition—as little family baggage as possible. The Jewish community of Rhode Island had agreed to embrace three more refugees from Soviet captivity ("Did you have running water in Russia?" a Jewish social worker in Providence later asked my mother). In the spirit of family harmony all six of us—my parents and I, my grandmother, my mother's younger sister, and my eleven-year-old cousin—signed up for a bus trip. The bus was to leave Ladispoli early in the morning and take us to Florence, where we would spend most of the day. We were to stay the morning of the second day in San Marino and by the evening arrive in Venice, where we would spend the night and part of the third day, returning to Ladispoli late in the evening.

"In some ways, rogues of different nations resemble one another," said the Russian émigré painter and poet Semyon Krikun. The name of the person who operated the refugee bus excursions out of Ladispoli was Aleksey Nitochkin. An ethnic Russian, in the 1970s he had emigrated from Leningrad with a Jewish wife. They went to New York by way of Vienna and Rome, just as we did. In New York, as Nitochkin claimed, he earned a Ph.D. at Columbia, writing a thesis on Eastern patristics. He told the refugees he did it all "on his own," a "man from the street," a "guy from the asphalt," as he liked to put it, and the refugees both believed him and didn't. Nitochkin said he was a professor of theology for six years at a college somewhere in upstate New York, but academic politics didn't agree with him—academic politics and jealous colleagues. So after not getting tenure he divorced his first wife, married an Italian woman he'd met in graduate school, and moved with her to Rome in search of new freedom and happiness. They settled in

Ladispoli, probably because former refugees, like former criminals, are drawn to their old haunts. When the floodgates of Jewish emigration were reopened in 1987, Nitochkin opened a tour service, taking former compatriots around Italy on the cheap. What Nitochkin had done for a living prior to starting the tour business was anybody's guess. He claimed he had published articles in leading Italian magazines, but we had no way of checking. I later found out that Nitochkin did publish sketches, stories, and poems in the émigré press, especially in the Parisian quarterly *Messenger of the Russian Christian Movement.*

During that summer in Ladispoli, Nitochkin offered three excursions: the one to Florence, San Marino, and Venice, which we had chosen over a trip to Pisa, Lucca, and the Cinque Terre, and also a third one, to the Amalfi coast, which mother and I took later in August. I highly doubt Nitochkin had a license to run the excursions or even took out insurance. But that's my present Americanized self speaking. We didn't give such matters consideration at the time—Nitochkin was taking us to see Florence and Venice! So who cared if he had proper permits and papers? His excursions were a fraction of what it would cost a foreign tourist booking a regular bus tour in Italy. There were no glossy brochures and not even flyers for Nitochkin's tours. They were by word of mouth only, and the trips left Ladispoli on short notice, when our roguish underground tour operator had recruited a bus full of refugees and collected advance payments. The tour guides, temporarily enlisted from the ranks of the overeducated Soviet refugees, lectured in Russian. Nitochkin also did some of the lecturing on the bus, about himself, politics, and life in America. He called it "conditioning of refugees."

Besides my parents, grandmother, aunt, cousin, and me, there were about forty refugees with us on the bus speeding to Florence. There was Nitochkin himself and two ancillary tour guides, Pyotr Perchikov, a former comedian, and Anatoly Shteynfeld. Perchikov's job was to provide entertainment at those times when both Nitochkin and Shteynfeld had exhausted their commentary. He told ethnic and political jokes and Moscow bohemian gossip, most of it quite stale. Andrea, our bus driver, was the only native on the bus. A Roman cat, Andrea represented authority, despising all refugees and foreigners and even treating his employer Nitochkin with a tinge of condescension. "Never met a Jew I liked," Andrea told me at the first pit stop.

We arrived in Florence past noon and were left to our own devices until five or six in the evening. After losing a sense of time on Ponte Vecchio and letting my eyes dreamily flow downstream with the slatternly water of the Arno, after levitating on Piazza della Signoria and standing in front of and inside Santa Maria Novella and Santa Maria del Carmine, I felt pulsating joy at being a part of these miracles. Imagine the way a twenty-year-old Soviet Jew feels cheated out of the inheritance of beauty when visiting Florence for the first time! This is something I could only describe after leaving this world and learning to speak not in words but in pure images. And the joy of being able to take stock of all this Florentine beauty can lead a Jew astray if he doesn't know who he is and where he comes from.

By sunset we were back on the bus, leaving behind Tuscany's undulating landscape and crossing into Emilia-Romagna, bound for the sleepless Bologna. As if by coincidence, not only was Irena, my Rigan belle, on the trip with her whole clan, but also Lana Bernshteyn. My former Moscow girlfriend was there with her new squeeze, who so excelled at math, with her father and grandmother who so resembled one another, and her younger brother who had quickly turned into an Italian urchin. Irena and I sat together on the bus, and I sent my hands on exploratory expeditions into the not-so-distant realms. This was a lot like our swims and walks on the beach under the punishing eyes of Irena's older brother or parents.

I would slide my arm down her waist and encircle the small of her hip. "Enough of a good thing," Irena would breathe in and pull back to her seat, before her mother had a chance to turn and give us a dour look. Irena and I hadn't yet accepted the cul-de-sac of our flirtation. At least I hadn't. On this trip I was hoping to get away from Irena's family.

On the superhighway to Bologna, weaving my fingers into Irena's and then unweaving them, I was thinking to myself: They are all here. My whole family. A Moscow ex-girlfriend and a Ladispoli almost-girlfriend. My restless Soviet past, my refugee Italian present, and the vague promise of a permanent American future.

It was past nine in the evening when the bus pulled into Bologna. "They call it 'Red Bologna,'" Nitochkin announced.

"And why 'red'?" my grandmother asked.

"The place is run by the Commies. Totally out of control," he explained. "We're only stopping for an hour. This is Piazza Maggiore, Bologna's biggest square. I want you all back on the bus in an hour."

Irena and I snuck away into a side street and grabbed some pizza. I don't remember very much of nighttime Bologna, especially as I saw it after Florence and a day of journeying. Some sort of a workers' rally was going on in Piazza Maggiore, slogans on banners, loudspeakers, and a chanting crowd. I remember illuminated porticos everywhere on the square, like a mesh of blackened silver that Bologna wore around its neck and shoulders. And there were performers and mimes, a great many of them. After pizza and a stroll, Irena and I stopped to observe two mimes at work. One, an open-armed Gorbachev, had a pale, powdered head with a strawberry mark. The other was a Reagan with bulldog wrinkles and his prosthetic smile. At intervals the two would come together, shake hands, and freeze in a historic embrace.

Then I bought us gelato from a stand in front of a large fountain bleeding red and green light. We weren't four hundred yards away from our tour bus, but the rallying piazza was a good place to become invisible. While the gelatonist packed into the cone the five flavors Irena had chosen—and she liked to start with chocolate and cleanse the palette with lemon—I composed myself and said, trying to speak as softly as I knew how:

"We cannot go on like this."

Irena received her cone from the hands of the gelatonist, dug into the chocolate demidome with her tongue, then licked her lips as if smudging dark lipstick.

"I agree," she replied, after having another go at the gelato. "Want a lick?"

"If not tomorrow—then when?" I asked.

"Yes," Irena replied.

"Are you going to say yes to everything?" I asked her, stroking her right elbow.

"Yes."

"Do you want to get away from the 'rents tomorrow in San Marino?"

"Yes."

"Will you come up with some excuse to disappear for a couple of hours?"

"Yes."

"Will I ever see you naked?"

"This is the best pistachio I've ever had," Irena changed the subject.

When we got back to the bus, my mother took me aside and told me that Shteynfeld had paid her an inappropriate compliment, and that father, furious, had held him by the throat, pinned to the side of the bus. Shteynfeld had threatened to report him to the *carabinieri* for assault and battery, and father had said, "One more squeak, and I'll put your head where your ass is." That's the last thing we need now, I thought, picturing my father, who had boxed seriously until his eyesight had rapidly deteriorated in med school, having it out with Shteynfeld in Bologna's main square. Just think of this: a Jewish-Russian poet-doctor defending the honor of his muse against the backdrop of a Communist rally in Bologna.

On the bus Shteynfeld looked livid and pretended to be reading an Italian paper. The rogue and the Roman cat argued over directions, and Pyotr Perchikov took over the mike and told Odessan jokes as we rode to some town on the outskirts of Bologna, where we stopped for the night. I was having to share a room with my grandmother, who seemed less tired than I was and started asking me questions like, "Who built Florence?" or "Do they still make raincoats in Bologna? They were so popular at home in the sixties." After I had already turned off the light on the night stand between our beds, my grandmother whispered like a kid sharing a bunk with me at a summer camp:

"What is this San Marino they are taking us to?"

"It's a very tiny state. A mountain-state, basically. But even Napoleon didn't conquer it. Sleep, *babulya*, please."

"Napoleon?" she asked. "Oh, I love Napoleon!"

"You do?" I asked her, from some place half the distance between wakefulness and sleep.

BY ABOUT TEN IN THE MORNING our bus was close enough to San Marino for Shteynfeld to point out the three peaks of Monte Titano rising from the plain ahead of us.

"This is the national emblem of the Republic of San Marino," he announced with pathos. "Three peaks surrounded by castle towers. You can see it on their coat of arms."

"And coat of legs," added Perchikov the comedian.

Shteynfeld didn't care for the joke and gave Perchikov a look of contempt. He had been lecturing about San Marino for about an hour—since we had passed the city of Forli, more or less the midpoint between Bologna and our first destination of the day. Half of the refugees slept; the others listened and tried to ask intelligent questions. One man, a flamboyant piano tuner from the city of Minsk in Belarus, even took calligraphic notes in a leather-bound notebook.

Shteynfeld had almost won me over again with his vivid account of Sammarinese history. And he had gained a keen audience member in my grandmother, who was for some reason very taken with the idea and image of a proud pocket-size mountain republic that hadn't bowed to her beloved Napoleon. Suntanned, wearing a white blouse embroidered around the collar and a rather tight cream skirt that my mother had begged her not to wear, grandmother looked young and renewed that morning. One could have easily thought her ten years younger. And she had just turned seventy-three that summer. It was grandmother, not Irena, who sat with me on the bus during the ride from Bologna to San Marino. In the morning Irena was cranky and went to sleep on the back seat where it was darker and a little quieter. Skeptical by nature, like most Jews who grew up by the Baltic Sea, Irena must have sensed the imminent disappointment of the day, whereas I, an adopted son of Italy, was still buoyant with romantic expectation.

Perhaps it was due to my radiant spirits that I was even ready to forgive Shteynfeld for his cowardly pass at my mother. After all, my father had already made him pay with fright, so why dwell on it? And listening to Shteynfeld's explanations felt like the old days when he used to lecture me about Etruscans as we stood on Ladispoli's street corners. Shteynfeld the classicist was illustrious when describing the legendary founding of San Marino by a Dalmatian hermit stonecutter by the name of Marinus in the fourth century. By the time he reached the Renaissance, Shteynfeld was getting bored with his own story, and he started playing games with his audience.

"The republic of San Marino was briefly occupied only twice in its entire history," he said. "Does anybody know by whom?"

Nobody knew.

"Figures," Shteynfeld said, mouth contorted. "First by Cesare Borgia, and then by Cardinal Alberoni's troops over two hundred years later, if memory serves—and it usually does. And then the pope recognized San Marino's independence. Well, I guess I should mention that in 1944 the German and then the Allied troops briefly came through San Marino. But that doesn't really count. San Marino tried to be neutral during the war."

"And what about Napoleon?" my grandmother screamed out, so loudly that she startled me.

"What about him?" Shteynfeld despised anything that happened after the French Revolution.

"Tell us about Napoleon," my grandmother pressed on, using her favorite "we the citizens" mode. She still hasn't unlearned it, even after almost twenty years in America.

"Tell them, Anatoly. The people want to know," Nitochkin the rogue interceded.

"What did Emperor Napoleon do when San Marino had no loo?" Perchikov came in with one of his impromptu jokes. A couple of people readily giggled.

"A typical Russian obsession with Napoleon," Shteynfeld remarked, wryly. "All right then. In 1797 Napoleon's most loyal general, Louis Alexandre Berthier—he later became marshal of France when

Napoleon became emperor, not the greatest of his generals, mind you, but an obedient executor of Napoleon's will—sacked San Marino."

"Oh, my God," grandmother loudly sighed.

"I would ask that you please not interrupt me!" Shteynfeld yelped.

"Berthier's troops stood at San Marino, threatening the republic, but its leaders protracted the negotiations for the terms of surrender for so long that one of the republic's captains regent reached Napoleon and secured his protection. San Marino was spared. A grand symbolic gesture, perhaps. And the Congress of Vienna recognized its sovereignty. There's your Napoleon story, my dear lady," he concluded, turning to my grandmother, who had become the center of Bonapartism on our bus of Soviet refugees.

"Beg your pardon, what did you say the population was?" the piano tuner asked, interrupting Shteynfeld.

"I repeat: About twenty-five thousand Sammarinese live within the boundaries of this small republic," Shteynfeld said, icily. "It's the third-smallest state in Europe, after the Vatican and the principality of Monaco. And remember, it's the smallest republic in the world. The Sammarinese love their freedom. Their constitution goes back to the year 1600, if you can you imagine it."

At this point Nitochkin tore himself from a conversation he was having with the Roman cat at the wheel—most likely about Russian versus Italian women—and said into the driver's microphone affixed to a metallic flexible neck: "That's right, folks, the whole place is less than one-third the size of Washington, D.C. I once spent six months in Washington on a fellowship advising Congress about the Orthodox Church." And he told another one of his unimaginable American stories that many on the bus refused to disbelieve. Whether or not he actually had a Ph.D. from Columbia was a different matter, but the rogue was, to give him credit, up on Italian politics.

"It's a fairy tale," he said. "A dictator's dream turned nightmare. Think about it: The Sammarinese have a sixty-seat parliament, called the Grand and General Council, elected for five years by direct popular vote. The parliament elects from among its own a twelve-member Congress of State. And every six months members of the Grand and

General Council choose the two titular heads of state, called *i capitani reggenti*. Both captains regent have to approve any decision of the Congress of State. Can you imagine this madness? And a military of about a thousand men to protect the republic from an invasion of wild goats."

"Is there a Communist Party here?" asked the piano tuner. The nighttime Communist rally in Bologna had impressed and terrified him and the other refugees.

"Funny you should ask," the rogue replied. "They do have what's called a Communist Refoundation Party—basically the former Communist Party. And a whole bunch of socialist parties. Plus Christian Democrats, Popular Alliance—the usual center and right of center stuff. And until 1943 they had a Fascist Party."

"Oh, my God!" my grandmother cried out. "What a shame!"

"The whole of Italy did," the rogue said with a melting smile, "which didn't prevent San Marino from being home to about one hundred thousand refugees, many of them Jewish. Things in Italy are more complex than some are willing to believe. Much more complex than in America, your future home, my darling lady."

The bus slowed down as we crossed the border of San Marino. "Welcome to the Land of Freedom," said the signs in Italian. The bus went up a winding road before turning into a large parking area labeled "Parcheggio 2." Other tour buses crowded the sight. The parking area was the bottleneck of a tourist trap we were about to enter.

Prior to opening the bus door, the rogue made an announcement.

"Be back here by three o'clock. And the driver tells me we've lucked out: It's the annual Sons and Daughters of San Marino parade. So the place will be crammed full. Allow additional time. Remember, ladies and gentlemen refugees, we will not wait for you. If you're late, you'll have to make it back on your own. *Buon giornata.*"

Our fellow travelers, including Irena and her family and my grandmother, aunt, and cousin, had already filed up the stairs going up to the town gates of San Marino. My parents and I were still standing in place, looking up at the three peaks of Monte Titano, each studded with a tower. We took slow bites of our red apples. This was our down time, a respite from collective activities.

"I would rather be looking at Byzantine frescos in Ravenna," father said. "Or visiting Rimini."

"My darlings," mother said, putting her arms around father and me. "We'll be in Venice tonight, can you believe it? In Venice! With the gondolas and the pigeons of San Marco. I can just see it all—like a dream."

"And I keep thinking of Pasternak's poem about Venice. 'Like a Venetian woman, Venice/From the embankments threw herself,'" father recited. "This is how I imagine her, Venice."

"Let's go, dreamers," I said to my parents. "San Marino isn't Florence, but let's make the best of it. I have to be somewhere at one, so we have about two hours together."

"Are you going on a date?" mother asked.

I didn't answer her.

We climbed a series of stairs and unwinding streets until we came to the Gate of St. Francis, through which we entered the limits of old San Marino. More stairs, streets, and elevators eventually brought us to the First Tower at the top of Monte Titano, from which we could see both the promise of Adriatic blue and the frowning hills, coiling vineyards, and verdant valleys surrounding the diminutive republic. The Sammarinese vistas were attractive but not breathtaking, and we didn't bother with the other two towers. Spiraling down on foot, we fell onto the historic center. Signs pointed to a basilica where the remains of the founder of San Marino lay buried, and we wandered in and out lazily. The most imposing building was the Palazzo Pubblico with its turreted tower and crenellated walls, the seat of San Marino's parliament and government. Looking back at San Marino I envision something out of a Disney theme park, or a pseudo-gothic castle like the one in San Simeon, California. The historic center had small museums offering the tired wanderer displays of old armor, various torture instruments such as the rack or the Spanish boot, and not a whole lot more. And there was the main square, Piazza della Liberta, choking with souvenir shops and gaudy stalls. On sale were mostly T-shirts, hats, bags, and various trinkets with the three fortressed cowlicks of San Marino. Shops also advertised sweet wines and cognac distilled from the locally grown muscat grapes. Advertisements in windows depicted a man with a full face wearing a bicorn hat, right arm tucked under his vest on his belly, left folded behind his back. "Lowest cognac prices in Europe," read the signs. The man on the advertisements had a coat with gold epaulets and an oversized star on his heart.

"We should probably get some cognac," father said dreamily.

"Good idea, papa," I said in a dumb voice.

"Have you two ever heard of good Italian cognac?" mother asked us.

Instead of the unheard of cognac named after the imperial protector of San Marino who needed only four hours of sleep and died in exile off the shores of Africa, we bought a bottle of water, a crumbly loaf of white bread, some fresh cheese, and a bag of golden grapes. Father washed the grapes under a water jet squirting out of a wall, and we picnicked on the steps in a shady side street off the main square, our provisions spread out on the pouty stones. A little before one in the afternoon I parted with my parents. We agreed to meet on the bus.

"Have fun, my dear," father said, giving me one his ironic half smiles. "Don't get carried away."

I kissed mother goodbye and headed up to the Palazzo Pubblico, where Irena and I had earlier agreed to rendezvous. Turning from the cool and dark side street into the sunlit Piazza Liberta I came upon a trattoria with outdoor tables, and just as these things usually happen in fairy tales of love, longing, and pursuit, there was a corner table with a brightly colored tablecloth, plates of pasta, and glasses of wine, where my ubiquitous aunt sat eating lunch with my cousin in tow, in the company of a gorgeous woman with long auburn hair, faintly Asian eyes and cheekbones, and a refined, if slightly naïve face.

I was right in front of their table. There was no escape from the family ambush, and a part of me was dying to know what the gorgeous woman with auburn hair was doing with my aunt and cousin. In her typical fashion my aunt introduced me as "a brilliant student" and "a young poet." The gorgeous woman spoke fluent English and also some Russian. She was Jewish, originally from Budapest, and she married a citizen of San Marino and moved there in the late 1970s. How my aunt and the lady met—and why my aunt and cousin got invited to lunch—I have no idea, although nothing would surprise me after the violinist she had smuggled out of Russia in the Manchurian trunk. The gorgeous woman asked me to join them at the table, but I couldn't, although I was tempted.

"Where's grandmother?" I asked my aunt in a half whisper.

"Oh, she's touring the museum of San Marino history," she replied, as though it was the most natural thing for a seventy-three-year-old refugee from the USSR to do instead of eating fresh pasta out of large steaming bowls. "We're meeting her in a little while."

I felt a vague sense of incongruence, knowing full well my aunt's stretchable notion of time, but I didn't say anything. I was going to be late to my date with Irena, and it would have been awkward to argue in front of the gorgeous lady, who had sprung onto this page of family absurdities from some other book of life. I just smiled, waved them all goodbye, and walked away.

In the dark middle archway of Palazzo Pubblico, where echos take refuge when the sun hits its zenith, Irena and I met like two conspirators.

"What did you end up telling your folks?" I asked, taking her hand.

"I told them I was going with you to the local history museum—to see Garibaldi's banner. My father seemed pleased with the choice. And my mother just rolled her eyes."

"And my greatest admirer, your vigilant brother?"

"Oh, he's just being a boy," Irena replied, tenderly. "Let's get out of here."

Irena and I strolled past the old city gate, veering somewhere to the right toward a long meadow abutting an olive grove. Under the trees the grass was cool and still a little wet with the morning dew. Or perhaps it had rained here the night before.

I spread out my faded denim jacket in the shadow of an olive tree. Shaking her head, Irena let her muslin curls loose. She was wearing a sleeveless blouse with pearly buttons in the front and a round, open neck of the sort that many young women were sporting in Italy that summer. A yellow skirt barely covered her lap when she sat down on my denim jacket.

"Finally," I said, relishing the moment of being alone with Irena and also thinking that we only had about an hour and a half.

"Finally," said Irena, making fun of my intonation. She pulled out a stem of ryegrass, and with it she tickled the back of my neck and behind my ears. "What are you going to do with me, Moscow boy?"

"What am I going to do with you?" I answered with a question, drawing nearer to her. "I'm going to ravish you right here."

"Hmm . . . How exciting," Irena said, leaning back on her right elbow.

I lay next to her, also resting the weight of my head and torso on my open palm and elbow.

"So you'll ravish me," Irena said, still playfully. "And then what?"

"And then . . . and then—"

"—and then you'll go to New England, and I'll go to California, and we'll probably never see each other again," Irena suddenly went from lighthearted to somber.

"But . . . but . . . what if . . . ?" I had a hard time coming up with a slick line.

"Scared you, didn't I?" Irena laughed, regaining her playfulness.

"You did."

"The thing is that I like you, Moscow boy. I like you a lot."

As we kissed my stray hand untied the string of the round collar and undid the top pearly button of her blouse. We're finally getting somewhere, I was thinking, as Irena's hands drew tighter round my neck. I rolled over from the side, kissing Irena's neck, which tasted of olives and summer mountain wind. It's finally happening, I kept thinking to myself. I was down to the last button, grasping for it, thinking to hell with all the buttons and hooks, almost forgetting that Irena was not just a part of myself clad in a bra and yellow skirt, forgetting where I was—not on a quartzy Baltic beach but within an olive grove in San Marino. Then I heard very loud hissing and screeching and Italian words erupting out of some place over our heads. "Attenzione! Attenzione!" streamed from the city walls up on high. "This is the

Citizens' Emergency Broadcast Service of San Marino. Please listen to this announcement. An old Russian lady is looking for her family. Come and collect her at the Palazzo Pubblico in the radio station."

"I think I have to go," I said, separating myself from Irena and sitting up.

"Go where?"

"I think it's my grandmother. I think she's lost or in trouble or I don't know what," I said, brushing off blades of grass and small dry olive leaves.

"How can she be lost?" Irena said, lips pursed. She buttoned up her blouse crooked, missing one button.

"I don't know. I'm sorry. I just have to go."

"How do you know it's your grandmother?"

"They said *'vecchia signora russa.'* I just have a bad feeling. I already had it when I saw my aunt at the trattoria in town."

"She's always with your aunt and cousin. They are . . . inseparable. I don't get it."

"That's the whole thing. I'm sorry, Irenochka. I'll see you later."

"Take your jacket."

Idler. Loser. The words ran through my head as I dashed across the meadow and hopped up the stairs toward the town gate. Loser, now you blew it! And another voice: She's your blood, your family, she took care of you and read poetry to you when you were little. Hurry up, you heartless rat. But her blouse was coming off, the first voice countered as I ran up the stairs and the steep road, she was all yours. How could you walk away from it?

Outside the Gate of St. Francis, I saw my parents sprawled out on a stone bench in the shade, eating more grapes.

"Did you hear? It's grandmother. We've got to do something. She's lost," I yelled to them from a distance.

Father unscrewed the top on a plastic bottle and calmly offered me some water. Mother also looked unperturbed.

"Mama, we've got to do something. We've got to rescue her."

"She's not lost," my mother replied. "She's just having a panic attack because your aunt isn't by her side."

"How? What happened?"

"After you went to your date, your father and I bumbled in and out of stores, bought a straw hat for him—the kind he's always wanted—and then we went to buy some fruit and we bumped into your grandmother. She was by herself and looked frazzled. She said your aunt and your cousin had gotten lost and we had to find them. 'We must go to the authorities,' she said. And also: 'They must do something.'"

"And you?" I asked, still catching my breath.

"And I told her first of all they weren't lost, but your aunt was probably late or had lost track of time like she often does. But your grandmother just wouldn't listen. 'I'm going to the authorities,' she said to us. So your father and I showed her where the Government House was. You know how intolerably stubborn she gets."

"She wanted your mother to go with her to see one of the captains regent," my father chimed in. "As her personal interpreter."

"But wait, I still don't understand what happened," I said.

"What probably happened is that they were supposed to meet, and your aunt and cousin were late, and your grandmother started freaking out," mother said. "And she probably wanted to torture my sister back for being late. It's all such nonsense. How can you be lost in a small town surrounded by walls?"

"We told her we would sit here and wait for her until two-thirty," father added. "The only way to the bus is past this gate. She knows exactly where we are."

Instead of collecting my grandmother at the Palazzo Pubblico, I ended up joining my parents on the stone bench and eating more of the golden muscat grapes.

About ten minutes later the loudspeakers came alive again: "*Attenzione! Attenzione!* This is the Citizens' Emergency Broadcast Service of San Marino. Please listen to this announcement. An old Russian lady is looking for her family. Please come and find her at the Palazzo Pubblico in the radio station."

"What are they saying anyhow?" father asked. "I only understood '*signora*' and '*russa*.'"

And then, in complete defiance of Aristotle's dictum, the most improbable thing happened. My grandmother's voice came through the broadcasting system, half the sentence in flight, as did also shuffling noises and sounds of struggle.

"My daughter is lost with my granddaughter. Possibly a kidnapping it is. They need to be rescued." Grandmother's hysterical Russian sentences flowed over the walls of San Marino.

"Aspettate, aspettate," the announcer's male voice came through, and with it more tussling and scuffling.

"Daite govorit'" (Let me speak!) said grandmother in her sonorous voice. "Fascists!"

"I don't believe this," father said, crushing a handful of grapes. "She's on the air. Live. I'll be damned."

"Save my children!" grandmother pleaded. "I demand that the government of San Marino do something right now. Immediately. A diplomatic scandal. This is outrageous. I will hold you accountable. *Dochen'ka, ty gde?"* (Darling daughter, where are you?)

How long did she last on Sammarinese air? Five, ten minutes? Besides delivering more or less incoherent sentences in Russian, fraught with fear for the lives of her lost daughter and granddaughter, my grandmother also tried the other languages she had once spoken or studied and since forgotten.

"Mayn libe tokhter" (My beloved daughter), grandmother said plaintively in Yiddish. *"Moia donka . . . kokhana moia"* (My daughter . . . my beloved), she sang out in Ukrainian. *"Zgoda, jedność, braterstwo"* (Concord, unity, brotherhood), she chanted in Polish. And finally she barked in German: *"Was ist das? Donner-wetter!"*

Having exhausted her supply of non-Russian locutions, my grandmother reverted to Russian and let her memory wax histrionic.

"I suffered under Stalin," her voice spread across the airwaves of San Marino. "I was an honors student at Kharkov University. I was invited to the Palace of Government for a reception, and Grigory Petrovsky himself, he was a powerful man, chairman of Ukrainian Central Executive Committee, awarded me a cash stipend. I had a picture taken where he was shaking my hand. And then in 1938 Comrade Petrovsky was purged, and I stayed up all night looking for the picture because I was afraid I too would be arrested. I cut him out of the picture with scissors. O, people of San Marino, how I've suffered."

Then grandmother's voice changed again, from lyrical to fuming. "Can you hear me, you vile thing?" she screamed. "I raised you and took care of you, and now you dump me in the middle of San Marino! Children are ungrateful locusts. Children are rascals, scoundrels. Doubly the rascals abroad."

The overheated voice of my grandmother was broadcasting all over San Marino on the emergency network designed to call the citizens of the small republic to arms when the enemy shows at the foothills of Monte Titano.

"Why is nobody doing anything? I demand to know!" grandmother screamed. "In the Soviet Union I was an economist. I was a prominent person at the Ministry of Energy. I had a staff of thirty. Two secretaries. The minister himself knew my name."

At this point my mother started dying of shame before my father and me, before the citizens of San Marino, before the whole world.

By now grandmother was listing all the famous Italians she had heard of back in the USSR, mostly film personalities, musicians, and left-wing political leaders and activists: "Fellini, Mastroianni, Sophia Loren, Claudia Cardinale, Verdi, Donizetti, Puccini, Robertino Loretti, Togliatti, Gramschi, Giuseppe da Vittoria, Sacco and Vanzetti." Then she remembered Mussolini, for better or for worse. "It's a Fascist nest here," she cried out. "Help, they are secretly rounding up Jews. Help. SOS SOS SOS!"

Then the announcer's words *"una vecchia Stalinista"* (an old Stalinist) and grandmother's *khooligany* spurted out of the two loudspeakers mounted on top of the city gate, and the San Marino public announcement system went dead.

For a few minutes we sat on the stone bench, mechanically munching on the muscat grapes and not speaking.

Father broke the silence. "Now that was one classy performance."

"This is not funny," mother said. "It's embarrassing. All of Ladispoli will soon know."

It was well past two o'clock when my aunt and cousin materialized in front of the gate, my aunt wearing the new Italian dress she put on that morning, all frilly and jittery like a dancing horse.

"Where is she?" she asked us.

"She's up at the Government House," mother replied. "You're over an hour late."

"I must go and fetch her," said my aunt, eyes a-sparkle. She left my cousin with us and cantered through the gate and up the road.

Minutes after she had disappeared we heard sounds of live music, a windy march. A small band emerged from behind the bend on the road to our right. It paraded past us and up the road that encircled the old town walls. Marching after the band came a procession of men in white coats, blue pants, and straw hats, and women in white and blue dresses. The men carried banners and the women waved little blue and white flags of San Marino with three turreted peaks inside the gilded coats of arms. The procession of Sons and Daughters of San Marino was followed by a platoon of soldiers wearing bicorns and carrying rifles with wooden bayonets. Were they all impersonating Napoleon on the Bridge of Arcol? Finally a row of accordionists playing some bouncy songs walked by, all the players dressed in white chambray shirts and britches and funny blue berets.

And then my grandmother appeared around the bend of the road, the last paradeer, traipsing behind. Her blouse was untucked, and her red and blue sun cap was turned to the side. She resembled an Italian market lady after the end of a long hot day of selling peaches and plums. But she looked even more like a tired general who had put down a mutiny, staring wildly at the sky above and at the town walls as if telling them, "You too will fall one day."

Clutched in her left hand was a bottle of cheap local Napoleon. Taking swigs from the bottle, grandmother sang "Moscow Summer Nights" as she walked down the hill after the procession.

"She isn't lost," she announced to us. "No, no, no! She abandoned me, the wretch. I hate her, I disown her."

Plunking down next to my father on the bench, she leaned her head on his shoulder, sobbing.

"I gave up love for her," she said, her voice losing strength.

"Mama, we all know the story," said my mother.

"No, let me finish. You never let me talk. After your father and I divorced, I met a man on the waters at North Caucasus, in Kislovodsk. We both had gastric problems. He was a widower, about ten years older, a Jewish gentleman. He lived in Leningrad."

Grandmother straightened her sun cap. She now held the bottle of cognac between her legs, no longer taking swigs.

"You probably don't remember this," she said, turning to my mother. "I went to visit him in Leningrad. You were seventeen, your sister was ten. I sent you both to stay with my brother for a week, during spring break.

"His name was Veniamin. A very elegant man. He was a professor at the Leningrad Polytechnic. With his own private automobile. I was forty-two. You understand? Forty-two. It was during the Thaw; Stalin had died, we all felt hope. So I visited him in Leningrad. He brought me breakfast in bed. Fresh cottage cheese and honey from the farmers' market. He sang for me and played the piano. It was out of a movie. I hadn't ever had it before, you know, with your father."

"What's 'it,' *babulya?*" my eleven-year-old cousin asked.

"Be quiet, kitten. It . . . it . . . well, it's ice cream, sweet ice cream," grandmother said, tears welling up in her grey-blue eyes that refused to age with the rest of her. "He asked for my hand in marriage. But I stepped on my throat. I had my daughters to put through school and university. So what now? What do I get back? This?" Pointing upward to the three peaks of Monte Titano, she lifted and shook the bottle.

"Mama," said my father, "why don't we all have a drink of your Napoleon. To your victory over San Marino."

"*Babulya,* it's going to be okay. We all love you," said my cousin, her shorn curls having grown out after two weeks in Austria and two months in Italy.

And then my aunt galloped through the gate, and there were tears of joy and reconciliation. The three of them were hugging and kissing and jumping up and down, and my parents and I just sat there on the stone bench. There was no room for us in this spectacle of family love, where art and life were no longer separable.

By this point a group of refugees from our bus had come through the Gate of St. Francis, among them Lana Bernshteyn and her new boyfriend in a striped polo shirt. I was praying Irena wouldn't be among the group.

My parents and I sat there looking down at the valley where Napoleon's army once stood in contemplation. The cognac burned and soothed but it couldn't wash away all the years of untherapied family problems. We were the last to get on the bus bound for Venice. Three hours later the purple pigeons of San Marco greeted Napoleon's victorious troops.

Literature is Love

Soon after arriving in Ladispoli, we discovered a Russian lending library at the local Jewish refugee center, which wasn't really a refugee center but a suite of catacombic rooms outfitted with two or three file cabinets, a fax machine, and a copier. Two Iranian Jews in aviator sunglasses took over the rooms and used them in the manner of a private office. Nobody knew what their business was; nobody asked questions. A slothful JIAS official from Rome visited once a week to sit in his cubicle and smoke; sometimes a lady friend on killer stiletto heels accompanied him. The refugees received their cash allowances at the local bank. Instead of serving as office clerks and cordial librarians, our Jewish-Iranian brothers (who, as it later turned out, were indeed brothers) discouraged us from coming in, and it was rumored that one of them once called a Jewish woman from the Belarusian town of Gomel "an unclean whore," except how could she (a) hear it when muttered under the Iranian's breath; and (b) understand it when spoken in Farsi. But the anti-Iranian resentment grew among the Soviet refugees.

The lending library wasn't even a room but actually five bookcases. The JIAS must have purchased a book collection from some émigré widow in New York and shipped it to Ladispoli without even bothering to check the titles. Why else would there have been, alongside stories and novels by émigré classics Bunin and Aldanov, a reprint of *The Protocols of the Elders of Zion,* issued in Paris in the 1920s? It was a predictably random assortment of books and incomplete runs of the New York–based magazines *The New Review (Novyi zhurnal)* and *Aerial Ways (Vozdushnye puti).* Besides fiction, nonfiction, and some poetry, there were also various books of the sort the émigrés of the post-1917 "First

Wave" continued to reissue in the places of their dispersion. Among them was a copy of *The New Complete Dream Reader.*

Daniil Vrezinsky, the playwright's son and former Gulag inmate who had helped us find our apartment, took me to the lending library on my second day in Ladispoli. There he found on the shelves a copy of *Spring in Fialta,* Vladimir Nabokov's third Russian collection of stories. The brownish cardstock cover was ripped and missing two corners, but the volume was otherwise in sound shape.

"This is the original 1956 edition," said the Daniil, stroking the cover. "Chekhov Publishing House. New York. Worth a bit of money. These beasts will destroy it."

The ex libris on the inside cover had been scraped off, probably in haste; the top part with the former owner's name and a logo were missing, but the bottom third of the sticker had survived. On it was an address in Rego Park, New York. At the time I had no idea that Rego Park was a section of Queens and vizualized it as a small town somewhere on Long Island.

It makes me happy to taste these words as I type them: While reading *Spring in Fialta* I experienced love. As far back as I remember it, my father liked to repeat Nabokov's motto, "Literature is Love." Father used Nabokov's words as an epigraph to a memoir-novel that he wrote in the mid-1980s in Moscow, after surviving a heart attack caused by KGB intimidation; it was a tribute to his literary youth in Leningrad during Khrushchev's Thaw. Already in America and in graduate school, I realized that the quote came from the very beginning of chapter 7 in the novel *Despair,* which Nabokov wrote in 1933 in Berlin. My father had been quoting Nabokov's aphorism incompletely. In the Russian text it goes like this: Во-первых: эпиграф, но не к этой главе, а так, вообще: литература это любовь к людям. (Literally translated from the Russian, the sentence reads: "At first, the epigraph, but not to this chapter, but in general: literature is love for people.") In 1936 in Berlin Nabokov himself translated *Despair* into English, and it appeared in London a year later. The opening of chapter 7 in the translation leaves out "love for people": "To begin with, let us take the following motto (not especially for this chapter, but generally): Literature is Love." The opening of the chapter remained unchanged in the second version of Nabokov's English translation; it was published in America in 1966 and further reworked the translated text of 1936. So my father had been quoting the phrase exactly as it appears in both Englished versions and not in the Russian original. How could father have quoted in Russian what he could have only read in English—and definitely hadn't? He hadn't started reading Nabokov in English until some time after we came to America. In fact, I'm quite certain father could have found the aphorism "Literature is Love" only in a smuggled 1978 Ardis reprint of the 1936 Berlin Russian edition of *Despair,* which someone must have lent him back in Moscow. In the foreword to the 1966 English-language edition, Nabokov speaks of "foreread[ing]," and I wonder if my father had somehow managed to "foreread" the American afterlife of Nabokov's Russian aphorism. But it's about time I closed this literary digression and returned to June 1987 in Ladispoli.

I took the copy of *Spring in Fialta* to the beach. Windswept round my neck, like a tricolor of some anarchist tropical nation on the mast of a schooner, was a striped towel of green, red, and black. My entire beach wardrobe consisted of three T-shirts and a pair of faded cut-offs. I despised suntan lotion and at the beach wore what my wife calls a "sack o' marbles" bathing suit. I was very skinny at the time, partly from a healing duodenal ulcer and partly from what was then an all-incinerating metabolism, and my abdomen still carried the remains of a "six pack" that I had developed the summer before during a two-month expedition to the south of Russia and the Caucasus. At the time I didn't need prescription glasses, and walking to the beach, the Nabokov collection under my arm, I must have felt like both a library nerd and a streetwise jock of the sort that library nerds secretly envy.

The Russian-overrun strip of the Tyrrhenian beach became my public reading room. Of course, I read in other places that summer: under the carved shadows of chestnut trees, on the balcony of our apartment, on the train taking me to Rome and back, and even while waiting for my Italian lover on the back seat of her rusty Mustang. But

I devoured the Nabokov collection right at the beach during the first days in Ladispoli, and in some ways the book changed my life.

When we left the Soviet Union, Nabokov's works, banned there until 1986, were just starting their triumphant literary return. Prior to emigrating, I had only read Nabokov's *Pnin,* in February or March of my last Soviet spring, staying up all night to consume a smuggled copy that a friend had lent to my parents for two days. At the time I read *Pnin* not in the original English but in Gennady Barabtarlo's good translation, to which the writer's widow, Véra Nabokov, had also contributed. Ardis, an American firm that reprinted many of Nabokov's Russian émigré editions, had published it in 1983. These Ardis paperbacks of various banned books reached the Soviet Union in the baggage of visiting foreigners and diplomats to begin their underground circulation. Reading Barabtarlo's Russian translation of *Pnin* until dawn, I thought that the prose was incredibly alive with something I couldn't quite pinpoint, some intoxicating sensation of verbal freedom. In places the translator's Russian overcontorted itself, like a eunuch fussing over this fair or another in the master's harem. But what a harem!

I also recall a separate episode: staying up past midnight in my room, reading in bed, and hearing wisps of conversation flowing in from my parents' bedroom: "She used to come to her sister's bed in the middle of the night . . . just died in childbirth in Italy . . . like brother and sister . . . wanted her . . . this happens, you see. . . . " I didn't know then but now I know that my parents were discussing a scene in Nabokov's *Glory,* now my favorite of his Russian novels and the book I read after *Spring in Fialta.* This is the scene where Sonia the serpent visits Martin the marmoset in her dead sister's bedroom, in her parents' London house. My parents must have thought I was too young to read about transgressing the borders of brotherly-sisterly love. Was I?

What were they like, the stories in *Spring in Fialta*? I did hear in them echoes of master Chekhov, especially of "Lady with a Lapdog" in Nabokov's title story. But at the time I thought—and it took living in America to realize I was wrong in my youthful nihilism—that unlike

Chekhov, Nabokov was supernally unmoralistic. I loved the absence in Nabokov's stories of talk about a "beautiful new life" that's about to begin, that lies just around the bend. Besides Chekhov, I could notice the influence of Nabokov's elder émigré rival Bunin in those places where Nabokov portrayed desire and took out the spent characters. And I wasn't at all thinking about the Russian classics and what Nabokov had learned from Tolstoy.

Western modernists? Of what I'd read in translation, in the Soviet Union, a Proustian something did waft in from Nabokov's pages, and perhaps also something of Kafka in the merciless clarity of diction. But most of all, the stories in Nabokov's *Spring in Fialta* were quite *unlike* anything I'd known before. I had suspected something like this could be done, existed somewhere, but not in the books by Russian authors I'd been reading. In my circle of friends, who feasted on anything they could find by Western writers in translation, I was an oddity, something of a Russophile. In those years my best Moscow friend Misha Zaychik would go all around town looking for old issues of *Foreign Literature* magazine, find a serialized translation of Musil, Thomas Wolfe, or Kawabata, and have the issues bound and preserved for posterity.

Reading Nabokov's Russian stories in Italy, less than a month after leaving the Soviet Union, was not unlike losing one's virginity. It was both riveting and emptying. A young refugee feeling out of his natural element, I needed to be taken away and seduced. Nabokov's stories did that to me. Having my first fill of them in a Mediterranean resort, on a beach possessed by Odessan circus wrestlers with their quarrelsome wives and noisy kids, contributed atmospherically to the sensation of leaving a three-dimensional world with black scorched sand, littered with cherry stones and crushed cigarette butts, of leaving this mundane place and going somewhere else, to another Mediterranean resort called Fialta where fate brings lovers together for just another exilic rendezvous, where writers drink "pigeon's blood" for immortality and middle-class marriages recede into the margins of time. A place where time itself could be stopped or even undone. I remember thinking that the story "Spring in Fialta" was absolutely perfect, couldn't be any better, and I also singled out another Nabokov story from the same period.

It's called "Cloud, Castle, Lake" and signed "Marienbad, 1937." Four or five years later, when I was doing research in graduate school, I found out that Nabokov wrote it after leaving Germany for good. He was in the middle of an affair with an émigré woman from Paris, an affair that threatened to ruin his marriage. In key moments Nabokov's storyteller joins the main character, a Russian expatriate referred to as his "representative," in leaping out of the narrative plane and calling someone "my love, my obedient one." The addressee is a lover, a wife, a distant beloved, a feminized Russia . . . and also the reader herself.

When I first read those stories, what I would now describe as controlled pleasure didn't seem controlled at all in "Spring in Fialta," "Cloud, Castle, Lake," and the collection's other best stories. And here's something of a paradox. Having just escaped from the Soviet police state, where my parents were hunted and harassed, I was brimming over with politics. And yet I was not interested in reading political fiction. I remember well that Nabokov's most overtly political story in the collection, "Tyrants Destroyed," a pamphlet aimed against Stalinism and also Hitlerism, didn't move me. But I loved "Cloud, Castle, Lake," which Nabokov wrote in response to Nazism, because in this story totalitarianism is treated as collective philistine violence against love's private, indeterminate nature, against the characters' romantic vulnerability. For me, "Tyrants Destroyed" lacked a certain lyrical quality when I first read it in the summer of 1987. A few years ago I had occasion to recall—and recalibrate—my first reaction to "Tyrants Destroyed" when reading through Nabokov's correspondence with his principal American interlocutor, the writer Edmund Wilson. Wilson makes a telling remark in a letter of 30 January 1947, in response to the publication of the dystopian *Bend Sinister,* Nabokov's first American novel: "You aren't good at this kind of subject, which involves questions of politics and social change, because you are totally uninterested in these matters and have never taken the trouble to understand them." When taken out of context of the Nabokov-Wilson epistolary dynamic, Wilson's verdict seems harsh; in the case of *Bend Sinister* it's rather on target. I've never taken to Nabokov's dystopian fiction, even the magisterial *Invitation to a Beheading,* which has both love and lyricism, and my partiality probably goes back to that Tyrrhenian reading room in Ladispoli. In retrospect I can see what struck me so much about Nabokov's stories, and also about his novel *Glory*. The love I experienced while gorging on those pages was double: of loving Nabokov's prose and of being loved back—or whichever came first. There was a double pleasure in recognizing the author's design and of being recognized by it, of becoming part of the text and in this way experiencing the mysteries of the universe that are revealed to the characters not through politics and ideology, but through sex, death, and intimations of other worlds.

How strange and yet how delectable it is to be remembering this now in English. Reading Nabokov's Russian prose in Italy—did I identify with him back then? With him or his texts? I hadn't even seen a picture of Nabokov. So perhaps not him but some wondrous, composite image of a writer-exile. Was it Nabokov with whom I felt such a bond almost twenty years ago in Ladispoli, the real Nabokov or perhaps some idea of him, seared upon the pages with this man's violent love of language. At the time I knew few facts about his life. I hadn't read a single critical essay about him. And the little I knew about his career came secondhand. I couldn't possibly identify with Nabokov's life when I knew next to nothing about it, could I? Did I know he left Russia as a young poet, a twenty-year-old aristocrat, trilingual from childhood? I believe I did, but it now seems I identified less with a real Nabokov and more with one of his fictional alter egos. One of them, the poet Vassiliy Shishkov in Nabokov's last Russian short story, performs a Rimbaudian somersault and vanishes from Paris in 1939, disappearing into the "sepulcher" of his verses. A cinematic superimposition of time has occurred, and I'm having trouble separating myself reading Nabokov in Ladispoli from myself remembering it today. It's a clear Boston morning in the middle of June, and the voices of playing children in the Catholic academy across the street are drowned out by lawnmowers and hedge trimmers. What did I know, back in Ladispoli, of Nabokov's American years? Only vague contours of his flight to fame: an émigré professor in some faraway place with a Homeric name, then Lolita's bestsellerdom. His Swiss years? Nothing.

Butterflies? Just a flutter of wings carrying his popular legend across the Soviet border. Did I know Nabokov had a Jewish wife? Probably not. And his glorious English, half-invented by him in a fête of self-compensation? It still drives Anglo-American authors madly jealous. I hadn't tasted even one morsel of Nabokov's English before coming to America, and I read *Lolita* for the first time not in English but in Nabokov's Russian translation. That summer in Italy I couldn't imagine giving up Russian and writing in English. I wanted to preserve everything I was and had—or I thought I was and had. This is why the story "The Visit to the Museum" in *Spring in Fialta*—about a Russian émigré who realizes there's no physical return to the USSR—resonated with me so much. This was about all of us waiting in Ladispoli. About our Russian (Soviet) past and what would become of it. In Ladispoli all of the refugees were trapped in museums of time, and the sooner came the realization that there was no going back, the less traumatic it would be to let go of the past.

I used to think that reading Nabokov was an antidote against the shock of leaving Russia and coming to the West. But I was wrong, I now realize. Reading Nabokov in Ladispoli was my culture shock. I was reading Nabokov and waiting for America.

8

Uncle Pinya, Visiting

One memory-melting afternoon during the first week of August I returned to Ladispoli from Rome with the usual market booty of turkey and acromegalic vegetables burdening my shopping bag, only to find my Israeli great-uncle Pinya sitting in our kitchen and having tea with toast, jam, and ricotta cheese. He got up to kiss and hug me, the pliers of his bony hands clenching both my shoulders. I felt his sandy cheekbones against my lips.

"Sit down, my boy. Have a glass of tea with us," Uncle Pinya said as though he had known me for eternity.

There was something disarmingly adorable but also encroaching and invasive about our Uncle Pinya, something I associate with the word *meshpucha*.

I should explain that we hadn't been expecting Uncle Pinya until the following day. He had sent us a telegram: "my dears arriving rome day after tomorrow yours pinya."

"As if he had waited for us to make up our minds about going to America," mother said after the downstairs signora had delivered the telegram, ashes flying off her slender cigarette onto her purple peignoir.

"He's not like that, my Uncle Pinya," father said. "He's an idealist. He used to be in the Socialist International. And he worked with the Arabs, in the desert."

So he did.

Mother had instructed me to buy more vegetables and greens this time: Uncle Pinya was a passionate vegetarian. Instead of spending the night at an airport hotel at Charles de Gaulle, Uncle Pinya had made an earlier connection to Milan and from there flew to Rome, eager to see us. His suitcase toured Italy for another two days, but

Uncle Pinya had a piece of light hand luggage with him, containing a toiletry kit and denture case, a change of underwear, an old Baedeker, a Russian novel, and a camera. He was a champion of traveling light, but he brought with him weighty family histories and an unnerving feeling of inescapability.

An "uncle from Israel" was a legendary cliché of our Soviet refusenik years. When submitting an application to emigrate, people would sometimes fictionalize stories about their mother's or father's long-lost and now miraculously found Israeli uncle or aunt. But ours was a real uncle, one of my late grandfather's older brothers, who had been living in the land of Israel since the 1920s. My father's legendary Uncle Pinya was not fictional, although some of the things we had known about him seemed a bit unimaginable to us back in Moscow. A left-wing Socialist (he called the conservative Israeli Prime Minister Shamir a "stinking dwarf"), a speaker of Arabic and friend of the Bedouins, an atheist and an eccentric, a lover of Russian literature and erotic art, Uncle Pinya was now sitting in the kitchen of our Ladispoli apartment, having come to Italy to embrace us. Perhaps even to talk us into going with him to Israel, where the family had lined up a medical job for my father, and where the government sponsored publication of repatriates' literary works.

I had first heard about Uncle Pinya from my father when I was about nine, and my parents were standing with one foot in refuseniks' limbo. My father, when he was growing up in postwar Leningrad, knew about Uncle Pinya from his grandmother and her other children who stayed in Russia. In the 1930s and 1940s, a *brif* from what was then called Palestine would have been a huge event for the whole family in Leningrad. After 1949 the regular letters from Uncle Pinya stopped coming; having relatives in Israel was becoming more and more dangerous.

By the end of Uncle Pinya's visit to Ladispoli, not only had we learned about his life, but we also had filled gaps in our family history, adding Uncle Pinya's story to what we had already known. Pinya and his two younger brothers (my paternal grandfather Izya being the middle child) were all born between 1907 and 1911 in or around

Kamenets-Podolsk, then an important regional center in southwest-ern Ukraine. The first wife of their father died and left him with two small children. A mill owner and successful entrepreneur, their father (my great-grandfather) married a woman who was already twenty-five, practically an old maid, and came from a poor Jewish family. She raised his two children, a boy and a girl, like her own, and bore him the three boys. In some ways the adopted children were closer to my great-grandmother than her biological children, and they stayed near her for most of their lives.

The family spoke Yiddish at home, and the children were also ex-posed to colloquial Ukrainian and Polish, and later, in *Gymnasium,* to literary Russian. As far as I can tell, Uncle Pinya didn't get along very well with his father, who didn't shun modernity but respected Jewish traditions. After his bar mitzvah Uncle Pinya never again prayed or went to synagogue, and when we met him in Ladispoli, he came across as an enemy of religion and its web of institutions.

As Uncle Pinya and his younger brothers came of age in Kamenets-Podolsk, regimes and occupation forces came and went: Provisional Government, Bolsheviks, Ukrainian Directoriat, General Denikin's White Army, Simon Petlyura's Ukrainian units, Polish troops, and Bolsheviks again (this time, to stay). By 1922 Uncle Pinya had become both a Socialist and a Zionist. He developed an interest in agronomy and agriculture. In 1924 he sailed from Odessa on board a Soviet ship bound for Jaffa. He never laid eyes on his parents again, nor on three of his four siblings. In the late 1970s he saw his youngest brother Pasha on a visit to Hungary, which was in the Eastern Bloc but had trade rela-tions with Israel.

In Palestine Uncle Pinya trained and eventually started working as a land surveyor. He married a woman from Ukraine; they spoke Russian and Hebrew at home. Uncle Pinya's two sons were born in the 1930s, his youngest close in age to my father. By then the family in Russia had relocated from Ukraine to Leningrad. Corresponding with relatives in British Mandate Palestine was still reasonably safe for the family in Russia, and both Uncle Pinya and my father's father, Izya, had known from the beginning that the other's wife was expecting and agreed to give the children the same or similar names. Both were boys and were named after a Jewish king.

In the late 1930s, for his leftist activism Uncle Pinya was fired from the British Department of Land-Surveying in Palestine. Much as he abhorred the idea of starting a business of his own, he had a family to support, and he opened a private land-surveying office. He spent months working in the desert. I've seen photos of him riding a camel, dressed in Bedouin garb. He was scrupulously honest and enjoyed a solid reputation with both Jews and Arabs. He was also known to underbid and to pay himself last. The land-surveying business didn't become profitable until the 1960s.

Uncle Pinya's first wife died in the 1970s, and he remarried. His older son never accepted the second marriage. Still, after his son retired from the Israeli military, Pinya made him a partner in his firm. Eventually the son took over the business, turning it into a modern high-tech operation. Uncle Pinya continued to come in every day for a few hours, supposedly to do the books. He outlived his second wife, who, like Uncle Pinya himself, had come from Ukraine in the 1920s. When we met him in Ladispoli, Uncle Pinya was single again—single and still hungry to live.

My father had been corresponding with Uncle Pinya since about 1980, when Pinya wrote to him against the wishes of his youngest brother, Pasha. There had been bad blood between my father and Uncle Pasha ever since my grandfather's death and funeral. The correspondence continued, despite efforts by Uncle Pasha to portray my father as a ruffian. About every four to five months we would receive from Tel Aviv a hefty envelope with a long letter and pictures. I can only wonder how many the KGB had stolen for its fathomless literary archives. The letters, at times bordering on a graphomaniac's outpourings and chapters from unfinished autobiographies, described our extended Israeli family and minutiae of Uncle Pinya's life. Uncle Pinya also sent us packages with German-made rubber-sole shoes and denim jeans. Some of his letters carried outlandish requests, such as to find out if any relatives of his childhood Ukrainian friend Pavlo were still living in Podolia. In the others he preached vegetarianism to us with such zeal that we wondered if Uncle Pinya had any idea how hard it was to procure even basic staples in a Soviet food store. In the letters he came across as a staunch liberal, as unprudish and self-denuding, and also a romantic, exactly as I found him in Ladispoli as we shared an afternoon tea and a snack of bread, ricotta cheese, and apricot jam. He treated us with such familiarity that it felt—or had initially felt—like the family had never been split after Pinya's departure in 1925. He immediately insisted that not only my father—his nephew and son of his "beloved brother Izya"—but also my mother and I address him with the informal *ty* (you) and drop the patriarchal "uncle."

"I used to play soccer with your dear papa, back in Kamenets," Uncle Pinya corrected my mother as she tried to resist a breach of protectively formal grammar. "He was a tall and handsome fellow, a bit narrow in the shoulders, but that was fashionable in those days. Lanky. Your son looks quite a bit like him."

"Kamenets" was how its natives and their descendants lovingly referred to Kamenets-Podolsk, the town of both my grandfathers' childhoods and youths. I can well remember my mother's father smiling dreamily when he mouthed the word "Kamenets." My father's family had been living in the environs of Kamenets-Podolsk for at least five generations. In the late 1840s, my grandfather's grandfather was allowed to settle on the land in the townlet of Dumanov. Situated near the border of the Austro-Hungarian Empire, Kamenets-Podolsk was the capital city of the Podolia Province. On the eve of World War I, nearly half of the city's population, about twenty-three thousand, was Jewish. By the 1930s the Jewish population had dwindled by half; only three thousand of the Jews in Kamenets had survived the Holocaust. During the Soviet period Kamenets grew more and more provincial and unimportant, and it was subsumed as a district center into Ukraine's Hmelnitskiy Province, the very name of which brings memories of atrocities committed against the Jews by the troops of Ukrainian Hetman Bohdan Hmelnitskiy in the 1640s.

"My boy, have you been to Kamenets?" Uncle Pinya asked me as we got up from our tea.

"No, I haven't," I answered, a bit on the defensive. "Didn't have the occasion. There was no family left."

"And what a beautiful town it is! The Smotrich, its looping banks, the old Turkish fortress. . . . I would like to go back and visit. My Ukrainian, you know, used to be much better than my Russian. And my best friend Pavlo—"

"Uncle Pinya," father interrupted him. "We did try to locate his family. We wrote to the town clerk, but we couldn't find anything."

"Ah," Uncle Pinya sighed. "Why have you never visited? Do you also believe, like those knuckleheads of ours, that Ukrainians are anti-semitic? Such hogwash!"

This is a good moment to describe Uncle Pinya. He was about five-seven, with a lion's mane of hair. Very dry, but still very animate—like a mountain river in summer that still remembers itself turbulent and full of spring torrents. The oval of his face and his distinguished, raven nose were shaped much like those of all our male cousins, uncles, and nephews on my paternal grandfather's side. However, Uncle Pinya's skin had acquired the permanent cinnamon stain of the desert. When we strolled on the boulevard in the days following his arrival, a refugee couple stopped to comment how much the grandfather, father, and son all looked alike; they had assumed that Uncle Pinya was my grandfather. Uncle Pinya was eighty-one when we met him, and under the metal frames of his unfashionable spectacles his boyish eyes led a convivial life of their own. He spoke excellent Russian, a bit outmoded and only slightly accented in the manner of educated Ukrainian Jews, and he sometimes used English words to refer to objects he must have first encountered after leaving Russia. For instance, he said *gelikopter* instead of the native Russian *vertolet*. There was something unexpectedly modern and progressive to this Israeli uncle. And he wasn't even trying to shock us with his revolutionary exhibitionism of ideas.

Before we had time to cover the most basic of the family terrains, Uncle Pinya announced to us that it had always been his dream to visit Pompeii and see the famous frescos and what remained of the Roman city. He had with him an old Baedeker of Italy, and he opened it to the section on Pompeii and showed us a reproduction of a fresco from a lupanarium.

"Look, look, such sophistication," Uncle Pinya said, pressing two fingers to the deeply arched back of the woman in the picture. "They knew more about love than we'll ever know," he added, turning to my mother, who was slicing a huge blush peach.

"I want to stay here a couple of days, and then I want to take you all to Pompeii and also to Sorrento," he explained, summing up his plans. "Sorrento and Capri were Maxim Gorky's stomping ground. Did you know that, my dear boy?" Uncle Pinya asked me.

"Sure, I—"

"—I adored Gorky when I was your age," interrupted Uncle Pinya.

Mother and father persuaded him to rest a bit before an evening stroll and dinner. Tumbling in and rising out of the delayed siesta in the living room that I would share with Uncle Pinya for the next few days, I heard him shuffling books, newspapers, and old issues of Italian and Russian magazines spread out on the coffee table. When I woke up Uncle Pinya was no longer in the room. The door to my parents' bedroom was still closed, and after washing my face I ambled to the kitchen, where I found him, clean-shaven and beaming with oomph, violently scribbling something in a pocket notebook. Under a Chekhovian ashtray on the kitchen table I saw three crisp hundred-dollar bills—a green oasis amid the table's arid surface.

"What's that, Uncle Pinya?" I asked.

"A troika of wild horses," he sang out, clicking his fingers like a Gypsy singer. "Wake up your lazybones parents. I'm inviting you all to dinner, to celebrate our reunion."

Looking for a restaurant on our first night with Uncle Pinya turned out to be an ordeal. At first he made us stroll on the boulevard to work up, as he put it, a "healthy appetite." Then he dragged us around half of Ladispoli's central quarter, going into restaurants, studying menus, examining the ambiance, and inquiring about vegetarian options. "Does your red spaghetti sauce have any meat?" Uncle Pinya would ask, plunging my father into a fit of embarrassment. Or, "Can we have that table facing the fountain?" (pointing to what was inevitably a reserved table). Or else, "Do you have a nonsmoking section?" (in the Italy of the 1980s?!). And Uncle Pinya did not seem to mind having to look further. Silver-blue hair shining in the setting sun, slacks and checkered shirt fluttering on his slight frame, his right hand affirming the principle of the open-ended future, Uncle Pinya led his tired relatives all around the main piazza and the commercial strip and then down Via Ancona, until we finally found refuge in an open-air restaurant just around the corner from our apartment building. We'd come full circle. It was an Italian restaurant with Chinese lanterns where music played at night and a Tom Jones lookalike sometimes performed standards. For some reason Uncle Pinya liked the place, and after switching two or three times we finally settled at a table that was "not too close to the street or the music, but with a view of the boulevard."

Uncle Pinya was very pleased with his choice, and he next proceeded to dispense advice on what to order, advocating for salads and other vegetarian fare. Uncle Pinya spoke English to the waiter who thought he had seen it all. Uncle Pinya also knew some German and French, which he put to use while communicating with the waiter.

"It's too hot to guzzle red wine, and beer is for people with no taste," Uncle Pinya declared. My poor father had to give up the hope of a drink.

The waiter brought us a sweating carafe of water, some bread, and portions of *insalata verde*. Uncle Pinya pinched off a piece of bread, chewed on a lettuce leaf, and leaned back in his chair.

"Now I need to tell you something," he said. "You know I don't like to beat around the bush."

"What's the matter, Uncle Pinya?" father asked, feeling trapped—as mother and I also did.

"Nothing's the matter. Why are you all getting so tense?" Uncle Pinya replied, putting another lettuce leaf in his mouth and chewing with maddening slowness. "I just wanted to tell you that I don't resent you for not going to Israel. Once again, let me say that you'd feel at home there, but I don't resent you. America is very nice; I've been there five times, to Washington, New York, Boston, Chicago, San

Francisco—all great and fine cities, but it's a desert. People are too individualistic."

We sat silently, backs pressed to our chairs. There's always payback time, I was thinking, as I waited for Uncle Pinya to chew up another piece of lettuce.

"You're my late brother's son," Uncle Pinya said, turning to my father. "You're practically like my son genetically, so I accept your decision. Unlike some relatives back in Israel, especially our cousin Zara, the one whose son was killed in '67. She was very upset you aren't coming to Israel. But let me say it one more time: If you change your mind, it's not too late."

A minute of silence felt like eternity in the outdoor restaurant, where music played and waiters scurried around like frenzied squirrels.

"Okay, I just needed to get it off my chest," Uncle Pinya said jovially, clapping his hands. "Let's not fight, my dears. Let's eat and celebrate our reunion." He lifted a glass of water, licked his lips as though preparing to offer a toast, but then put the glass down.

"But there's one more thing," said Uncle Pinya. Something inside me felt like a huge toad trying to leap out.

"I wanted to explain something to you, my dears, because this has come up in our correspondence, when you were still in Moscow. And already once today, when we were having tea. It's about my political beliefs."

That was vintage Uncle Pinya: choosing salads and pasta dishes one minute, confessing his Communist sympathies the next.

Mother, father, and I laid down our forks and knives as a sign of surrender. We were Uncle Pinya's. He held us prisoner.

"I came to Israel—you probably know this—in 1925," he began. "I had left Kamenets because I couldn't stay there. I was in a youth Zionist organization. We were all idealistic boys and girls, and a Jewish acquaintance whose son worked in local law enforcement had tipped off my father that there was a signed warrant for my arrest. In haste I fled to Odessa, where we had cousins. I was eighteen. I didn't know what I wanted to do. My great passion was reading. I had five or six notebooks full of stories, poems, openings of novels. I wanted to write about working people, to be a Jewish Gorky. It sounds childish today, but back then. . . .

"In Israel I spent some time in an agricultural commune near the Sea of Galilee. Life was very hard. I missed home and my family. I still wasn't sure in my heart why I was there. I became an apprentice to a land surveyor. In 1926 I joined the Department of Land-Surveying. The office was run by the British. The bosses were disciplined workers with a colonial mentality."

The band started playing "O Sole Mio." Uncle Pinya had barely touched his food. Where does he get his boundless energy? I remember thinking. Only molten speckles of the sunset had remained on the faraway horizon.

"Very soon," Uncle Pinya continued with his story, "I was branded a left-winger and Soviet sympathizer. I was also openly critical of the British and what they were doing in Palestine. The conniving. The pitting of Arabs against Jews. Broken promises. The White Papers. My bosses at the Department of Land-Surveying also had difficulty making sense of my politics and my friendships with Arabs. I was also seriously studying Arabic. I didn't fit common profiles. I was a Zionist, but I was never a Jewish chauvinist. And mind you, I was never a member of the Communist Party, although I did vote for their candidates for years in the municipal elections. Eventually I joined a Socialist party, Mapam, although not until after the war and the founding of Israel. But that's another story for another dinner."

When our pasta dishes arrived, Uncle Pinya wrinkled his youthful brow, gave the waiter a stern look, and asked if the singer could sing a little softer. The waiter spread his arms, mumbled something, and left.

"I was already married," Uncle Pinya continued. "We were living in Tel Aviv, and I was still thinking of repatriating. I want you to understand how I felt. In 1932 I petitioned the Soviet consulate in Istanbul to allow me to return to the USSR. My petition was denied—otherwise who knows how things would have turned out? We might not be sitting here today. You know, there was a fellow I met when I worked in Upper Galilee; he later took the pen name "Mark Egart," but he was still called Mordekhai Boguslavsky when I knew him in 1925. He was originally from Krivoy Rog in Ukraine. You know Krivoy Rog?"

"My mother had a first cousin there," mother replied, politely.

"Aha! Well, this Boguslavsky went back to the USSR in 1928 or 1929, I believe. Some did go back, you know. Not many, but some did. He later published books in Russian. *Scorched Land* was his big novel, a bit propagandistic, but the sections describing the hard life of the young men and women from Russia on agricultural settlements, they were quite accurate, you know. I remember because I was there."

Uncle Pinya finally tasted his penne with tomatoes and zucchini, too impatient to eat more.

"So I stayed in Israel, and we had two boys. But I continued to read Soviet papers and magazines and follow the current events. It still had a grip on me. Then, in 1938 I was fired from the Department of Land Surveying. They had found a convenient excuse—'staff reduction' they called it—but it was for my political sympathies all right."

"Pinya, Uncle Pinya, you're not eating your food," said mother.

"The food will wait. It's not interesting." (Uncle Pinya used the words *interesting* and *not interesting* all the time in place of *good* and *bad*.) "I just want to finish with politics, and then we can drink and laugh like children of doubt and disbelief," said Uncle Pinya to my mother, appropriating Dostoevsky.

"What I wanted to explain to you is that it took me longer than many even among my comrades to shed illusions about the Soviet Union. Not until after the death of Stalin. And still I couldn't quite believe the things we were hearing. In 1968 a second cousin of mine, Manechka—you probably didn't know her—came to Israel from Odessa. She was the first relative to leave the Soviet Union since the 1920s. I spent a week interrogating her. I exhausted her with questions about life there. She was an obstetrical nurse, a very fine and sane person. She never married, and she died of cancer just a few years after coming to Israel. I had known her, Manechka, since childhood, and seeing her and talking to her weaned me from my last illusions. But I still miss Kamenets, still today, after so many years. Terribly."

Uncle Pinya reached for a large, sky-blue handkerchief and wiped the corners of his eyes. The waiter, who came to offer us coffee and dessert, fractured the silence that had descended upon our table.

With the bill arrived the most dramatic moment of the evening. First Uncle Pinya put on his spectacles and examined the contents of the bill, line by line, like a schoolboy still learning to read cursive. Then he removed a pen from his breast pocket and proceeded, right under the stare of the apoplectic waiter, to cross out lines in the bill. He crossed out a line and then paused, lifting his head and commenting: "What cover charge? Bread and water should be free with dinner." Then he crossed out another line and exclaimed: "What cheese? You think we should be paying for the crummy piece of cheese you brought for the four of us? In any case, in civilized restaurants salads come free with the entrees."

The headwaiter and two other waiters had now joined our server in front of the table, and the four of them argued with Uncle Pinya in some transnational restaurant argot, interrupting each other.

"Uncle Pinya, I beg of you, please stop," my father moaned.

Undeterred, Uncle Pinya added up what he thought the bill should have been, counted out the money, and put it on a little plate on top of the severely edited bill.

As we walked out of the restaurant, the headwaiter yelled something along the lines of "Don't ever come back here, thieves." All we wanted to do was leap over the two blocks separating the restaurant from our building and disappear. But our curious and benevolent Uncle Pinya wasn't quite ready to go home.

Exiting the restaurant, he noticed two men, a white one and a black one, sitting at a corner table under the blue and green shadows of Chinese lanterns. Both soused, their chairs pulled close together and facing the street, they sat embraced, arms locked around each other's shoulders. A jug of Chianti stood on the table in front of them, and they sang a droning, drunk, multilingual song about love and friendship. The two men were Sasha Sheyin, a former Moscow peace activist and refusenik whom we knew quite well, and an Eritrean immigrant by the name of Efrem. An elementary school teacher by training, Efrem became Sasha's bosom buddy in Ladispoli. Efrem started taking Sasha on various gigs, usually unloading or loading trucks with fruit and vegetables. Compared to the other refugees, Sasha was flush with cash, and he and Efrem would sit at night at cafés, drinking beer and wine and greeting other Russians as they passed by on their evening walks. Now Sasha waved to us and raised his glass, and we had no choice but to approach his table. The Eritrean knew one Russian word, *druzhba*, which means "friendship," and he and Sasha screamed "Comrades, *druzhba*, comrades, *druzhba*" in the helium voices of cartoon characters. Uncle Pinya was very intrigued by the friendship of Sasha Sheyin and Efrem, and on the way back he kept asking us about racism in the Soviet Union.

"I never believed the rumors, you know," Uncle Pinya told me after I'd switched off the light to go to sleep.

That night I had a torturous dream. It starts on a late-morning train to Rome. The train is unclean and oppressively hot. I'm headed to Rome for my weekly shopping, feeling quiet premonitory rage. The fancy Roman crowd on Via Nazionale, where I walk from the train station, is vain and vaudevillian, and the window displays of clothing stores give me an inferiority complex. The Round Market irritates me this time—the way a country fair sometimes annoys a tired visitor with its vapid amusements.

By the time I get off the train at Ladispoli-Cervetori, it's already past three in the afternoon, the deepmost hour of the siesta. Rolling and dragging my plaid East German-made shopping bag through the cottonball heat of Ladispoli's main street, I feel like a family pack mule, and no thoughts of filial duty can extinguish my stored-up ire.

In our apartment discord hangs in the air like acrid smoke. My mother is sitting at the edge of the living room sofa, absently fingering an air mail envelope that lies, ripped open, on the coffee table. When she turns to me, I see how the corners of her lips tremble, how alone she looks despite my father's presence in the room. I want to run up and hug her, but my angry self pulls back and resists the impulse.

"Your father has something to tell you." Mother is speaking so quietly that the words come out breathless, like dead butterflies.

Father stands in the frame of the balcony door, dressed, for some reason, in his good city clothes: a pair of tan gabardine slacks, a candy cane–red long-sleeved shirt, and his new cordovans, as though he was getting ready to go out. The shirt is buttoned all the way up, but there's no tie or jacket. I follow him to the balcony, wiping sweat from my brow with the bottom of my T-shirt. Against the thick tangerine light of the sun, moving westward over the sea below, my father's face looks pale and foreign to these southern latitudes. These words run through my head: He's my father. He was born in Leningrad. He's a Jewish doctor. He writes incredible stories. He's hopeless.

Father kisses me on the cheekbone and slides his prickly cold cheek against my lips. "Son, I've decided to go to Israel. It's better this way." His voice treads on the verge of sobbing, and I too feel I'm going to burst out crying.

"America's too difficult for me. And English . . . ," father pauses, composing himself. He isn't a smoker, but he walks over to the coffee table, takes one of mother's cigarettes—she herself barely smokes anymore—and lights up. He holds his cigarette with three fingers, like a pinch of salt. I just stand there on the balcony, not saying anything, not trying to dissuade my father, just waiting for him to finish.

"I got a letter from Uncle Pinya this morning," father says to me. "Uncle Pinya writes that they're still holding a job for me at a hospital in Tel Aviv. I can start working and use Russian with patients. And I'll have my readers there, too. You and your mother will go to America. And you will visit me every summer, my darling."

Father looks at me without meeting my gaze, and I turn and look at mother, who is now standing at the threshold of the balcony door, almost translucent, like an old fresco.

"Talk to papa. Maybe he will listen to you." Mother reaches over and strokes my arm just below the elbow, but instead of embracing her, I step back, not even too dismayed by the dearth of my response to my own parents. All I want to do is get away from them. I want to be with

Italians, I want to forget that I am myself: a Russian, a Jew, a refugee, and my parents' child.

"You two figure this out," I scream out. "You can go to Israel or Madagascar or the end of the world."

I don't know if it's possible to feel shame in a dream, but I feel it now as I type these wretched words onto the screen of my laptop.

"I'm not part of this," I say to my parents. "It's between you two. I don't want to be part of this. I've had it being the peacemaker my whole life."

I grab a towel and swimming trunks and dash to the door.

"Whatever you two decide is fine with me," I add. Turning to take another look at my parents, I see in their eyes not anger, but only guilt. How paradoxical. It doesn't even take them a few seconds to forgive my heartlessness!

I run—literally run—to the beach. It's usually quite empty this time of the day. I change by tying a towel over my waist, leave my things by the water, and throw myself on the waves. I want to wash off the sweat of Rome, of commuter trains and the market. I want to wash off all memories. After the swim I lie face down on the hot black sand and sleep for an hour—or at least it feels like a long time in my dream. Then I have another swim, wipe off the sand, and walk to a concession stand on the parapet. I eat a disgustingly sweet oily piece of fried dough covered in confectioner's sugar. I don't have too much trouble killing another hour. I people watch, and then it's almost six, time to go to the weekly movie screening at the American Center. They serve pink punch at the screening. After the movie I meet Leonardo, Tomasso, Sylvio, and the others in our regular spot but only stay about an hour, squirming in my aluminum chair and not doing a very good job of stringing together the Italian words I've learned over the past weeks. Restless and still not ready to face my parents, I walk back and forth on the boulevard, hearing the boozy echoes of two bands blaring on the waterfront.

When I open the door, I see my parents having tea in the living room. They have the happy faces of children playing together after a fight. I've missed the tears of reconciliation.

"I've persuaded papa to go to America," mother says, and gets up to kiss me.

I HAD LOST MY PATERNAL GRANDFATHER, Uncle Pinya's younger brother, in 1972. I was four. He was in his sixties. He had stomach cancer and was living with his third wife. I couldn't have known him well, not only because of my age but for the simple reason that we were living in Moscow and he in Leningrad. My mother's father, the one with whom Uncle Pinya used to play soccer in the days of their Ukrainian youth, passed on when I was eight. Him I knew very well. From my mother's father I heard many stories of his youth, of Kamenets-Podolsk, of his "dear sweet Ukraine," as he still referred to it despite everything. But of my father's late father I can only recall ripples of occasional footage: a faded, darkly water-colored veil of the cancer ward where my father and I visited my grandfather not long before his departure, and his large grey head on the propped-up pillow. Striped pajamas of the sort that, I swear, now make me think of nothing but Auschwitz. But I also remember my grandfather's visit to Moscow. This must have been in the fall of 1970. I'm three, and my grandfather has a nice charcoal suit and white crisp shirt and looks Italian. He smiles like a diplomat who wants peace at any cost—land, reparations, whatever you say. He smiles and lights my mother's cigarette while his third wife, a slender woman in a floral dress, hands me a present from across the coffee table: a bow and arrow set.

"Be noble like a knight," grandfather tells me.

My mother always remembered her father-in-law as "charming and indifferent." When I was growing up, my father said four things of his own father: He was a brilliant engineer and could detect what was wrong with a car just by listening to the engine; he loved history and especially the Napoleonic wars; he never raised his voice; he told the best jokes in the world. I think I remember the telling of the jokes—my grandfather's measured cadence and soft timbre that women are supposed to find sexy. My mother laughs hysterically at his jokes and my father also laughs, but cautiously, a bit nervously. When my father was eight, during the war, grandfather, then a naval lieutenant commander, had left him and my grandmother to start another family. The wound of abandonment has never closed.

LUCKY IS THE AUTHOR in whose pages Calliope, the muse of epic, Clio, the muse of history, and Thalia, the muse of comedy and light poetry, all sing in concert. I'd left Calliope behind the Iron Curtain. Clio abandoned me already in Ladispoli, taking refuge in a seaside trattoria. And only Thalia, an immigrant like myself, is still by my side as I write these pages in America.

Uncle Pinya stayed with us in Ladispoli for six days, and they felt like six months. Those draining, eye-opening days. From Uncle Pinya I heard more trivia than I ever wanted to know.

"Answer quick, my boy, what's the difference between a village *(derevnya)* and a small rural town *(selo)?*" he would ask as we walked back from the beach toward our siesta and the promise of quiet.

"I don't know, Uncle Pinya. You tell me," I would reply.

"See, you don't know, and I still remember: A small town must have a school and a church," he delivered, triumphantly.

For me, seeing Uncle Pinya was like being able to connect the lines of our family past. And it must have been the same for both my mother and father. Uncle Pinya had known their fathers before my parents knew them. This is why being with Uncle Pinya in Ladispoli finally felt like moving from a Euclidian narrative world, where stories of our family in Russia and stories of our relatives in Israel ran parallel to each other without ever intersecting—a barely two-dimensional world sustained by an occasional letter and photo—to some other space of family present and future. In this Lobachevskian world where we dwelt during Uncle Pinya's visit, the parallel lives had suddenly and unthinkably intersected.

But the excitement of crossing the family storylines came at a price. The name of the price was nosiness. It was at times unbearable. How Uncle Pinya interrogated people! And his obsession with the love life of people and animals. At the Ladispoli beach, when I had gone off to buy a roll of film, he sought out Irena, my Baltic girlfriend who never was, and questioned her about our "relations," as he put it. He was disappointed.

And the worst part was when in the span of two days Uncle Pinya developed a romantic interest—first in my grandmother, a widow, and then in my aunt, a divorcée. Grandmother flatly rejected his advances. He was too old, she said, and also, what was she going to do with a retired land surveyor from Israel, twice a widower, who used to play soccer with her late husband? As for my aunt, she didn't reject Uncle Pinya's attention outright and even accompanied him on a half-day tour of Etruscan tombs. Later that evening my mother had to have a little sisterly chat with her, and my father with Uncle Pinya. One of the arguments that my father used in trying to quell Uncle Pinya was that the two families were distantly related—my parents were second cousins twice removed or something like that. He had "serious intentions," Pinya answered in his defense, and most Ashkenazi Jews were second or third cousins twice or thrice removed, so what's the big deal anyhow?

That night I dreamt about looking for an oasis in the dessert and running into Uncle Pinya dressed as a Bedouin.

"Water, water," I tell him in the dream.

"Are you a member of the Second International?" he asks.

"No, I'm not. Why?"

"The cheese in the restaurant was not interesting," says Uncle Pinya and starts singing "La Marseillaise" in Russian.

AFTER LADISPOLI I only saw Uncle Pinya one more time. He never visited us in America—he had his own reasons. Father and Uncle Pinya occasionally corresponded, and they saw each other in the mid-1990s in Israel, when my parents stayed at an artists' colony in Jerusalem. It wasn't the same Uncle Pinya, my parents later told me. He was physically still strong, but his memory was beginning to fade.

In the summer of 1998, less than a year before I met my wife and my life changed forever, I took my last long trip as a bachelor. I was on my first sabbatical, and I didn't have to teach for the whole year. On the road for almost seven weeks in August and September, I had visited my dear Estonia and also stayed in Poland, where Jewish memories were for sale in Kraków's Jewish town, but only a handful of elderly Jews remained. After that I went to Israel for the first time and spent two weeks touring the country. I found it no less than enthralling. Was it a mistake we hadn't come here in 1987? I kept asking myself as I traveled around and met our relatives on both my father's and mother's sides.

After spending time in Haifa and Upper Galilee I made my way back to Tel Aviv. On my second day there Uncle Pinya's younger son, a sculptor and poet who was close in age to my father and would have looked even more like my father had the sculptor-poet grown a mustache, took me to see my great-uncle.

"Phoning my father is pointless," the sculptor-poet warned me. "He won't remember you. We'll just go visit him in the morning."

Uncle Pinya was living in the same apartment in the eastern part of Tel Aviv, not far from the Cinerama and the Sport Palace, where he had moved with his family in the early 1950s. He refused to go to assisted living, and a Russian lady from the post-Soviet wave of *aliya* looked after him. Framed by the black apartment door and wearing his signature striped short-sleeved shirt and unwrinkled trousers, Uncle Pinya looked desiccated like matzos. (I've borrowed the metaphor from the inimitable Odessan poet Eduard Bagritsky.) No short-term memory remained in his almost weightless body.

"Who are you?" he asked after we kissed and embraced.

"I'm Izya's grandson, Uncle Pinya. Remember Izya?"

"Izya? My brother? What do you take me for? Of course I remember him."

And he pulled me by the T-shirt to his den, where family photos crowded the walls. I recognized many of the faces. After Uncle Pinya had left in 1925, his parents would paste his photo into the formal family portraits, so his head always looked bigger than the heads of his four siblings.

"See how far apart the buildings are?" Uncle Pinya said proudly, opening one of the windows. "Tel Aviv's overcrowded, you know. And there's a waterfall nearby."

It turned out Uncle Pinya used *vodopad,* the Russian word for "waterfall," instead of "fountain." There was a large fountain erupting out of a rock in a public garden across the street.

Russian books—classics but also paperback thrillers about the Russian mob—lay scattered all around, abandoned on the sofa, the window sills, the kitchen table.

"You see how spacious this apartment is?" Uncle Pinya said. "Yes, well. Who are you again?"

"I'm your younger brother's grandson," I answered.

"I have two, which one?"

"Izya. Do you remember Izya?"

"Of course I do," Pinya replied as I pressed my hand to the cold wall under a framed picture where the three brothers—Pinya, a teenager, his brothers Izya and Pasha, ten and nine—were captured by a Kamenets photo artist who dashed his name across the right bottom corner.

"Of course I remember Izya," Pinya repeated. "Tell me again who you are."

But then he suddenly remembered my father and asked, indignantly, "Why doesn't he send me his new books?"

So his memory hadn't all expired.

Two days later, on a Friday afternoon, the youngest of Uncle Pinya's granddaughters picked me up near Dizengoff Center, and we drove through the swampy heat of Tel Aviv to fetch Uncle Pinya and take him to her father's house by the sea. It was Uncle Pinya's weekly ritual to spend Friday nights with one of his sons and their families.

Following in the steps of her father, the sculptor-poet, my cousin was studying art and had just spent a semester in Florence. She was wearing a white linen dress with slits in the back. She had short black shiny hair and hazel eyes, and she never stopped smiling.

In the car on the way over I'd started telling my cousin about Uncle Pinya's visit to Ladispoli. We barely knew each other and both became very excited to have a love in common—Italy. Uncle Pinya sat silently in the back for most of the ride.

"I never learned Italian," he finally said. "But I speak Arabic fluently." And he said something as a way of demonstrating it.

Over a vegetarian dinner in a dining room overlooking the Mediterranean, Uncle Pinya and I spoke in Russian, which the others, native Hebrew speakers, didn't understand.

"My first wife and I used Russian as a private language when we didn't want the boys to know something," Uncle Pinya said to me. "But my older son picked up quite a bit. My younger son—just a couple of words here and there. My second wife and my girlfriends after her have all been from Russia."

"Papa, how's Verochka?" the sculptor-poet asked Uncle Pinya in English.

"Who's that?" Uncle Pinya asked, not one bit bewildered.

"Verochka. Don't you remember?"

"Ah, Verochka," and Uncle Pinya turned to me and switched back to Russian. "Verochka is my girlfriend. She's younger by quite some years. We tried doing it, you know, but it didn't work."

The recent past had ceased to exist, but the distant past was a vast sea, on whose waves Uncle Pinya still cavorted. I was asking him about his youth in Kamenets and how he, son of a wealthy bourgeois family, first became interested in socialism. Uncle Pinya responded with a confession of feeling guilty for something he did—or rather didn't do—as a young man. This was just before he left home for good. His father had asked him to come to synagogue with him on *shabes,* and Pinya adamantly refused.

"I remember this day like it was yesterday. You understand, I've regretted it my whole life. I never saw my father again. I should have come with him. I should have said the hell with the principle," Uncle Pinya said.

Does memory feed on unabolished guilt? Or is it guilt, like a lamprey, that feeds on memory?

Uncle Pinya lived for five more years. He was almost one hundred when he cashed his check.

Uncle Pinya, an inveterate believer in telling the truth even if it means violating another person's privacy, is more alive than most of my deceased relatives.

On the fourth day of his Ladispoli visit Uncle Pinya woke me up at six in the morning. "Rise and shine, my boy. I'm taking you all to Pompeii. Right now."

Over breakfast mother said her blood pressure was low and she didn't have the energy, and I said I didn't want to leave mother alone. Panic in his eyes, father went to Pompeii with Uncle Pinya. The travelers returned by the end of the next day, Uncle Pinya bubbling with impressions, father looking exasperated. A week later mother and I ended up going to Pompeii with a group of Soviet refugees on a bus tour operated by the rogue Nitochkin.

From Pompeii Uncle Pinya brought us a gift, a book I still have in my home library. I pick it up from the glass bookcase in the "red room," where it shares a narrow berth with Modigliani, Malevich, and Chagall. I look at the frescos of copulating people and animals and think of the ebullient Uncle Pinya and of what my father told me, under his breath, as we came out to the balcony.

The sun had already sunk into the Tyrrhenian Sea outside our windows. Uncle Pinya was in the kitchen enumerating to my mother all the amazing things he had seen in the House of the Vestals and the Villa of Mysteries. While Uncle Pinya leafed through the book he brought us, showing my mother the "interesting" frescos, my father described to me how they took the Naples train from Termini and how Gorky, the patron saint of proletarian writers, must have been turning in his grave at the thought of his admirer Uncle Pinya crossing almost everything off the bill at an open-air restaurant in Sorrento, the luminous Sorrento where my father and Uncle Pinya had stopped for the night before they took a boat to Capri the next morning.

"Capri was something out of this world," father said. "And Uncle Pinya, Uncle Pinya was his own natural self."

La Famiglia Soloveitchik

A tall, hefty woman with a double bun of russet hair came up to us at the beach and introduced herself. We had spread our towels over by the water's edge, right next to her family's beach encampment with its multiple tote bags, piles of clothes anchoring the corners of a floral bed sheet, and an assortment of beach toys and flippers. In her right hand she held by the neck a plastic bottle, as though preparing to strangulate it.

"Soloveitchik's our name," she said to my mother, with a Ukrainian accent. "We're from Lvov. And no, we are not related," she added, cryptically, and kicked her head back, like a mare shaking off a horsefly. Then she took a long swig of some carbonated nonsense from the plaintively squealing bottle. Her unsparingly perceptive chocolate-brown eyes had finished drilling holes in our foreheads and turned to the water, where three children frolicked together in a way that suggested they were siblings. The eldest, a girl of about twelve, supervised the other two, boys of about eight and four. The girl and her youngest brother looked very much alike, both with kinky black hair and pale skin, bearing a close resemblance to their angular, sluggish father, who sat on the floral sheet reading a thick tome. The older boy was different—bouncy, boisterous. .

Over the summer my parents and the Soloveitchiks became quite friendly, and I saw them almost daily. Alina Soloveitchik did most of the talking in her family, leaving to her quiet husband Leonid the multiple tasks of carrying their belongings, supervising the children, and also being a silent witness to what she called "telling it like it is." Leonid, or Lyonya, had the furry, smallish ears and tender, protruding face of a giant anteater.

"I took after my Ukrainian papa," Alina liked to repeat. "He always told people what he thought of them. Some didn't like it. But they surely respected him. My *Yiddishe moma,* now that's a different story for you."

Before Alina's larger-than-life personality takes over this page, I should explain that each time she would introduce herself, Alina mentioned that her husband's family "were not related." Related to whom? The people she was talking to? Very few understood what she meant. I had no idea until my father, at the time my principal source of Jewish spirituality, had explained that Alina was talking about none other than Joseph Soloveitchik, the great American rabbi and philosopher. The word *soloveichik* means "little nightingale" in Russian, and it's not an uncommon Jewish name. "There's more than one little bird by that name," was Alina's aphorism for the occasion. How this woman from Lvov even knew about Rav Soloveitchik, and why she felt compelled to say this to strangers, was a mystery. There were other mysteries to Alina Soloveitchik.

Alina immediately designated my mother as her beach mate and confidante and made it her mission to rescue her from loneliness. My mother, who is by nature both timid and sociable, tended to dominate over her Moscow female friends in an understated, trendsetting fashion. But she was so emotionally drained during the first few weeks after leaving Moscow that at the beach she let Alina take charge of her spirits. Lyonya and my father would occasionally play a game of chess. A couple of times they went fishing off the jetty, but the bond was really between the women, the mothers.

The Soloveitchiks, Alina and Lyonya (forgive the accidental dactyls—iambic feet can be too small) were each forty, significantly younger than my parents. They were headed for Cleveland, where Alina's brother had immigrated eight years earlier with his wife, children, and Alina's mother.

"You know, this is how God likes to kid us," Alina explained on the second day of our acquaintance. She was holding a plastic bag half-filled with cherries, apricots, and plums, to which she helped herself while also smoking a cigarette out of the left corner of her mouth.

"Now my darling brother practically sleeps at the synagogue, and he had himself circumcised and all that nutty business. And he used to be the greatest assimilationist in all of our beautiful city of Lvov. Strangely enough, that's my mother's blood, her influence. My Ukrainian father—would you believe it—he used to yell at my brother when he tried to tell nasty Jewish jokes he'd pick up from his street pals. Oy, I tell you, nothing's fair in this world. My brother didn't even want to go—and he got out in three months. We got stuck for almost ten years. And my papa's lying in the grave outside Lvov."

Alina spoke with pride and tenderness of her Ukrainian father, a former ace pilot and air force colonel.

"He would have been made a one-star general—he was already in charge of an air base. But we got it into our stupid heads to leave, and the bastards forced him to retire. You can imagine what they told him upstairs. And through the whole brouhaha he never said so much as one word of reproach to us. Just suffered silently. Didn't last one year in retirement—a stroke. Not even sixty-two he was, my papa."

I wondered about Alina's friendship with my mother, considering that Alina didn't have one good thing to say about her own mother, with whom she was to be "reunited" in America. One got the feeling that Alina blamed her Jewish mother for all their family troubles. Was she borderline antisemitic, in the domesticated way Jews sometimes allow themselves to be among other Jews? Today I might say she was self-hating, but back in Ladispoli my vocabulary lacked such terms. I simply sensed Alina's unease about being Jewish. Yet Jewishness, and particularly Yiddish words and phrases and also those jackdaw intonations, were as much a part of Alina as a lining is part of a coat.

"I tell you, my papa—may he rest in peace instead of flying those crazy loops at their shitty Victory Day parades—my papa did this imitation of my mother's Aunt Golda who lived in Czernowitz after the war—most of that side of the family were killed in the camps in Transnistria, but Aunt Golda had escaped to the hinterland in '41. *Oy Gottenu,* so you could lose your stomach laughing! Papa was generally very nice to my mother's meshpucha, but there were times he also couldn't bear it."

Having had a Ukrainian, non-Jewish father gave Alina a feeling of superiority. Torn between Ukrainians and Jews, she was of two minds about emigrating, even after ten years as a refusenik.

"You Muscovites wouldn't understand," she once told us as we added our tomatoes and cucumbers and scallions and melting cheeses and slices of bread to the Soloveitchiks' provisions for a picnic-style lunch at the beach. "I love Ukraine. I love the folk songs, their bittersweetness. 'Come out, *kokhanaya,* but for a minute, but for a minute come out,'" she sang out. (*Kokhanaya* in Ukrainian means "beloved"—the feminine form.)

Alina was also the first Jew from Ukraine I'd met who was so ardently pro-Ukrainian and so anti-Russian. "Ukrainians and Russians are so different," she liked to repeat. "You know what my late papa used to say? 'The Russians are all drunks. Only Ukrainians and Jews can get along.'"

And at times she seemed lukewarm toward her own adoring Jewish husband, who, at first glance, walked the dotted line separating a true mensch from the stereotype of a gentle Jewish husband that Slavs sometimes wish for their daughters to marry, in spite of congenital biases against Jews.

"My Lyonya may seem like a wimp compared to your darling boxer of a husband," Alina said to my mother on one occasion, so loudly that not only father and me but half the beach could hear, including Umberto Umberto, who was standing watch in his usual spot on the parapet by the concession stand. "But don't you assume he cannot stand up for me. You should have seen him when the KGB came with a search warrant in '83. I felt he would have ripped their throats out if they'd so much as touched the children or me." Suddenly Alina shouted, "Careful, Lyonya, don't drop them," and waved to her husband as he carried both of their boys out of the cresting waves.

It was, for the most part, a daytime beach friendship. Alina followed ironclad rules of child-rearing, according to which children had to be in bed by eight. On rare occasions Alina and Lyonya would go out and join the other sunset *flâneurs* on the boulevard. Their digs, two tiny rooms in a cottage they shared with two other refugee families, were too cramped to receive visitors.

Of the two or three times the Soloveitchiks came over for tea on our balcony, I was home only once, and a long evening it turned out to be. At first my father read a new short story he'd just written. It was set in a refugee hostel outside Vienna, and Alina loved it. Afterwards I read a story of my own, called "The Austrian Ballad," about an Austrian innkeeper and her lover, a Jewish refugee from Ukraine. Alina didn't like it at all.

"Young man, you've got a long way to go. In your father's story I could feel those words, those colors. It was exactly how I would have described it," she said without a shade of embarrassment. Lyonya kept silent, munching on an almond cookie.

"Well," she continued, lighting a cigarette, "I'm no writer, but I also have a story to tell you. It's about love. And about me. Here you go." She uncrossed her legs and continued.

"You know how these things start. Lyonya and I went to university together. He became a research chemist at a classified facility, and I a chemistry teacher. Then came the mid-1970s, the wave. Papa was still living; Ninochka, our eldest, was only one. Which means I was almost thirty—I didn't want to have more kids right away, you know, kept thinking I'd go back to school for an advanced degree. So we applied for exit visas. Lyonya was fired and also told at the visa office we would never leave. We became refuseniks. Two years later my brother Senya got out. Papa was already dead, and mother went to America with my brother. Like a wagon in autumnal mud, we got stuck. The year was now '82, Lyonya worked at a fertilizer factory as foreman, I was still teaching chemistry. They couldn't get rid of me. Students adored me, and I had the best test scores in the school district.

"I was about half my present size and not so bad-looking—wasn't I, Lyonya? Wasn't I?"

"You're still gorgeous, Alinochka," Lyonya replied placidly.

"Sure I was, before I had Sashka. I just haven't dropped all this weight," she said, and dashingly slapped herself on the hip.

"I'm trying to tell you about paradoxes of love," Alina continued. "I'd known this man for many years—since high school, actually. He was my first. Later we got seriously involved at the university. He became

a Komsomol leader, quickly rose through the ranks. He had everything going for him: origin, looks, smarts. Your classic Brezhnevite
golden boy from the provinces. He's now sort of trapped as second
secretary of the regional party committee. He would've gone much,
much higher if he weren't such a dirty dog about women. I'd always
known what he was all about, but I was drawn to this man, first in
high school, then at the university. And especially drawn to him when
we hooked up again, already after Lyonya and I became refuseniks.
This man has a wife, also Jewish—he has a thing for Jewish chicks.
Some fixation. We used to rendezvous in the Olympic gym, where his
buddy was the head gymnastics coach—all three of us had gone to
high school together. So he let us use his private locker room with a
shower. This poison lingered on until March, when we finally got permission to leave. I told Lyonya. He got down on his knees and begged
me. Begged me for hours, to stay with him. For the children's sake, he
said. And so here we are, going to Cleveland."

As the wife and husband Soloveitchik were getting up from faded
canvas chaise lounges on the balcony, I looked at Alina as discreetly as
I could, out of the corner of my eye. Large ropy veins, like aquamarine
lizards, climbed up her heavy legs, bared beneath her hiked-up bright
green skirt. But her face was still young and startling in its dark, brood-
ing, Ukrainian beauty. How can this be possible, I remember thinking, that I feel attraction for this overweight and loud forty-year-old
woman from Lvov?

The Soloveitchiks left Italy before us, and it wasn't for two years
that I saw them again. In 1990 I stopped for the night in Cleveland
on my way to Bloomington, Indiana, where I was to teach summer
school. Alina was working as a lab tech. Lyonya already had an advanced Soviet degree but went back to school to get an "American
Ph.D." On the inside, their ranch house in Cleveland Heights had the
look of a Soviet apartment, and the wife and husband Soloveitchik
both still looked very Soviet, especially so in contrast to their own
Americanized children. The oldest, Ninochka, was already in junior
high, and the two boys, Sasha and Vovochka, were going to a Jewish
middle school.

Almost twenty years have gone by since we all met in Ladispoli. My mother and Alina still occasionally exchange a phone call—lately an e-mail, without having once seen each other in all those years. This has happened with other families we befriended in Ladispoli. Immigrant lives toss people about the country, and they lose touch, for no specific reason. Yet certain memories and certain persons are most alive and vibrant when left in the past, exactly as we parted with them. I cannot imagine the Ladispoli beach without the Soloveitchiks in the center of the shot. Standing on a floral sheet under the stupefying midday sun, Alina is changing out of her black bikini with gold buckles.

"Lyonya, get the *bebeches* and the children and let's be going," she commands, referring in Yiddish to their things, the bags and beach toys.

"Alinochka, hold the towel. They're staring!" The usually phlegmatic Lyonya loses his nerve.

"What's the big deal? Let them stare all they want. You should be glad your fat wife still has something to offer to the world."

She turns to my mother and winks to her and guffaws so contagiously that my mother cannot help it and shares the laughing room with Alina Soloveitchik as the rest of us languish on the black sand of Ladispoli. There we're all still waiting for America.

9

Refuge in Paradise

We arrived in America at the end of August 1987, on board the now-extinct Trans-World Airlines. It was a plane full of immigrants—from the Soviet Union, from India, from Pakistan, from Egypt—and we all applauded when the plane touched down on a runway at Kennedy Airport. Ahead lay our new lives in the New World. When I turn forty in the summer of 2007, I will have been in America for half of my life—no small feat for the Jewish boy from Moscow that I once was.

The summer I spent in Austria and Italy in 1987 had paved the way for the detachment of the Russian "I" from the American "me." Like a time buffer, the three months described in these pages divided my life, separating my Russian (and Soviet) past from my American present. However, this story of emigration would not be complete without one more adventure, which occurred almost at the tail end of our stay in Italy. It was the first and only time in my life, not even in all the twenty years of living in the Soviet Union, that I felt desperately poor.

Now picture the second week of August in Sorrento. The day's sweaty palms were beginning to ease their grip on our throats. My mother and I were taking a three-day tour of the south of Italy. My father had stayed behind in Ladispoli, since he had seen Pompeii and Sorrento with Uncle Pinya a week earlier.

In Naples, after a tour of Castel Nuovo, where cobblestones smelled not of the fine dust of ancient Europe but of cheap red wine and sardines, the tour guide had insisted that we visit a church with the relics of St. Januarius. The name of this patron saint of Naples made me think of snow. Standing in the cool vault, enveloped by stale, aromatic air, I was transported to a nostalgic recollection. I saw a wintry land-scape from my native country: snowdrifts, a frozen river, hoarfrost on power lines. In my daydream, I was kissing a girl whose face I couldn't recognize; the lips, however, tasted warm and familiar. My vision came crushing down against the stone slabs of the church floor when an el-derly guard pulled me by the sleeve:

"Take off your hat, mister. Take your hat off. You're in a sanctu-ary!" The guard pointed his black finger at my boater with a blue rib-bon. He was enraged by my obliviousness.

In my streetspun Italian—still heavily indebted to botanical Latin, although now buttressed by near-native gesticulation—I proceeded to explain to the guard that Jews didn't uncover their heads in the pres-ence of the Almighty, but rather kept them covered at all times, espe-cially inside a temple. I don't know what had come over me.

The guard apparently discerned just one word from my lengthy explication—"synagogue"—and his face turned purple.

"Synagogue! But this is a Christian church! Take your hat off, you . . . " and here the guard fell short of words. "You're standing near the relics of St. Januarius. Take your hat off or leave the sanctuary!"

I should have taken my hat off. I shouldn't have laughed at the old zealot. But I was thinking of snow and of kissing girls in my native country.

The next stop on our excursion had been Pompeii. My knowledge of the place came from a Russian classical painting by Karl Bryullov, "The Last Day of Pompeii," depicting the eruption of Mt. Vesuvius in 79 c.e. I remembered the panic-stricken Roman women and men in crimson togas running out of their homes and being swept off their feet by swirling lava. There was nothing tragic or solemn in what I ac-tually saw. Fancy a twenty-year-old who examines, in the company of his own mother, frescoes of men copulating with women, other men, and animals. Picture dwarves with hooves and enormous members. Imagine the dry heat of an early afternoon in August in Pompeii. Try to visualize us: two refugees from Russia standing on petrified lava under the dome of an azure sky amid what used to be the walls of the Temple of Venus.

I had a backpack in those days, the only backpack I've ever owned. It was a present from an American girl I had courted in Moscow the winter before leaving Russia for good. The blue backpack, now dangling behind my back, contained my wallet, a folded anorak, and an address book with the names and addresses of everyone I knew in the whole world. The old wallet was made of yellow pigskin; it was bulky and didn't fit in any of my pockets. In it were seventy U.S. dollars—our spending money for the trip—and two refugee travel documents, my mother's and my own. To be precise, they weren't even proper refugee documents. We'd been stripped of our Soviet citizenship and had to surrender our passports before leaving Moscow, and our Soviet-issued exit visas had served as our identity papers when we traveled to Vienna and Rome. And now these transit papers of sorts had disappeared along with most of my links to the past stored inside my blue American backpack.

I'll never find out what actually happened. A group of us was heading back to the tour bus. I told my mother I would go look for a drinking fountain. Modern Pompeii is a grid of petrified memories—narrow streets lined with roofless houses. I turned into a nearby lane and, sure enough, it brought me to a fountain. The rest was like a mirage: I remember putting my backpack down on a bench a few feet away from the source, then drinking my fill and letting tepid water pour over my head and shoulders. Then I turned to the wide bench of pink granite where my backpack had been just a few moments before, but there was nothing there. I stood alone amid what used to be a Roman city of pleasure. I searched in vain for signs of the bright blue that would have been clearly visible against the backdrop of Pompeii's pale stones. Only the late afternoon sky of southern Italy was a deep blue over my head, a deep blue of omniscience.

What was I to do? Which side street to take in that labyrinth of crumbling walls? I began to doubt my own sanity. Might I have left the backpack in the Amphitheater? The House of the Tragic Poet or the House of the Faun? The Forum? The Temple of Jupiter? I dashed back and forth, trying to orient myself. I struggled to recall a point of reference, a fresco, a phallic relief, a garbage can, anything. Now all

Pompeiian houses looked the same to me, all men on the frescos alike, ugly goat-men with dirty manes of curly hair. In my panic, I could still remember that I was late, that a whole bus was waiting for me at the parking lot. I ran for all I was worth. My poor mother took the news stoically. But our fellow refugees on the bus showed no signs of compassion. It was almost as though they'd left their goodness behind the turnstile of the Soviet passport control.

"Enough is enough," a piano tuner from Minsk yelped right in my face. "We'll be late to Sorrento" (as if one could ever be late to Sorrento!).

"You will never find your little backpack," grumbled a dentist from Pinsk. "You'll get yourself a new one in America."

"Will your mama spank you?" asked a little girl from Dvinsk, traveling with a mother and a deaf grandmother.

I begged Anatoly Shteynfeld, whom rogue Nitochkin had placed in charge of the trip, to give me a little extra time. "Ten minutes," he squeezed out through his rotten teeth. And Shteynfeld looked triumphantly toward my mother, who sat in the back of the bus, hands pressing her temples. Like a jackal after a firebird, Shteynfeld still lusted after my mother, but after the trip to the north of Italy he was hesitant to show it. He now channeled his lust after another man's wife into open hostility toward me, her son.

I ran to the museum office, hoping they would have a "lost and found" room. There were three men in the office, the Italian park rangers as it turned out, dressed in half uniform, half fiction, and speaking less English than I Italian. They asked to see my identification.

"I don't have any. It was in the backpack."

"But we need to see your papers before we can initiate a search in the national park," said one of the three officers. "How do we know that you're not attempting to collect someone else's possessions?"

"Please understand, my papers are in my wallet. The wallet is, or was, in the blue backpack, and the backpack is missing."

"We're sorry, mister, but there is nothing we can do under the circumstances. You can try calling here to see if something turns up. But if I were you," and the second officer gave me a mortician's smile, "I would go to the *carabinieri*. They deal with foreigners." The third officer didn't utter a single word.

On the bus leaving Pompeii, mother and I both felt completely alone among the other Russian refugees. Now without transit papers to America, we were reduced to being mere figures of the past. Our predicament was especially absurd because we had two more days of sightseeing that were paid for, and we couldn't just disembark and head back to Rome, where new transit documents would be issued less than two weeks before our departure for America.

Printed on the letterhead of JIAS, the replacement documents showed our black-and-white photographs, seared in the upper right and lower left corners with a JIAS stamp. The newly minted documents attested to the fact that the pictures were indeed of my mother and me, and also listed our birth dates and the names of our respective parents. The replacement documents were even less official than the original Soviet-issued exit visas that had been stolen in Pompeii. On these makeshift papers, beneath the text in Italian attesting to our identities, a stone-faced immigration and naturalization officer would later stamp, "ADMITTED AS A REFUGEE PURSUANT TO SEC. 207 OF THE I&N ACT. IF YOU DEPART THE U.S., YOU WILL NEED PRIOR PERMISSION FROM INS TO RETURN. EMPLOYMENT AUTHORIZED," and scribbled below "JFK 8/26/87" and also his badge number. The immigration officer stamped our travel documents, took our U.S. visas, and also gave us each a white index card with some numbers and letters in red.

"Going to Rhode Island," the immigration officer said as he let us into the country. "Nice place. Great beaches."

In a daze we proceeded to a restaurant, where our old Moscow friends, now living in New Jersey, fed us sandwiches and then walked us over to a different terminal, where we boarded a tiny plane. It was one of those propeller planes that, I believe, no longer service passengers in national commercial airlines, and on its wobbly wings we flew from JFK to the pocket-size capital of the country's smallest state. From the tiny plane I looked down onto the city where I would spend my first two American years and where, by a fatidic coincidence, my wife grew up. I looked down on my first American home and thought: My God, how can Providence be so small?

But all of that wouldn't happen for two more weeks after our near-disastrous trip to the south of Italy, and as the tour bus carried us away from Pompeii and the site of the stolen blue backpack, the prospects of coming to America seemed bleak. Between the two of us, mother and I had about twenty dollars in our pockets, and no one was our helper. Now, as we approached Sorrento, Anatoly Shteynfeld informed the group that on a clear day one can see Capri off the tip of the Sorrento peninsula. The island of Capri was the final destination.

How can I describe that evening in Sorrento? A scratched print of a Technicolor film that I both shot and acted in. Faded colors and blunted sensations. And one acute feeling: longing. The Sirens lured and tempted Odysseus from this harbor. Sorrento was an eternal tune I'd known since my Russian childhood, yet I was a stranger in its squares and thoroughfares. Growing up behind the Iron Curtain, I had yearned to see Sorrento. I had been drawn to this place and its lore. I knew that many great writers had trod these streets and sat in these trattorias. I used to picture them in my head as I gazed at February-gray snowdrifts from my bedroom window in Moscow. What were they thinking about as they smoked their *papirosy* and sipped Chianti? Did they miss their native lands? Gorky's Volga, flooding far and wide in the spring; Ibsen's foggy and mysterious Christiania. I didn't miss Russia. I mean, of course I missed it, but I knew that there was no going back. What I longed for in Sorrento was some stability; my future was so uncertain, and now it seemed even more unsettled without papers and money.

On the main promenade, store windows loomed with silver and turquoise. Young glamorous couples devoured each other's mouths right in the middle of human traffic. Bands played "Come Back to Sorrento," and my mother and I were doing our best not to think of the meaning of the song's words.

A smug Anatoly Shteynfeld, in a new hat and sunglasses, sauntered past us. Then he turned back and caught up with mother and me.

"I don't suppose you'd be interested in sharing a romantic supper with me?" he said to my mother.

"Listen, Shteynfeld," my mother replied so quickly and so crisply, that a son's pride rushed to my cheeks and ears. "Second of all, can't you see that I already have a date," she said, resting her hand on my arm. "And first of all, didn't my husband tell you in Bologna to stay away from us? Well, guess what? He'll be meeting us at the piazza when the bus returns to Ladispoli. And he never warns twice." And mother turned on her heels and pulled me into the stream of Sorrento's richly emblazoned crowd. How I loved her in her strength and bluntness!

Eventually we bought ourselves two slices of the cheapest pizza we could find and wandered from one outdoor café to another, listening to bands playing, but too shy to grab a table. Finally, we found a café that did not intimidate us as much as the others and occupied a corner table away from where the band played and other tourists sat over large plates of salad and pasta. When the waiter finally spotted us, we asked to see the menu as though we had the intention of ordering a meal. When the waiter came back, I asked to see the dessert menu. "We changed our minds. Not hungry," I explained. We ordered two scoops of gelato, a pistachio and a watermelon, and requested some tap water with it. The waiter measured us with his eye the way a patrician looks at a beggar. He brought a dish with two tiny scoops and one spoon, and didn't bother with the water. No ice cream ever tasted as good as the one mother and I shared in Sorrento at sunset.

THERE WAS A TIME when paradise was accessible by land. One could leave behind Sorrento with its worldly hustle and bustle, the vanity of its fancy crowds, the overpriced restaurants and haunting gelato stands. One could simply abandon this domain of pickpockets and jewelers and walk across a narrow isthmus to the most perfect place on the face of the earth. And then one day a natural catastrophe sank the rocky link with the mainland, making Capri into an island, now reachable only by water. But all the same, one can still get there somehow!

In the morning, after a meager breakfast, we boarded a ferry run by Navigazione Libera del Golfo. The ferry was an identical twin of the one that used to circulate between the left and right banks of the Moskva River during my childhood. An old invalid of a ferry: peeling paint, squeaky doors, retirement-age crew. As the ferry slowly approached the island, mother and I sat on the upper deck, recounting the misfortunes of the previous day. The closer we got to Capri, the lighter we felt, the easier it was to let go.

We had eight hours to explore Capri, a little over ten dollars between the two of us, and half a roll of film in an old camera my father's father had brought from East Prussia among other trophies of 1945. Our eyes did most of the shooting, and those photographs are still fresh in my memory. Mother and I walked everywhere that day. First, a turbulent tourist crowd carried us to Piazza Umberto I, with its busy cafés and shops, and with German and English humming in our ears. We read daily menus—scribbled down on black slates—as if they were concert programs. An overture: *insalata caprese* (mozzarella, tomatoes, and basil). Enter first violin: rabbit cooked with vinegar and rosemary. Sweet lemon pastries, *limoncelli,* like trills of piccolo.

The island of Capri, as we soon learned from a public map, consists of two towns, Capri and Anacapri, and a few smaller communities. We decided to ascend as high as our feet would take us; we knew we wouldn't have the money to pay for a chairlift from Anacapri to Monte Solaro. We strolled through a public garden with almond bushes and a few couples of blonde, well-groomed men. My mother noticed a counter with hundreds of dark green bottles: perfumes made with local ingredients.

"What scents do you have?" I asked a rangy salesgirl, clad in soft yellow.

"We have everything," and her fingers lifted one of the bottles, opened it, and let my mother, and then me, sniff it.

It smelled like blossoming almonds. The salesgirl then picked up another vial and let us smell its contents. The coolness of an ocean breeze wafted through the air. The Italian girl now held almond blossoms in her right hand, ocean breeze in her left, and smiled at us.

"We can mix those scents in your favorite proportion," she said.

I thought of asking whether they could recreate scents from a description—a fresh haystack, a woman's hair after a long-drawn bath—but I didn't have the words to explain this either in English or in Italian.

There are places every Russian longs to visit. Paris is one of them, Rio de Janeiro another, Capri the third. Once you've visited those places, you can die a happy person. Mother and I found an open café on a mountain terrace with a view of the entire Bay of Naples. We ordered one tea and one piece of lemon pastry; the tea came in a little pot of stainless steel, with a choice of lemon or milk. We weren't sorry to part with seven more dollars.

"Do you remember Heyman?" mother asked, matter-of-factly, as she took a sip of tea.

"Yes, I do, very well. Why?"

"It was always his dream to come here one day. He knew every detail about this island. From reading."

Heyman taught music theory at the Moscow Conservatory. He was of Jewish-Polish stock, and he never spoke of his past. We knew he had grown up in Kraków in the German-speaking family of a psychiatrist, and we also surmised that his parents were killed by the Nazis. Music and poetry were the only countries Heyman hadn't disavowed. He was married to his former graduate student, a gentle Slavic blonde with cat eyes and ever-blushing cheeks. Their son, Kesha, had been my best friend in middle school. As a kid, he had the kindest, sincerest smile I've ever encountered. In high school, after we had already drifted apart, Kesha became a boxer and won several major tournaments. He was drafted into the military out of university and returned a different, damaged person. After a semester he dropped out and got mixed up in shady affairs. He would surface, every so often, asking mutual Moscow friends for an infusion of cash to support a "business venture" or to help pay off debts—the ones his father hadn't paid off. Then he disappeared altogether.

As far back as I can remember, Heyman was always working on the same book, an interpretation of Stravinsky's career. He would come home after a day of teaching music, drop his weathered briefcase in the hallway, and proceed to the piano in his winter coat and rabbit fur hat. He would play for an hour, usually from Stravinsky's fugues, sometimes pausing in the middle of a phrase. On a late afternoon in March, over a year before we left Russia, Heyman's wife found him dead at the piano.

"I'm sorry he never got to see Capri," mother said after a long silence. "I mean in his lifetime. I wonder what he would have thought."

There we were, mother and I, sharing a cup of tea almost at the peak of this mountain-island. It seemed that the whole world lay at our feet. We were penniless, without any proof of our identity. Moreover, we were between countries. Our lives were in flux, but we felt remarkably tranquil, as though destiny held its weightless hands on our shoulders.

At the table next to ours, an American couple sat down to lunch. He had a great belly and wore a red baseball hat. She had a triple chin and large modeled silver earrings with turquoise stones, probably purchased from a local vendor. The waiter brought them two plates with club sandwiches, two bottles of Coca-Cola, and two long, narrow glasses. The sandwiches were gargantuan and emitted the fine smells of smoked meats and honey mustard. Silent and content, the Americans were biting into their sandwiches and gulping Coca-Cola.

They were so blissfully comfortable in their own skin, so untouched by fears and inhibitions, so unworried about their future. They were so incredibly American, as though they carried around them invisible bubbles filled with the air of their native Ohio or Pennsylvania. The Americans were calling each other "hun" and "luv." They were exchanging weighty comments about the quality of Italian foods: "their" sandwich bread, "their" cheese, "their" turkey. It was getting harder and harder for us to dwell on incorporeal subjects.

"What do you think America is like?" mother asked me. Of course we were speaking Russian, and the couple with sandwiches couldn't understand us. "I mean, what do you think it's really like?"

"I think it's grand. It's like a game where no one knows the rules and everyone plays by them. I think it's an easy place to be. Lots of room. How about you, mama? What do you think it's like?"

"I'm not sure. I hope it's a place where you don't have to take part in anything if you don't want to. Beautiful beaches. I don't know. I think I've been waiting for America too long. I'm ready to go there."

"I think American girls are very sexy."

Down below we could see a sandbar girding the island of Capri. A narrow sandbar swarming with life and color and sun rays.

"Mama, let's make a promise, a compact. Let's come back here one day—you, papa, who knows? Maybe I'll fall in love and get married. And the four of us will sit in this café and look at Sorrento across the bay, and order club sandwiches, many club sandwiches, and of course champagne. And we'll talk about our new life in America and remember our old life in Russia. What do you think?"

"I think it would be wonderful. And especially your American wife. I can almost picture her."

A light cloud flitted by over our heads. A seagull screamed. A gust of wind blew a napkin off the table.

Mother looked at her wristwatch. "We should go. They won't wait for us this time. And we don't have any money to pay for new ferry tickets."

"Well, mama, perhaps we could just stay here. What do you think about moving to paradise for good?"

"I don't think I'm ready. And, besides, your father won't like it here."

As we were getting up, I turned to take one last look at the happy American couple now consuming powdered doughnuts and coffee.

After almost twenty years in America, when I sometimes feel low, I recall the end of that day on Capri, how mother and I walked back to the ferry down a serpentine road. All of a sudden it started to rain. We passed an old woman with a pink donkey, then a couple of men holding hands, then a boy with a fishing rod. Mother and I only exchanged glances. No words could describe our paradisal poverty.

1996–2006